Politics.
The Basics

Politics: The Basics gently introduces the reader to the world of politics. It is a comprehensive and clearly written introduction for those studying the subject for the first time. Each chapter considers a key area of politics, explaining and exploring the basic ideas and terms.

Politics: The Basics will trigger the imagination of readers and encourage them to look for politics beyond the usual narrow definition. Rather than confining itself to the national government level, the book includes work and social situations in its analysis – looking at tribal, feudal and dynastic societies and at local and international levels. Basic concepts such as power, liberty and justice are explored from a variety of political perspectives; different models of democratic government are compared and the place of political parties and the media in the democratic process is discussed. The book also looks at the policy process, focusing on health, welfare and education. It includes suggestions for further reading and an index highlighting key concepts.

Assuming no prior knowledge of politics, this book should be of interest to both the general reader and the student considering studying politics for the first time.

Stephen D. Tansey is Senior Lecturer in Public Sector Information Systems, Bournemouth University.

Other titles in this series include:

Philosophy: The Basics
Nigel Warburton

Language: The Basics
R. L. Trask

ROUTLEDGE

LONDON AND NEW YORK

Politics

The Basics

■ Stephen D. Tansey

ROUTLEDGE

First published 1995
by Routledge
11 New Fetter Lane, London
EC4P 4EE

Simultaneously published in the
USA and Canada
by Routledge
29 West 35th Street, New York,
NY 10001

Reprinted 1996

*Routledge is an International Thomson
Publishing company* I(T)P

© 1995 Stephen D. Tansey
Stephen D. Tansey has asserted his
moral right to be identified as the
author of this work

Typeset in Frutiger and Times by
Florencetype Ltd, Stoodleigh,
Nr Tiverton, Devon

Printed and bound in Great Britain
by TJ Press (Padstow) Ltd, Padstow,
Cornwall

*British Library Cataloguing in
Publication Data*
A catalogue record for this book is
available from the British Library

*Library of Congress Cataloguing
in Publication Data*
A catalogue record for this book is
available from the Library of
Congress

ISBN 0-415-10262-6 (hbk)
ISBN 0-415-10263-4 (pbk)

Contents

5 Issues   107

6 Mechanisms   131

7   Democracy   151

8   Policies   187

Preface

Who the book is for – and what it is about

This book is designed as a basic introduction to politics which will be useful not only immediately but also in the forthcoming century. I do not claim to be able to predict with certainty the political shape of the new century – but it is already clear that many of the old perspectives of superpower rivalry and class and ideological warfare which dominated the period from 1945 to 1991 – the era of cold war – seem to be of reduced relevance, whilst issues such as ecology, feminism and the role of what used to be described as the third world (referred to as 'the South' in this book) and of the 'new' information technology, are likely to move centre stage. An introduction to politics which takes a parochial single-country approach no longer seems sensible in an era of increased international interdependence – if not entirely of harmony!

The reader I had in mind was someone without a systematic knowledge of, or rigid attitudes towards, politics. This book is intended both to enable such readers to make up their minds about politics and to understand more about the academic discipline of politics (or, as it is more grandly described in the United States, 'political science'). In particular, it is hoped that pre-university students, whether or not they have studied politics at school, will find this book a useful indication of the ground covered by university courses. The book should also be useful for undergraduates beginning a course in politics or with a substantial politics content. However, I hope that open-minded and intelligent older and younger readers will also find much of interest in this approach. Nor would I have any objection to the occasional practising politician quarrying something useful from the work!

I have not taken the view that a 'social scientific' approach requires the assumption of an attitude of detachment from the politics of the day. Nor have I tried to sell a short-term political programme. The approach here is to search for long-term principles which can help guide political actions. 'Politics' has been taken to mean the essential human activity of deciding how to live together in communities. This activity has been put in a long-term and wide geographical context. Frequent reference has been made to both Europe as a whole and the USA. The focus is on the future of all the relatively prosperous industrialised countries of the 'West', but this cannot be detached from those of the rest of the world. In considering such an ambitious agenda I have drawn extensively on the work of many academics, whose ideas have in many cases already been borrowed (often in caricatured form) by politicians.

In a book designed to help readers to make up their own minds about politics, no attempt has been made to hide the author's particular liberal point of view. This has inevitably been reflected in such matters as the choice of topics for discussion. But it is hoped to give a fair representation of all other major points of view and to give an indication of where the reader can find accessible versions of alternative perspectives at first hand.

How the book is organised

The book begins with a discussion of the nature of politics and the variety of academic approaches to its understanding. The next chapter illustrates the variety of contexts in which political activity takes place. Two chapters then survey competing ideas about the aims of that political activity. Turning to an examination of what politicians actually do, we then consider some of the basic conflicts which divide humanity.

The next three chapters of the book consider in more detail how political decisions are reached: first in a very broad sense – when should the state decide and which state should that be; second, focusing on how modern democracies make decisions; third, considering more specifically some particular areas of public policy making and applying some of the ideas introduced earlier in the book.

The final chapter is an attempt to consider how and why political change takes place and what politics is likely to look like in the twenty-first century.

The book is not divided up in the same way that many politics courses are into subdisciplinary areas, but clearly in these terms Chapter 1 is about methodology, Chapters 3, and 4 are mainly political theory, 2, 5 and 9 are mainly political sociology, Chapters 6 and 7 mainly political institutions/comparative government, Chapter 8 public policy and administration.

At all times the intention is to assist readers to make up their minds about issues, rather than to argue for some predetermined conclusion.

How to use this book

There are many ways to attempt to introduce students to a discipline, and in this book I have chosen to concentrate on introducing some of the major arguments within politics and the concepts associated with them. Logically I have begun with the methodology and boundaries of a discipline. Complete novices to the subject may find this introductory chapter of limited interest at first and can be forgiven for skipping through it at first reading.

Students who have already started a politics course should find that this broader perspective on their studies stimulates more thought than many more detailed and limited textbooks. It should prove useful especially at the beginning of such courses and by way of revision at the end. It is also intended to help those contemplating such courses to decide if politics is the appropriate subject for them. By encouraging an evaluation of the reader's own political position and evaluating many basic political concepts as part of a sustained argument, I hope to encourage a critical and individual approach which is more valuable than a more 'factual' approach both in the examination room and in practice.

The Appendix 'Sources on politics' will be found useful in locating additional material in an academic or public library, including the use of newer electronic information sources. Many years' experience of teaching at this level has shown that most students greatly underestimate the library resources they have available.

References are organised on the Harvard system so that a date in parentheses after an author's name indicates a full reference in the Bibliography. Such dates normally indicate the edition used by the author for references but the latest edition for items recommended for further reading. In addition to the Bibliography, there is a section at the end of chapter listing recommended reading, which includes brief notes describing the works selected. Pairs of dates in square brackets after a person's name indicate dates of birth and death – approximate in the case of early figures.

A feature of the book which readers should find particularly useful is the definition of key concepts found in boxes at intervals in the text and indexed in bold type at the end. Students will quickly find that any work they submit which does not clearly define its terms will obtain an unfriendly reception and, conversely, such definitions contribute greatly to clear analysis and communication.

Acknowledgements

A word of thanks is due to my former students and colleagues on the former Dorset Institute (now Bournemouth University) courses entitled 'The Political Perspective' and 'The Social Dimension of Decision Making' which were the precursors of this book, to my current students on our 'Public Sector Management Systems' course for their comments and suggestions on this material, and to my wife for much patient proofreading, many useful suggestions and no little toleration and encouragement.

I would also like to thank my friends and colleagues Philip James, Tom Gillibrand, Jim Muir, Mike Rendell, Stuart Sanders and Bernard Smales, as well as several anonymous referees, and my editors at Routledge, Gordon Smith, Diane Stafford and Caroline Wintersgill, for their many useful and encouraging remarks about all or part of the manuscript. The blame for infelicities and errors remains, of course, with me. I would very much welcome comments from readers with a view to improvement in the next edition.

Chapter 1

Approaches

Politics in everyday life

Forms of government Let Fools Contest
What 'ere is best administered is best

Dryden

Is the study of politics a sensible activity, when any watcher of television news can see that democracies vary in quality through the peaceful Swiss and the brash American to the chaotic Italian model, whilst dictatorships seem to thrive at one time like the former Soviet Union, sending the first satellite into space and dominating half the world, only to crumble away as the result of forces which few seemed able to predict? There are times when it is difficult not to sympathise with the view that such matters are both out of the control and beyond the understanding of ordinary people.

And yet we have seen ordinary people bravely dismantling regimes which seemed immovable, and dying for abstract ideas about 'forms of government' – for democracy in Tiananmen Square, for national

1

identities, of which most people in the rest of Europe were previously unaware, in the former Yugoslavia and Soviet Union. It seems wrong, in the face of such evidence of the capacity of ordinary people to effect, and be affected by, political change, not to both consider the nature of political institutions and what action we should take in relation to them.

Leaving aside, for the time being, the dramatic examples of political action and change in faraway places, it is worth examining our own lives and considering the impact of politics upon them.

Suppose you are an eighteen years old living in the United Kingdom, working temporarily for a McDonalds, and hoping for a university place in the autumn. Waking up you may realise that the government (strictly Parliament) has legislated to convert what was a local time of 6.33 or so (depending on the latitude) to 7.30. Turning on the local radio station, whose franchise was granted by a quango (*q*uasi *a*utonomous *n*ational (or *n*on-) *g*overnmental *o*rganisation), you may hear the weather forecast from the government-financed Meteoro- logical Office; after hearing several CD tracks (payment of royalties to the authors and performers must be made by law by the radio station), you drag yourself out of bed (legally mattress materials must be non- flammable), down to your cornflakes (ingredients listed on packet in due form by another law). If you unwisely reach for a cigarette the government (/European Union) has both insisted on a Health Warning on the packet and taken a large rake-off in the form of tax. Without going through every minute of your day, it is clear that government is likely to be affecting almost every one of them in similar ways (air quality, traffic regulations, employment law – fill out the story yourself).

The bigger issues are, of course, affected in the same way: can you afford to go to university? What grants and loans has the govern- ment made available? What places are available in universities? What financial provision has been made by the government? How many other students have been educated by the state educational system to university entry level? If, on the other hand, you are unable to make it to university, then your prospects for permanent employment will depend upon the government's management of the economy; prospects for continued employment with McDonalds are dependent on, among other things, government policy towards foreign companies and the extent and effectiveness of health education campaigns!

So far we have only considered you and the government. Going back to our imaginary example, suppose on reaching the kitchen your father snaps at you, 'Can't you clear up the beer glasses and pizza cartons you and your friends littered the place with last night?' Arguably, this is a political situation too. Within the family fathers are sometimes thought to have 'authority' – some sort of legitimate power over children. As an eighteen year old, you might react to the speech as an assertion of authority and react negatively on the grounds that you are no longer a child to be given orders. Conversely, father may merely feel that in a community all should play their part and clear up their own messes. But in any case, if he wants you to clear up and you do not, this can be seen as a clash of wills in which only one can prevail.

Similarly, when you arrive at McDonalds it may well be you have discovered that the Assistant Manager (who is temporarily in charge in the absence of the Manager on holiday) is busy establishing in the eyes of the Area Manager that he can do a better job than his boss. Here we have a struggle for power in which people within the organisation may take sides (form factions as political scientists might say) – in short, organisational politics is being practised!

It soon becomes clear that 'politics' is used in at least two senses, both of which are immediately relevant to everyone's everyday experience: in the narrowest conventional (dictionary) usage – what governments do – it is affecting us intimately, day by day and hour by hour; in the wider sense – people exercising power over others – it is a part of all sorts of social relationships be they kinship, occupational, religious or cultural.

What is politics?

If we now try to define 'politics' more formally and precisely, we run into the sort of problems which will be found to recur again and again in this book. It is actually quite tricky to define scientific disciplines like physics and chemistry, but if you do so, you are not so likely to be accused immediately of failing to understand the problem, of lacking scientific objectivity, or of making unwarranted assumptions, as is a writer on politics. One of the problems is associated with whether we are talking about politics the human activity or politics the academic 'discipline' – or, in American, politics or political science. In principle, it might be thought that the search for truth about how human beings exercise power might be expected to be completely separate from the activity of actually seeking to exercise that power. But in practice, as we shall see, political ideas are some of the most important weapons in the politician's armoury. Attempts to ignore this are either naive or, quite frequently, a deliberate attempt to present a controversial political ideology as an indisputable political fact.

In this light it is worth considering rather critically the implications of some of the standard academic definitions of politics and of power as shown in Box 1.

Without giving a detailed analysis of each of the definitions in Box 1, it is obvious that they show very considerable differences which reflect the viewpoints of the authors. Most political scientists' definitions of politics are much broader in scope than the first, dictionary, definition which focuses on the state (although admittedly 'part of a state' could be interpreted widely). In effect, they largely endorse the view suggested above that politics is about the social exercise of power, rather than just the state. However, this may to some extent reflect the natural 'imperialism' of academics on behalf of their own discipline. Sociologists might argue that 'man moving man' would be more appropriate as a definition of their concerns.

Consider also, though, the unit of analysis in terms of which these definitions are couched. Weber, Lasswell and de Jouvenal appear to be thinking primarily in terms of individuals exercising power; Crick and Parsons focus upon whole societies; the *SOED* talks about governments, whilst Poulantzas views classes as the primary political 'actors'. This reflects a split between individualistic and collectivist theories which will be discussed in greater detail in Chapter 3.

Another contrast in these definitions which is also worth bringing out is that between what has been described as 'zero-sum' and 'non-zero-sum' theories of politics. This terminology is derived from the mathematical theory of games. A zero-sum game is the usual sort of game, such as chess or draughts, in which a win by one player is, by definition, a loss on the part of the opposing player or players. There

Box 1 Definitions of 'politics' and 'power'

Politics

> The science and art of government; the science dealing with the form, organisation and administration of a state or a part of one, and with the regulation of its relations with other states.
>
> Shorter Oxford English Dictionary

> a way of ruling divided societies by a process of free discussion and without undue violence.
>
> Bernard Crick (1964)

> who gets what, when, how.
>
> H. Lasswell (1936)

> man moving man.
>
> Bertrand de Jouvenal (1963)

> the authoritative allocation of value.
>
> David Easton (1979)

Power

> the production of intended effects.
>
> Bertrand Russell (1938)

> the probability that one actor within a social relationship will be in a position to carry out his own will despite resistance regardless of the basis on which the probability arises.
>
> Max Weber (Gerth and Mills (1948)).

> the capacity to mobilize the resources of society for the attainment of goals for which a general public commitment . . may be made.
>
> Talcott Parsons (1957)

> the capacity of a social class to realise its specific objective interests.
>
> Nicos Poulantzas (1973)

is a fixed amount of 'winnings' which means that the gains of one side are, by definition, losses to the other. Obviously many politicians, and political scientists, see politics this way. Thus Weber and (implicitly) Lasswell both seem to suggest that the political success of one individual may well be at the expense of others who oppose them. It is also a feature of Marxist theories like Poulantzas' that the interests of classes are opposed and are gained each at the expense of the other.

However, not all games are of this sort. In collective make-believe children's games, for instance, new themes introduced by one player can enrich the enjoyment of the game for everyone – in a game of Cowboys versus Indians, the introduction of Aliens may lead to everyone having a better time. There is not a fixed amount of 'winnings', by co-operation both sides can achieve more. In a similar way, Parsons explicitly argues that, by co-operation, different groups in society can each obtain greater benefits than would be the case if they worked in competition. Thus different theories place radically different emphases on consensus (agreement) and conflict in their theories of politics.

The author's sympathies lie with Maurice Duverger (1972) who argues, 'The two-faced god, Janus, is the true image of power'. In other words, both conflict and consensus are essential elements to the creation of a political situation. The imposition of one person's or group's interests on another by force and without any element of consent seems far from what most people understand by 'politics', as Crick (1993) argues. On the other hand, a situation (perhaps unlikely) in which a group in total agreement (as to goals and methods) proceed to achieve more and more of their objectives does not sound like a political process either! Where Crick is arguably in error is in failing to see the elements of consensus in what he describes as 'totalitarian' regimes like those of Nazi Germany and the Soviet Union.

Thus 'politics' encompasses a broad range of situations in which people's objectives vary but in which they work together to achieve those aims they have in common as well as competing where aims conflict. Both co-operation and competition may involve bargaining, argument and coercion. The art of politics may often lie in seeing the potential for alliances rather than antagonisms amongst differing groups.

Approaches to the study of politics

As our discussion of the nature of politics has suggested, one of the joys, and also one of the frustrations, of the study of politics lies in the variety of approaches adopted by academic writers to the subject. This is a joy in the sense that within one course of study you will be introduced to a rich spectrum of writing ranging from classic philosophers like Plato [427–347 BC] (1866) and Aristotle [384–322 BC] (1946) through radical sociologists such as C. Wright Mills (1956) and Pareto (1976) to dedicated modern social scientists wielding statistical tests of significance to analyse huge volumes of computerised data (e.g. Robert Dahl (1971)). It is frustrating in that the conclusions of such varied writers cannot be simply accumulated to form a certain body of knowledge representing the political scientist's view of politics. Students of politics must be ready to live with uncertainty, to sift through varied sources and accept what seems to them to be relevant and valid.

In the remainder of this chapter an attempt is made to offer some tools to enable students to do their own 'sifting', and to recognise why writers on politics differ so radically. We shall look at three main approaches to the study of politics, and within these at various schools of thought. This section should be thought of only as a sort of preliminary crude map of the terrain to be covered, not as a rigorous analysis of what kinds of writing on politics is possible or as a series of water-tight divisions. However, it will be found that two writers within a 'school' generally have more in common and are more likely to agree on what has already been established, and perhaps to refer to each other, than two writers in different schools.

· The three main contemporary academic approaches to the study of politics which are distinguished here can be described as 'traditional scholarship', 'social science' and 'radical criticism'. With an element of exaggeration they might also be thought of as the British, the American, and the French approaches (although the 'American' approach has gained much ground in Britain and internationally in recent years).

'Traditional scholars' often approach matters political on a rather piecemeal basis, looking at one specific country, political institution, theoretical concept or writer in depth, often with the tools and preconceptions of another academic discipline – especially history or philosophy. Thus, the core of the politics curriculum, at least until recently, in Britain has been the study of individual British political institutions in their historical context, the great political philosophers and what was misleadingly titled 'comparative government'. The latter being largely the study of American, French and Soviet government and politics separately. Often British courses have been part of a humanities-oriented programme such as the Oxford PPE (philosophy, politics, economics) programme. (For more on British politics courses see Appendix). A recent article compares the leading UK and US journals and shows that the leading UK journal, *Political Studies*, has 91 per cent of its articles focusing on institutional, descriptive, conceptual or philosophical topics (including history of political thought), whilst the *American Political Science Review* has 74 per cent of its articles in the behavioural/empirical or deductive/rational choice categories (Norris (1994) 15). In continental Europe politics has often been a subsidiary of faculties of law, sociology or history.

'Social scientists', in contrast would denounce the traditional approach as 'idiographic' (a word derived from Chinese writing – ideograms – and meaning representing one thing at a time), espousing instead a 'nomothetic' or generalising approach in which the endeavour of scholars of politics must be ultimately to derive general theories or laws about the nature of political behaviour. Thus, a typical American-style curriculum presents political science as one of a group of related social science disciplines, including Sociology and Economics, all using modern quantitative/computer-oriented methods of 'analysing data' scientifically.

'Radical critics', whilst not denying the need to produce useful generalisations from the study of politics, have denounced the conservative bias of US-dominated political science. Often their primary allegiance has appeared not be to an academic discipline but to a general doctrine calling for the radical change of existing (Western) societies – most frequently some variety of Marxism, but similar criticism can be produced from an ecological or feminist perspective.

The basis of the distinction being drawn is mainly in terms of what writers see their task to be, the methods they employ, the level and type of their analysis and the values they espouse, rather than the details of specific theories advanced. In addition though, a comparison of the specific theories advanced by different schools and approaches does show a concentration on different areas of human experience, broad patterns of difference in their content and a tendency to draw upon similar models and to use the same concepts within schools. On examination it will often be found that where writers from different approaches and schools deal with what is apparently the same topic (e.g. 'democracy', 'elections', 'society') their concerns and assumptions are often so different that no real dialogue can be said to have occurred. Box 2 offers an overview of these major approaches and schools which will be explained in more detail in the rest of this chapter.

Traditional scholarship

The first academic writers on politics – Plato (1866) and Aristotle (1946) – whose works are still studied in detail in most British universities were unaccustomed to the modern practice of compartmentalising knowledge into separate disciplines. Hence, they were not afraid to combine insights from history and current affairs with discussions on the big moral issues such as 'What is the best form of government?' or 'What is justice? This somewhat 'eclectic' approach (combining insights from various different sources) was also adopted by some of the more readable classic writers in the nineteenth century, such as John Stuart Mill (1910), Bryce (1921) and de Tocqueville (1966). These writers saw the rise of democracy as the major political development of their time and sought to analyse not only the idea, but its contemporary manifestations in different countries, and to suggest improvements and accommodations with the emerging reality of democratic government.

Because serious writers on politics now tend to be university lecturers, who have to have specialist interests and lists of articles in professional journals and/or monographs published by respectable academic publishers, they tend to adopt a much more limited conception of their role, with philosophically trained writers exploring concepts and the history of ideas, historians limiting themselves frequently to small periods of time and limited geographical areas, students of

Box 2 Major contemporary approaches to politics

	Traditional	*Social science*	*Radical*
Task	Piecemeal explanation	Science of politics	Radical social change
Methods	Descriptive, historical, philosophical analysis	Quantitative or theorising illustrated	Ideological criticism
Values	Liberal democratic	Pro US democracy and 'development'	Anti-establish-ment
Level of analysis	Political, psychological philosophical	Political and Social	Multi-level
Scope	Individual institutions or countries	USA or area studies	Global and historical
Content	Constitutional consensus disturbed by cataclysmic events	Pluralism	Class/ gender/ species conflict
Schools	(a) Liberal-Institutional (b) Historical (c) Philosophical	(a) Functionalist (b) Economic (c) Systems	(a) Marxist (b) Feminist (c) Ecologist
Typical	Constitutional convention, political culture, contradiction		
Concepts	Great man	Market, feedback	Patriarchy

SOURCE   Tansey (1973)

political institutions specialising in electoral systems, UK parliamentary select committees or the politics of privatisation. There is no doubt that such academic specialisation may reap benefits in terms of specific new discoveries (and in terms of obtaining rapid publication in academic journals), but this gain is also undoubtedly at the cost of a certain loss of perspective and certainly loss of a non-academic audience who often fail to see the relevance of much of this work to current policy issues.

Within British university politics departments much admirable scholarly work continues to be produced on political theory and 'political institutions' without any systematic attempt to relate findings to general theories of political behaviour or 'social science'. Some holders of professorial chairs are still wont to describe themselves as historians or philosophers rather than 'political scientists'.

Students of 'political theory' in this mode have tended to divide roughly into two main camps: the philosophers, who see their main task as the elucidation of political concepts (such as justice and democracy) with at least an eye to their relevance to contemporary concerns; and the historians of ideas, who have been concerned to trace the evolution of writings on politics, the intent of the writers of these texts and their influence on events.

Those who have written on 'political institutions' have often been less explicit in their theoretical intent, but writers such as Ridley (1975) have articulated the rationale and assumptions of much of this writing. In established and relatively stable democracies like Britain and the United States, it is evident that much of what we call politics centres around important governmental institutions like parliaments, elections, government departments, local authorities and the like. The study of how these institutions have evolved, the rules and practices surrounding them, and consideration of how they may be improved, is clearly of the utmost importance – particularly to writers (and readers) who share the general assumptions upon which they can be said to be 'based'. As citizens, and possibly future public employees or even politicians, we may feel that such activities scarcely need elaborate justification.

However, the sceptical and the ambitious may combine to throw doubt upon the academic credentials of such activities. Is the result really 'knowledge' which can legitimately be examined in universities

– or merely pragmatic common sense which can be used by those who agree with its (conservative and liberal?) assumptions? The sceptical will argue that the operations of representative institutions are merely a deceptive mask for the real politics of exploitation below (see 'Radical Criticism' later), whilst the ambitious see only scientifically established theories as the acceptable basis of knowledge at the end of the twentieth century.

Social science and politics

The proposition that our knowledge of politics should be scientifically derived seems, at first sight, undeniable. The applications of scientific method in many other spheres – physics, biochemistry, astronomy – has yielded not only a broad consensus on the truth of various scientific 'laws', but also practical results in the shape of space ships and 'miracle' drugs. If the application of systematic observation, computerised analysis of data, the testing of hypotheses through experiment and the painstaking building of small bricks into enormous edifices of knowledge can work in one sphere, why not in another? Since human beings are currently at such loggerheads over the nature of politics, it might be thought, indeed, that the construction of a science of politics is the most urgent intellectual task of our time.

The problems of creating a valid science of politics seem, however, to be so enormous as to place the whole project in some doubt. They include problems of value conflict, of complexity, of method and of philosophy.

It is tempting to dismiss conflicts of value as irrelevant to scientific investigation. The conventional argument is that science is morally neutral ('value-free'), but can be used for good or evil. Thus, the structure of the atom is the same everywhere, whether our knowledge of this structure is used to destroy civilisations, to fuel them or merely to understand their most basic constituents. True, it is easier to apply a knowledge of biochemistry to creating individual health than it is to use a knowledge of politics to create a healthy society – because there is more agreement on what an ill person looks like than on what is an ill society – but such ethical problems of objectives are seen as separate from scientific problems as to how things work.

In principle, the author would accept this proposition, although this then drastically reduces the likelihood of increasing social consensus by creating a science of politics. In social analysis so far, however, it has been impractical to create a 'value-free' vocabulary acceptable alike to social democrats, Thatcherite free-marketeers, Marxists, and feminists. Suppose we try to describe a faculty meeting: a social democrat might observe academic democracy at work; the Thatcherite see only a series of individuals asserting their interests; the Marxist may see wage-slaves ideologically dominated by the imperatives of the capitalist system; whilst a feminist sees a series of males exerting patriarchial domination. The concepts we use to observe social reality have values built in to them which make 'objective' analysis difficult if not impossible.

An additional problem in applying scientific analysis to the social/political arena is the complexity of the phenomena being studied. Scientific method has so far been most successfully applied to physical systems, less successfully to biological systems composed of physical systems, and with only limited success to human psychological systems composed of biological systems. So it should be no surprise that social systems comprising a still higher and more complex level of system are most resistant to analysis. Typically, science is seen as characterised by the testing of hypotheses through experiment. The experimental method is largely closed to political scientists since they do not possess the power to dictate to whole human societies how they should behave. In any case, experiments require identical control groups for comparison which, it is arguable, cannot be created. Some small-scale laboratory simulations of human power situations have been attempted with interesting results (e.g. Milgram (1965)), but the applicability of the results of these to whole societies is disputable. Statistical manipulation of sets of data about human societies may be a partial substitute for experimental techniques, but few convincing data sets have been gathered. Some attempts at this include Taylor and Jodice's (1983) *The World Handbook of Political and Social Indicators* and work by Kurian (1985) and Lane (1991) One very basic problem is that many countries do not have reliable population figures (e.g. Nigerian census figures have been politically contested because of their influence on the ethnic balance of power). It is also difficult to compare financial values in different currencies because of artificial exchange rates and differences in purchasing power. On the problems of this sort of exercise see C.L. Taylor (1969).

On a philosophical level, it has been argued that the sort of causal explanation that would be perfectly satisfactory in physical science would be unsatisfactory in explaining social phenomena – social explanations need to explain the motives of the persons involved, not just predict successfully what will happen (Runcimam (1969)). Additionally, if we accept that human knowledge and motivation are an important part of every political system, every advance in political knowledge is potentially available to the members of the systems we study. Therefore the knowledge we produce by analysing political systems becomes potentially a part of those systems and may, of course, upset any predictions we make about them (Popper (1960) and see Chapter 9).

Schools of political science

Some of the problems of establishing a social science of politics become evident if we examine the writings of some of those most committed to the enterprise. It quickly becomes clear than even amongst these writers there is no consensus on the concepts and methods to be employed, nor on the theories which can be assumed to have been already established.

Perhaps the most influential group of 'political scientists' are those centring on Gabriel Almond and the deliberations of the Committee on Comparative Politics of the American Political Science Association in the 1960s. Although much criticised on theoretical grounds, the terminology and approach adopted by these 'functionalist' writers is still widely prevalent in empirical studies of American, British and comparative politics.

In a vastly influential early work Almond and Coleman (1960) argued that we should speak of:

'Political system' instead of 'state'
'Functions' instead of 'powers'
'Roles' instead of 'offices'

'Structures' instead of 'institutions'
'Political culture' instead of 'public opinion'
'Political socialization' instead of 'citizenship structure'

Their argument was that by studying the processes necessary to maintain any political system in a variety of environments, rather than conventional liberal democratic institutions, they were creating the basis for a scientific approach: 'This is not only a matter of conceptual vocabulary [sic]; it is an intimation of a major step forward in the nature of political science as science ... towards a probabalistic science of politics'.

In some ways this attempt has been very successful in that thousands of writers have employed the vocabulary suggested, virtually every modern country has been described in these terms, and a vocabulary separated from that of everyday political discourse has been widely adopted by professional political scientists. Unfortunately there is little evidence that the vocabulary is used any more precisely than its 'old-fashioned' predecessors (Sartori (1970)) or that the assumptions implicit in the approach are any less arguable than (or, indeed, very different from) the liberal institutional approach. For instance, there has been no substantial agreement on what functions are necessary to maintain a political system (Dowse (1972)) or on the desirability of understanding politics in terms of the maintenance of the stability of existing nation states (Luard (1990) argues for a global perspective – see final chapter).

A good illustration of some of the problems of employing this newer vocabulary is to consider the concept of 'political system', used rather loosely by most of the functionalists to indicate that politics is not merely limited to traditional constitutional institutions but that they are influenced by social and economic conditions within a country. As Nettl (1966) and others have pointed out, this usage often *assumes* that the system is an entity which exists and carries out some defined role – such as 'the allocation of value'. Alternatively, the idea of system may be used more as a conscious analogy with engineering systems as with Deutsch (1963), who sees the political system as a steering mechanism for society – a flow of information through decision-making mechanisms which can be improved.

More systematic sociological thinkers such as Talcott Parsons (1957) see clearly that 'functions' are highly theoretical processes analytically distinguished from a messy empirical reality. The problem then becomes to see what predictions such a theory is making. The 'emptiness' of system theory is perhaps most clearly seen if the writings of David Easton (1979) are considered. He clearly states that 'political system' is a purely analytical concept which can be applied to any collection of entities the theorist finds convenient. He then suggests the possibility of the system responding to 'input' from the outside 'environment' by 'outputs' which in turn may affect the environment so as to stabilise it. In such a case, a stable 'homeostatic' system has been achieved. However, such an outcome is by no means inevitable – the problem then is to know when such an analysis is appropriate and when a breakdown of the system might occur.

Thus, many writers now claim to be adopting a 'system' approach, but it is often unclear whether they believe that political systems are observable entities, analytical frameworks, useful analogies or problem-solving devices.

By way of contrast, let us consider a more recent and perhaps trendier group of political scientists – the 'rational choice' theorists (or as we will usually refer to them, the 'economists'). As the names used to describe them suggest, they have adopted an alternative approach which, instead of starting with the behaviour of whole societies, focuses on the behaviour of individual political 'actors'. Mainstream economists have analysed markets starting with the behaviour of individual consumers and entrepreneurs who are assumed to rationally pursue their own interests (maximise utility or profit). The behaviour of individual voters, bureaucrats or legislators can be considered in the same way (e.g. Tullock (1965) etc.). As with economics, it is not asserted that all actors are rational – only that the system functions on the basis that most actors will be rational, and that irrational actors will cancel each other out/go 'bankrupt' etc. (Nor does maximising utility exclude the proposition that some actors will derive utility from altruistic actions.) Thus, for instance, the behaviour of bureaucrats, instead of being seen in constitutional terms as giving impartial policy advice to ministers, or in functional terms as part of both the interest aggregation and rule enforcement functions, is described as seeking to maximise their agency budgets in order to maximise their own power, salary and prestige.

Theories, models, paradigms

Faced with a thicket of rival approaches and theories (and the reader is warned that the variety of theoretical approaches has only been hinted at in this section) readers may be tempted to demand who is right and who is wrong, or despairingly to conclude that they will return to the subject in 30 years' time when the 'experts' have made up their minds. Alas, neither approach is likely to succeed, since no omniscient oracle is available to answer the question and, from past experience, thirty years of waiting will only increase the complexity of the choice. What perhaps may help to clarify matters is to try to separate out a number of activities which are frequently confused in the effort to generate a science of politics. To do so we need to consider how scientists normally work.

Popper (1961) has convincingly argued that scientific laws are useful general predictive propositions which have been extensively tested and not disproved. Few of the propositions advanced by political scientists seem to meet this test. As we have already seen, many of the propositions advanced by 'empirical political theorists' are difficult to apply to the real world of politics, do not make unequivocal predictions and certainly have not yet been extensively tested. Some more limited propositions might be regarded as testable hypotheses, the production of which constitutes a preliminary to the creation of usable theories.

It used to be thought that scientists derived their hypotheses for testing from the observation of as many 'facts' as possible (the 'positivist' view of science), but more recent historians of science have observed that, in fact, most innovative hypotheses come from a combination of acute observation and the application of 'models' of reality often derived from another area of science. Observers need to have an idea of what they are looking for. A 'model' is a simplification of reality which enables us to suggest relationships between the things we observe.

In politics numerous different models have been, and still are, applied. For instance, as we shall discuss at greater length later on, one of the dominating models in early modern (liberal) thought was the legal model of a contract applied to relationships between citizens and rulers or the state. Medieval thinkers tended to prefer an organic model of the state – e.g. the parts of a state as being like the parts of the human anatomy. Easton/Deutsch's application of a cybernetic (information system) model in the age of the computer thus becomes unsurprising in the ' post-modern' age.

Clearly, as Deutsch (1963) points out, models are not in themselves right or wrong, merely helpful or unhelpful. Choice of models will normally depend upon their relevance, economy and predictive power – the latter encompassing ideas of rigour (do theories based up on it give unique answers?), combinatorial richness (the number of patterns that can be generated from it) and organising power (can it be applied in many different circumstances?).

Really successful general models can be at the heart of what Kuhn (1970) terms a scientific paradigm. Thus the Newtonian model of matter as a series of particles whose relationships could be described in terms of a series of simple mathematical equations dominated physics for several centuries, just as the model of evolutionary development proposed by Darwin continues as the dominant paradigm in modern biology. Despite the positivist view of scientific development referred to above, Kuhn argues that most scientific endeavour ('normal science') consists in the further application of existing models to new areas or the explanation of apparent deviations from the dominant model in terms derived from it. Nor should this be despised; a great deal of modern technological and scientific progress has rested upon this process of 'pygmies standing on the shoulders of giants' – ordinary knowledge workers amassing detailed information within the dominant paradigm.

In these terms, political studies can be seen as an academic discipline in the pre-scientific stage in which no dominant paradigm has yet emerged. What are described here as 'schools' can be seen as aspirant paradigms, and the main question which has to be asked of them is how useful a source they are of applicable models to new situations, of testable hypotheses and of concepts for helpfully describing and analysing events, rather than their absolute truth.

In considering more 'empirical' work by writers on politics, the question is not so much whether they are employing some orthodox approach but more specifically:

- Is the approach they employ appropriate to the problem in hand?
- Are they clear and consistent in the way they employ theories, concepts and models?
- Are they careful not to mistake theoretical assumptions for established conclusions?
- Are they careful to examine all the evidence on the issues they examine – not just looking for evidence for a proposition derived from their model or approach?

In the present state of knowledge, it will often be found that a combination of insights derived from different approaches throws the most light on an issue.

Radical criticism

One characteristic of a scientific theory is that it should be value-free – there is no left-wing physics and right wing physics, just good physics and bad physics. It is not that 'ideological' (see later, Chapter 4, p.92) distortions are impossible or unlikely – theological and political considerations have hindered the acceptance of the Darwinian paradigm in biology, for instance – but that in the long term the insistence on observational, statistical and above all experimental verification of theories, and probably too the existence of relatively united world professional organisation of scholars in particular areas, has enabled a consensus on paradigms, theories and concepts to emerge.

Consideration of many of the approaches put forward by political scientists reveals that the models upon which they are based, the concepts they employ and the theories they espouse frequently imply a clear set of values which others might well wish to dispute. If we consider Almond's functionalist model, for instance, despite some protestations to the contrary it seems clearly to view politics as a matter of maintaining political stability by enabling political interests in a system to be conciliated ('interest articulation and aggregation') by a state which functions through a traditional liberal pattern of legal rules ('rule-making, rule enforcement and rule adjudication'). This model of politics then stresses values of 'pluralism' (see later Chapter 5, p.125–9) and consensus which may be uncontroversial in the United States (where most political scientists live) but which were clearly not acceptable in the old Soviet Union or amongst left-wing thinkers in Paris or even London. Similarly, a glance at the individualistic model put forward by the 'economists' reminds one of Margaret Thatcher's famous remark that 'there is no such thing as society – only individuals'. Such theories clearly imply a fashionable suspicion of big government and a stress on the 'profit motive' in the broad sense.

The obvious rival approach in political analysis to the stress on individualism and consensus found in many of the theories of political science is to consider the collectivist and conflict-oriented view of politics put forward by Marxists. There are, in fact, as we shall see in Chapter 4, as many varieties of Marxism as there are of political science. But the basic model, stemming back to Marx and Engel's *Communist Manifesto* (in Marx and Engels (1962), Marx, Engels and Lenin (1960)), is of a society divided into large collectivities (classes) whose interests are in basic conflict. The only long-term resolution of such conflicts, which stem from the basic relationship of exploitation between the capitalist bourgeoisie (the owners of the 'means of production') and the proletariat ('wage-slaves'), is through a socialist revolution. Although to readers in the Western world such an approach seems clearly biased, is this any more than a taking-for-granted the values of our own society? Many Soviet citizens took these assumptions for granted in the same way that most British or American citizens assume that 'democracy' means a society in which everyone can vote at periodic elections at which the rich can buy unlimited media exposure for their views.

A number of recent writers (Miliband (1969), Gramsci (1969)) have approached the analysis of modern politics through a variety of Marxist models with, in some cases, enlightening results. Conventional assumptions have been questioned and further economic and political dimensions to problems exposed. In the Western world, for instance, the cultural and media influence of capitalism has been emphasised, whilst in the 'Third' world Marxist emphasis on the international economic environmental influences (Williams (1976)) seems much more realistic than analysis of political parties who are liable to disappear overnight in a military coup (Sklar (1963), Weiner (1962)).

As with conventional political scientists, the work of Marxist writers is of variable quality and interest to the ordinary reader. Here too, a tendency to mistake assumptions for conclusions or to jump to conclusions favourable to the initial model adopted, can be discerned. In addition, perhaps, there may be a greater tendency to engage in 'theological' disputes within the school about the proper use of concepts and to take explicit policy positions. It is not always clear how academic (in accord with the canons of conventional scholarship) some books are intended to be. Conversely, of course, some Marxist works – particularly the *Communist Manifesto* itself – have been subjected to an orgy of academic criticism despite their explicitly polemical role.

More recently a number of radical feminist writers have emerged who have also questioned the assumptions implicit in conventional political analysis. They too have seen society primarily in terms of an exploitative relationship ('patriarchy') between collectivities (adult heterosexual males versus the rest). (It should be emphasised that this is a discussion of radical feminist writers – many feminists adopt a more liberal, moderate stance.) Like later Marxists, they have stressed cultural and media aspects of political relationships, but they have also stressed the political aspects of personal relationships. Whereas conventional analysis has looked at explicit political conflicts reflected in conventional party divisions, these writers have seen potential (seismic) splits repressed by conventional politics. Some animal liberation and ecological writers could also be seen in the same methodological light as the Marxist and feminist critics discussed here. However, for convenience, they are discussed in a later chapter.

Lest the idea of repressed political divisions be dismissed out of hand, it is worth considering the case of Afro-Americans in the United States. As recently as the 1950s in many parts of the USA, as Bachrach and Baratz (1970) remind us, although deprived of basic human rights and discriminated against, living in a 'democracy' and resenting their condition, sometimes even in a majority in their local community, Afro-American concerns did not even feature on the political agenda.

Bachrach and Baratz put forward an interesting general model of political activity, combining insights from both the pluralist and Marxist models, which suggests that an apparently free play of political interests in a 'democratic' system may coexist with suppressed conflicts in which the interests of certain groups often fail to reach the political agenda; in which policies favouring them, even if nominally adopted by governments, will not be implemented fully by the machinery of government. In which, in short, what Schattschneider ((1960), 71) calls a 'mobilization of bias' built in to the system operates against them. Whilst Bachrach and Baratz are mainly concerned with racial biases, clearly these biases can equally well be those of gender, ethnicity (see Chapter 5, p.120–5), religion or capitalism. Models of this sort – which integrate insights from a number of existing approaches – may well represent the way forward for political analysis.

Recommended reading

Crick, Bernard, 1993, *In Defence of Politics*, 4th edn, Harmondsworth, Middlesex, Penguin. A stimulating and readable essay which defends Crick's own concept of politics against totalitarians, experts, nationalists and other false friends.

Leftwich, Adrian, 1983, *Redefining Politics*, London, Methuen. Interesting for the breadth of examples employed from the Aztecs to the World Bank.

Zuckerman, Alan S., 1992, *Doing Political Science: An Introduction to Political Analysis*, Oxford Westview Press. A contrasting US view which stresses the study of politics as an academic social science.

Chapter 2

Systems

Varieties of political system

In this chapter we shall elaborate upon a point already raised, namely, that politics is not an activity confined to modern liberal democratic national governments. We have already seen how politics can be seen in personal and organisational activity – a point to be developed further in relation to our later discussions of feminism, anarchism and ecology. We shall also see how political activity can be found at levels of government other than the national (local, regional and supranational) and in systems with very different styles of government to our own. Political 'system' is being used here in a loose sense to denote a complex of interconnecting political activities in a society or societies – it does not imply the adoption of any particular system model.

For a graphic illustration of the thesis that politics is not just about how states are run, let us consider the case of societies without a state to see if we can

23

identify anything resembling what we would normally think of as 'politics'.

This, in turn, raises the issue of what is meant by a state. At this stage, let us ignore some complicated academic arguments and settle upon a working definition from Max Weber, a nineteenth-century German liberal sociologist (Box 3).

Box 3 Definition of 'state'

An organisation having "the monopoly of the legitimate use of force in a given territorial area".

Weber (in Gerth and Mills (1948))

This reflects the way most people probably see the world today: as in most atlases, it is seen as divided into a series of exclusive geographical areas (countries or nations), each of which has a government whose people recognise its authority to maintain order amongst them, by force in the last resort if necessary. This government may, of course, be divided into central, regional and local levels and executive, legislative and judicial arms, but all these bodies are seen as a system for taking decisions on behalf of the nation (or society) and maintaining law and order.

Politics without the state: tribal societies

This is a picture we shall be questioning in more detail later, but for now let us point out that until very recently 'tribal' groups have been 'discovered' in the forests of Papua New Guinea and Brazil living apparently undisturbed by the governments which purport to represent them at the United Nations. Of course, such tribal groups may be thought of merely as traditional 'mini-states' and as only a minor deviation from the picture (or what social scientists tend to dignify as a 'model') previously presented. However, social anthropologists who study such groups in detail, have shown convincingly that tribal societies may differ radically from the state model of government.

The use of 'tribal' in this context is often avoided by social anthropologists as implying a condescending view of the peoples concerned as primitive – this is not the author's intention. Many of the groups concerned have sophisticated cultures, high levels of artistic achievement and admirable ways of life. 'Tribal' is used here as an easily intelligible synonym for what anthropologists frequently term 'simple societies' – those having common cultures (e.g. one religion and language), undifferentiated role structures (most people do a small range of similar jobs) and with strong emphasis on kinship and custom (Mitchell, (1959)). Following Weber, the defining characteristic of such societies may be taken to be a claim to common ancestry.

One obvious way in which these groups differ from the state model of government is in terms of territory. Whilst many such groups do have what they regard as their own territory, some are so nomadic that they can make no such claim (perhaps herding cattle through lands cultivated by other groups like the Fulani of northern Nigeria or ranging broadly over deserts or forests also used by other groups like the Kalahari Bushmen). Most such groups, in any case, think of government as a property of what sociologists describe as the kin group – all those people descended from a common ancestor or married to such persons. Hence the idea of the 'blood brother' (familiar from cowboy films) – to become a member of the group it is necessary either to marry into it or be adopted as a member of a particular small family group.

Still more startling to the modern Western citizen than such groups' relative indifference to the idea of a territory being subject to a particular code of law is the absence in some of them of anything resembling a fixed governmental organisation. Whilst the absence of a chief or council might not be regarded as so strange in tiny groups such as the !Kung bushmen of the Kalahari desert (Marshall (1961)), it seems almost incredible in groups numbering as many as a million or more such as the pre-colonial Tiv of Nigeria (Bohannan (1965)).

How can centralised political institutions be avoided in such societies? One explanation lies in the attitude to law found in most tribal societies. Whilst Western societies (following the nineteenth-century English jurist Austin) tend to see law as the creation of a sovereign representative legislature (or at least of some group of citizens acting through recognised constitutional procedures), tribal societies see law as a part of the way of life inherited by the group from its ancestors. Thus living human beings only interpret and enforce the authority of the ancestors. Hence no legislature is necessary. Such a view is clearly only tenable in relatively stable societies – although, as Gluckman (1965) points out, rebellion against those interpreting the law is perfectly possible in such a system. What is unthinkable is the revolutionary process of replacing existing laws with new ones. The inflexibility of such a system can easily be exaggerated since, in practice, as with English common law, old laws can be reinterpreted in new circumstances or quietly ignored as being no longer appropriate.

But does not the enforcement of law and the defence of the group require centralised government? The example of the Tiv suggests one way round this problem. They operated what the social anthropologists term a 'segmentary lineage system'. This means basically that every Tiv's place in society is governed by the lineage to which they belong – i.e. how they are descended from the ancestor of the group, 'Tiv'. It is not that the more closely related you are to the founder of the tribe the more important you are – there is no royal family since all are held to descend from the same source. Thus, every Tiv is equal and a fierce egalitarianism reigns. Instead, in any dispute people claiming descent in the same line are expected to take sides together. Naturally, should non-Tiv attack Tiv, all members of the group would be expected to assist if need be (starting with those most closely related to those attacked). If fighting or quarrelling takes place between Tiv, however, support would be due to people in 'your' lineage.

Such a system seems, at first sight, merely to encourage conflict and disorder. If everyone can rely on a host of supporters in a dispute with others, will not disputes be the order of the day, especially in a situation where there are no established permanent tribal chiefs or headmen (in the sense this is usually understood)? There seems to be no doubt that the Tiv are inclined to stick up for themselves fairly aggressively (in modern Nigeria they have frequently come into conflict with their more conservative neighbours as well as formerly being a traditional recruiting ground for the British colonial armed forces).

In fact, though, the system seems to have worked well in practice. One reason for this was the existence of a considerable consensus on the customs (laws) to be applied. Disputes were not automatically the subject of violence or warfare but settled through meetings (or 'moots') of those concerned in the broad, Tiv, sense. After a certain amount of more or less violent posturing, the form was for all to have their say on the rights and wrongs of the dispute with relatives helping the aggrieved sides to present their case. Then a resolution of the dispute was attempted by mediation between the two lineages. If a solution could not be found, the two groups would remain 'at daggers drawn' until a solution could be found. In such a situation a premium was placed on a bargaining and reconciliation rather than mechanical law enforcement. Many of those on either side might not feel too deeply affronted by (say) an alleged case of adultery, failure to pay up on a dowry payment or words said in a drunken brawl – but they would be severely inconvenienced if the other lineage in the village was not prepared to cooperate in the next hunt or harvest. An additional subtlety which modified any tendency to take disputes too far was the consideration that your opponents in this dispute might be needed in a larger dispute with more distantly related Tiv at some time in the future!

The Tiv are only one example of numerous tribal societies which existed without centralised governmental institutions. Many have used some variation of the combination of 'feuding' and informal reconciliation systems practised by them. Additionally though, disputes might be settled by resort to oracles like the famous classical Greek oracle at Delphi, in which disputes were arbitrated upon using magical signs resulting from sacrifices. The ambiguity of some of these pronouncements may well have been a sensible political device on the part of the oracle or medicine man to avoid identification with either side and promote a negotiated settlement. Other societies practised a division of functions on an 'age grade' basis in which, for instance, the oldest men might collectively manage relationships with the Gods, another male age group constitute the leaders of the hunt, the oldest women practise medicine, and so on. In some groups important functions connected with warfare, law and order, or magic might be vested in secret or title societies, membership of which had to be earned by feasting existing members, undergoing initiation ceremonies and performing subordinate roles in a trainee grade. In such societies skill in magic or warfare might be rewarded by promotion 'on merit' or promotion might depend upon seniority. Authority in such societies might thus rest upon a variety of foundations – a reputation for wisdom in settling disputes, knowledge of traditional remedies for illness or magic, ability as a war leader or merely being the grandfather of a very large (polygamous) family. Such authority figures might well be known by a title which translates into English as 'chief' – but their powers were often far from the absolute despotisms imagined by many early Western writers on these subjects. (Of course, chiefs in some tribal societies did have what we might regard as 'despotic' authority, e.g. Sharka the Zulu chief who ordered whole battalions of his men to commit suicide as a demonstration of his absolute authority.)

In these tribal 'stateless societies' then, there is law rather than anarchy (in the everyday sense of no guarantees of law and order); equally, collective decisions on self-defence and economic co-operation are also made, but in a decentralised fashion. Many members of these societies would also emphasise that collective activities also occur on a spiritual level. In short, life continues and even apparently prospers without the state with its accompanying mechanisms of professional armies, bureaucrats, prisons and the like.

It is not surprising that, consequently, some modern thinkers – anarchists in the technical sense – have argued that the same is possible in a modern context. We shall examine their views at more length in Chapter 3. First, however, it is interesting to look at another example of what might be described as 'politics without the state', although this is perhaps a slightly more arguable case.

Politics without the state: feudalism

This second example is the feudal system – particularly as it was practised in Europe in the eleventh and twelfth centuries. Feudalism has also been observed to apply in many other parts of the world, most notably in pre-modern Japan (Reischauer (1956), Prawer and Eisenstadt (1968)). European feudalism is of interest as being perhaps 'nearer to home' for contemporary European readers and as showing the state as we understand it to be a more recent innovation than some may have imagined. It may also suggest some lessons for the future of Europe.

At first sight, feudal Europe was full of states and mini-states, rather than stateless. Did not England, France, Poland and other familiar states already exist in this period – admittedly accompanied by extra 'players' on the international scene like Burgundy, Saxony and Venice? The appearance of kings, dukes and doges on the scene would seem to indicate the presence of strong centralised decision making institutions for these territories. The similarity of names with institutions and territories of later periods may well, however, be quite misleading. Outside of England and France particularly, it soon becomes clear that the idea of a number of territories each with its own legal jurisdiction is quite inappropriate. This is clearest in the area round about what is now Germany – where what was misleadingly called the Holy Roman Empire (accurately described as neither 'Holy', 'Roman' nor an 'Empire' by Voltaire [1694–1778] ('Essai sur les moeurs et l'espirit des nations', LXX) masked a confusing array of jurisdictions. The 'Holy Roman Emperor' was the nominal supreme ruler of a hotpotch of kingdoms, dukedoms, sovereign bishoprics, independent or federated cities and the like. His powers over each were different and ill-defined, the heads of some of these territories having the power to elect the Emperor's successor. The Catholic Church, in the shape of the Pope, claimed powers over the Emperor and his 'vassals' (those who had sworn allegiance to him), which in later times were felt to be 'sovereign' prerogatives. Equally, the Church claimed exclusive jurisdiction over all the clergy and over many matters of family law – as well as rights to censorship and the levying of separate clerical 'taxes'. In some cases, incumbents of independent kingdoms such as France and Spain held territory within the Empire as nominal vassals of the Emperor or some other 'ruler'. Similar confusions were to be seen in relationships between the King of England in his capacity as Duke of Normandy and the King of France.

In effect, law enforcement and defence were the subject of a patchwork of rights and privileges, which were mainly the consequence of a pyramid of personal relationships between lord and vassal, with each vassal, in turn, being lord to an inferior group of lords, until one descends to the level of the ordinary knight in his manor. At the aristocratic level, the possession of land entailed not only something like the modern idea of ownership but, perhaps more, the notion of government. In principle, in the early feudal period, land could only be held by those prepared to administer and, most importantly, defend it. Hence, only adult fighting men could hold land. If, for instance, the King gave land to a duke, the only way he could hope to hold it was by sub-contracting the administration and defence of much of it to a group of earls or counts, who in turn would obtain the allegiance of knights to hold particular manors, or fortified villages.

One consequence of this is, logically, an overlapping of jurisdictions in that the same area would be under the control of (in our example) a king, a duke, a count and a knight. Undoubtedly, the church would also claim jurisdiction in some cases. For that matter, it was common for hard-up lords to grant jurisdiction in commercial matters to town councils through charters – the terms of which some councils in Britain are still preserving and attempting to enforce!

In practice, lords were interested primarily in matters relating to their feudal dues – the equivalent of modern taxation and rents originally primarily payable in labour services. The lord might quite frequently originate from a different part of Europe, linguistically and culturally from his serfs – so that they would often prefer to seek justice through informal community channels. Amongst lords, appeals to judgement by legalistic tribunals were often eschewed in favour of trial by combat or, as Bloch (1961) describes, through the pursuit of feuds or vendettas which could operate in very similar ways to the system described earlier in relation to the Tiv (though in a more bloodthirsty manner on the whole).

Thus, it is clear that in the feudal period, as in tribal stateless societies, individuals could be in conflict over the allocation of resources and these conflicts be resolved; communities also made decisions about their defence and economic welfare; but no effective and centralised state machinery existed to carry this out.

It is worth, at this stage, also suggesting some of the origins of this system since this will be found to be of considerable relevance to a number of disputes we will consider later on. On a broad political level, this system can be seen as the product of a tribal invasion by groups like the Vikings, Goths and Huns of a Europe previously governed as a part of a vast and sophisticated Empire (Rome still dominated the European imagination – although the Western Empire was long gone at this period). Economically, the disruption of constant invasions had led to declining production and a lack of currency, so that a cash economy could no longer be sustained. In terms of military technology, an important factor is the importance of the heavily armoured man on horseback – the medieval equivalent of a tank – who required the economic resources of the best part of a village to support, and intensive and long training.

Culturally, it is also worth pointing to the dominance of Catholicism – which helped to unify Europe round common standards. For instance, the Crusades brought people from all over Europe together and helped to generate a consensus on knightly behaviour – which admittedly had little to do with Gospel standards. 'Chivalry' may have had rather more to do with common understandings about making warfare and landlording more secure and desirable occupations than they might otherwise be, than with gallantry towards the female and weak, but clearly shared standards of behaviour were evolved which enabled medieval Europe to function.

States without nations: kingdoms

At a later stage in European history, some individual feudal territories evolved into something much more like a modern state. Kingdoms emerged with distinct boundaries within which central authorities claimed exclusive jurisdiction, sophisticated judicial systems with rights of appeal from local courts up to the centre, a taxation system divorced from the rents payable to the owners of land and, in some cases, representative legislative assemblies. Part of the attraction of the Protestant Reformation for princes was the opportunity to assert both legal control over matters such as family law which had previously been Church matters, and to reassign extensive Church property holdings to themselves and their supporters. Henry VIII's example in these matters was accompanied by similar phenomena in countries such as Sweden, whilst even Catholic monarchs such as Louis XIV began to assert control over religious orders and to negotiate greater influence over the Church in their territory. (Warning: several centuries of European history have been telescoped into one paragraph here!)

In essence, similar political institutions to these kingdoms were also be found in many other parts of the world. For instance, in what is now Nigeria at about the same period it seems likely that sizeable kingdoms existed in Benin, Yorubaland (Oyo) and in Hausaland (Kano etc.), whilst earlier such kingdoms were to be found in India and Central America.

By definition, a kingdom can be regarded an example of *dynastic* politics. That is, they are not so much governments by individuals as by families. In the European examples this usually meant that the state was regarded as all the possessions of a single family regardless of geographical sense or the ethnic or national origins. Thus, the United Kingdom included Scotland, all or parts of Ireland and Wales, as well as Calais and the Channel Islands (ignoring for the moment the more far-flung colonies), because the Kings of England inherited these areas from the Duchy of Normandy, succeeded to the separate throne of Scotland, or conquered adjacent lands. The Kingdom was not united by linguistic, cultural or religious similarities. For some time other members of the family were frequently expected to take a major role in government – queens ruling in the absence of kings, the eldest son of the Crown of England being designated Prince of Wales. Similarly, the Low Countries could be regarded as a possession of the Spanish royal family. Within a royal family, rival claims to the succession could arise and conflict between young supporters of the heir to the throne and established counsellors of the king were virtually the norm.

In the African examples mentioned, the family's role took drastically different shapes. Within the context of polygamy there was more scope for dispute as to succession, such disputes taking the most drastic form in Zululand where it was usual for the king to execute any brothers who failed to go into hasty voluntary exile (LeMarchand (1977). In the Yoruba kingdoms a more constitutional version of the succession crisis involved 'kingmakers' selecting the heir from the ranks of a number of princely families who each provided a king in turn.

Most of these monarchic political systems shared a 'court' style of politics in which the administration of the royal household and its estates were inseparable from the business of the kingdom as a whole. Power in such systems might well reside primarily with those who most frequently had the ear of the monarch regardless of official position – and including the king's mistress, confessor or hairdresser! The politics of such a system is primarily conducted within a consensus on fundamental values (those of the tribe or ruling aristocracy) with an emphasis on individual advancement through patronage; a powerful patron rewards his supporters and followers with benefits derived from his control or influence over government which might well be regarded as corruption in a contemporary democracy.

The assumption may often be made that a monarchic state is a 'despotic' one in which the monarch's will is final. This seems to be far from the case in practice. First, the monarch's position is usually a traditional one. The same tradition which places the king in power frequently sets distinct limits upon the exercise of it. The king may be seen as divinely sanctioned and protected, but this implies that he respects the religious feeling of his people. These may be expressed by religious authorities – archbishops, high priests or synods – who are regarded as equally legitimate within their spheres as the monarch is in his. A good example of the sort of limit which might apply is to consider the important area of taxation. In the African kingdoms mentioned, Hausa kings were traditionally entitled to levy taxes, but the Yoruba kings could only rely upon a traditional level of offerings on specified occasions. Even the strongest English monarchs required the approval of the Houses of Parliament, particularly the House of Commons, to levy taxes – although they might be able to manipulate a favourable majority by the use of patronage.

The practical limits on the exercise of royal power also include the frequent lack of any strongly developed administrative machinery, particularly at local level, so that the king might effectively have to persuade nobles/gentry and municipalities to cooperate. The political capacity of the occupant of the throne was, obviously, also a vital consideration. When minors succeeded to the throne, such a system might, in effect, become government by a committee of prominent court members, whilst the chief minister of a foolish or lazy king might easily have effective power. In the Japanese case, the Shōgun or prime minister became the effective power for centuries, becoming in turn an hereditary office.

Although kingdoms of the type described are now rare, they are not extinct (see for instance Kuwait, Nepal and Saudi Arabia) and the dominance of this type of political organisation for many centuries in many parts of the world is a caution against assuming contemporary state forms are inevitable. Furthermore, many of the concepts we have introduced here, such as political patronage and even court politics, can still be applied in contemporary political systems; consider the Reagan White House in which the Chief Executive's wife's astrologer is alleged to have been vitally influential!

States without nations: empires

Perhaps still more remote from contemporary experience is the concept of empire. Yet this is a form of rule which has dominated large parts of the globe for millenia, let alone centuries. The most notable examples upon which we shall concentrate at first are the ancient empires of China and Rome. But similar structures were to be found in India (e.g. the Moghul Empire), in Africa (amongst the Egyptians and in Mali) and in Central and South America (e.g. the Aztecs). Nor should it be forgotten that, more recently, each of the European nations sought to create colonial empires in Africa, Asia and the Americas, whilst the USA and the former USSR could both be accused of having colonial possessions by other names.

It is tempting, and not totally misleading, to attribute the longevity of many empires to the military advantage of a large and powerful state surrounded by much smaller states or tribal territories. Whilst empires may be briefly built on military advantage alone as, perhaps, was that of Alexander the Great, the longer-lasting examples can be attributed not only to size but also to the advantages of a 'civilised' culture in the literal sense of a society centred upon relatively large urban centres containing specialised personnel who contributed technical and organisational advantages to the empire. The prestige and and self-esteem associated with such systems may well help them to survive. Certainly the ruling groups of the Chinese, Roman and British Empires were all firmly convinced of the superiority of their cultural inheritance over that of the rest of the world and successfully imparted this ideology to many of their subjects and neighbours. However, this conviction did not prevent such systems from adopting and adapting to useful features of surrounding societies. The history of China is particularly noteworthy for the way in which the Empire was militarily subdued on a number of occasions by warlike tribes from the periphery, but the conquerors on each occasion came to be merely a new ruling group operating a very similar political system to the one they had defeated (Eberhardt (1977)). The adaptability of the Romans is well illustrated by their reactions to Greek culture in the early period and the transformation from the Classical Empire based on Rome into the Byzantine Christian Empire based on Constantinople. One vital feature of such systems is the way the rulers must be prepared to tolerate linguistic, cultural and religious diversity, providing subjects are prepared to make the necessary political compromises with the primary needs of the empire.

Such empires have generally been characterised by the development of an extensive cash economy, permitting complex economic exchanges over long distances. These same distances have required efficient means of communication amongst the 'civil servants' of the empire, who must also be capable of working together in a coordinated fashion. The empire can only survive militarily by deploying its military resources over long distances to optimum effect. Thus, literacy and bureaucracy as well as good roads (or a navy) and professional soldiers, become a necessity.

The Chinese Mandarinate is a good illustration of many of these themes (Gerth and Mills (1948, Chs VIII and XVII)). China was unified for centuries by an administrative pyramid of Mandarins, linking the court and the rural districts, who were required to pass examinations in a common core of knowledge. This was centred upon literary and historical texts and was mostly concerned with developing an educated gentleman with a good knowledge of ritual. Good government was mainly seen in terms of political stability rather than social and economic progress. Some writers stress the role of the

Chinese bureaucracy in regulating the drainage and waterways system of China just as the Egyptian priesthood served the Pharaoh, sacrificed to the Gods, and controlled the waters of the Nile through an elaborate drainage system (Wittfogel (1957) 17–18, 26–7). Whatever the usefulness of the services they performed, it is clear the cohesion of the system was vastly assisted by the common origins, knowledge and attitudes of these administrators who were amongst the first who could reasonably be described as 'bureaucrats'.

Empires and bureaucracy

Weber (Gerth and Mills (1948, Ch. VIII)) convincingly described some of the key characteristics of bureaucracy (literally government by offices) which, he said, 'compares with other organisations exactly as does the machine with non-mechanical means of production': (see Box 4).

Although bureaucracy may have originated in the needs of empires for the efficient administration of huge territories, it is clear that it has flourished most mightily in more recent times in meeting the needs of massive industrial populations, all of whom need to be treated alike in the name of democracy. The analysis of bureaucratic administration in such circumstances must be one of the major preoccupations of political studies in our own time, and we will consider this further at a later stage.

Empires and race

Returning to the analysis of empires, one final point is worth emphasising – the contrast between the ancient empires and the nineteenth- and twentieth-century European colonial empires in their attitudes towards their subjects. Basically, this may be encapsulated in one rather nasty word – racism. The European empires increasingly were based upon a core metropolitan state which claimed to be a nation and often a democracy. The empire was a separate area of colonies whose dependence on the metropolitan area could only be easily justified by an allegation of the incapacity of their inhabitants to rule themselves. Nineteenth-century anthropologists' findings were used

Box 4   Bureaucracy

Characteristics:

(a) Fixed and official jurisdictional areas
  – official 'duties', stable rules, methodically carried out
  (Specialisation)
(b) Official hierarchy
  – pyramid of officials each reporting up to level above
  (Integration)
(c) Use of files
  (Organisational memory)
(d) Official activity as full-time work
  – no conflict between private and public interests
  (Dedication)
(e) Expert training of officials
  (Technical competence and ésprit de corps)
(f) Corpus of rules
  (Predictability)

Likely context:

(a) A Money economy
(b) Large political units with extensive functions
(c) Developed communications

and abused to justify a doctrine of the racial or cultural inferiority of 'coloured' people compared with the 'white' race. In theory, official attitudes might not quite go so far as to allege permanent inferiority on the part of the governed. British policy in principle was based on grooming colonies for self-governing 'dominion' status (like the white ex-colonies of Australia, New Zealand and Canada), whilst the French, for instance, were much more prepared to accord equal right to 'natives' if they assimilated French culture and behaved as black

Frenchmen. However, the Nazi view of the permanent inferiority of 'non-Aryan' races probably reflected the practice of European colonial residents more accurately for most of the nineteenth and early twentieth centuries. The near extermination of the aboriginal inhabitants of Tasmania and the South African colonists' doctrine of Apartheid being cases in point.

In contrast to this, the Chinese restricted their empire mainly to groups who could be assimilated into the Chinese way of life, though viewing groups outside the empire as racially and culturally inferior, and the Romans extended Roman citizenship to a number of other urban centres and made no systematic discrimination between Italian, Greek or African subjects.

Nations and states

Earlier we took the state to be, in Weber's words, an organisation having 'the monopoly of the legitimate use of force in a given territorial area' but suggested that the model of government and the state which this may suggest – of a world dominated by sovereign 'nation-states' – is a relatively arguable and new one. Europe did not look much like this until about 1919 after the Treaty of Versailles, and Africa, not until the 1960s. Countries like the United Kingdom (as we saw earlier) and – until recently – the Soviet Union and Yugoslavia are (or were) clearly multinational. The Antarctic remains the subject of (frozen!) conflicting claims to jurisdiction.

We shall examine questions of national and ethnic identity at greater length in Chapter 5, but it is worth noting here that states with a one-to-one relationship with an unambiguous 'nationality' are difficult, or impossible, to find. Thus, even France, one of the originators of the doctrine, is still faced with regional identities such as Breton and Basque, some of which would prefer an independent existence. Conversely, Switzerland, Belgium and Canada all contain considerable French minorities to complicate their national identities. Nor are these isolated examples; virtually every African country is the product of the more or less arbitrary drawing of lines on the map in the nineteenth century so that, for example, modern Nigeria contains three major – and many minor – population groups, with two of the major groups – the Yoruba and the Hausa – being found in substantial numbers in neighbouring states. In the Middle East many Arabs aspire to the union of all Arab, or – which is not the same thing – Islamic, states. Many post-colonial states thus have a relatively fragile sense of national identity.

The nation-state and sovereignty

Although nation-states are thus difficult to come by in practice, the predominant theory of the state today, as incorporated in the concept of the United Nations and in international law, is that of 'sovereign states' whose legitimacy is based mainly on the idea that each nation has a right of self-determination. The people of a nation thus are seen to consent to the establishment of a government over them which supports a system of law appropriate to their culture and traditions. This idea came clearly to the fore in human history only with the French and American revolutions at the end of the eighteenth century.

The model of government in which a nation makes decisions through a state machinery, although helpful in justifying the establishment of self-governing democratic systems in opposition to alien or autocratic rule, arguably becomes an obstacle to understanding the working of a modern sophisticated liberal democratic state. As noted earlier, these are usually divided into executive, legislative and judicial arms, and central, local and regional levels, of government. The outcome of the constitutional working of these specific institutions of government can – and should – be regarded as the 'nation's' decision. An oversimplification which is, however, often put forward is that some individual element in the constitutional structure is the body which incorporates the national will. In the French tradition there has been a tendency to see the national assembly as that body. In the United Kingdom the government has sometimes tried to take the same line – as in a recent official secrets case in which it argued that for civil servants the national interest and the government's interest are the same thing. The Soviet tradition, of course, was to see the Communist Party in an analogous position. In the liberal tradition, however, the distinction between the government of the day and the state – between opposition and treason – is a clear and vital one.

Types of state

Clearly, modern states vary a great deal in their organisation and in their concept of the role of government. Bernard Crick (1993) has suggested a good starting point for the classification of states which brings out some of these differences. He distinguishes between republican, autocratic and totalitarian states (Box 5).

These categories, are, however, extremely 'broad-brush' as can be seen from the variety of examples quoted in each.

Autocratic regimes were probably more common in the past than today, but they are far from extinct , particularly in the 'South'. Derbyshire and Derbyshire (1991) classified 165 states by regime type and concluded there were 16 'nationalistic socialist', 12 'authoritarian nationalist', 14 'military authoritarian' and 11 'absolutist' regimes – total of 53 (or 32 per cent) in the mid-1980s. These regimes were mainly in Africa, but with three from Asia and one each from South America and Oceania.

Most modern 'republican' regimes could be described as 'liberal democratic' in that they are not only constitutional but also have representative institutions based on universal suffrage (one man or woman, one vote). However, historically, there were many states like eighteenth-century England which had some respect for individual rights and a constitutional form of government, without being fully democratic. Classical Athens was not in our sense fully 'democratic' since women, slaves and resident foreigners did not vote, although all full citizens could participate directly in debate and voting on matters of public policy. Similarly, Renaissance city-states like Venice had participative, but not fully democratic, forms of constitutional rule. As is evident from the use of eighteenth-century Britain as an example, Crick is not using 'republican' in its usual sense of 'not monarchic' but in the broader sense of a state whose affairs are public. Derbyshire and Derbyshire (1991) classified 50 states as liberal democratic systems (mainly in Europe (16), Central America and the Caribbean (13) and Oceania (9)), together with 51 'emergent democracies' scattered broadly across the globe. Thus, roughly 61 per cent of modern states can be seen as 'republican'

The category of 'totalitarian' state has been criticised as too

Box 5   Autocratic, republican, totalitarian states

Autocratic

Public interest defined by government. Subjects' involvement in politics seen as suspicious/subversive. Government's role mainly limited to taxation, foreign policy, etc.

In 'private affairs' citizens pursue their own happiness without interference.

E.g. monarchic governments of eighteenth century etc., many third world military regimes.

Republican

Government as a constitutional process in which disparate group views on the public interest are reconciled through a political process of discussion.

Government may intervene in economic and social affairs to maintain public interest and minimum welfare standards for all.

In 'private affairs' citizens pursue their own happiness without interference.

E.g. eighteenth-century Britain, classical Athens, modern liberal democracies.

Totalitarian

Government defines public interest which is all-inclusive. Political opposition is treason.

No private sphere – good citizens participate enthusiastically in rebuilding society. Official ideology defines happiness.

E.g. Hitler's Germany, Stalin's Soviet Union.

SOURCE After Crick (1964)

tightly drawn to contain or at least to usefully describe any modern states 'Totalitarian' state was not a term coined by Crick, nor do all authors using the term emphasise those elements of Crick's treatment which have been highlighted here. For more on the controversy surrounding the term for political analysis see Freidrich (1964). 'Totalitarianism' is usually used loosely to describe communist, fascist and racist regimes. (For further discussion of this concept see Chapter 4, pp.78–9) But clearly the intention of such a category is to include both extreme right (fascist) and extreme left (communist) regimes. The former Soviet Bloc (eight states in the Derbyshires' study) and Apartheid South Africa might be candidates for this description totalling approximately 5 per cent of states but a much higher proportion of the world's population in the 1980s.

Democracy, the welfare state and the market

In recent years the number of liberal democratic states has dramatically increased, with the disintegration of the Soviet Bloc and a marked trend to democratisation in Latin America. The Derbyshires (1991, 237) note a 25 per cent growth in the number of liberal democracies from 1989 to the end of 1990. We could go further and assert that free elections along with a competitive free economy (modified by some commitment to a welfare state) has become in some sense the norm for a modern state. In Europe, for instance, the members of the European Union are all states of this type and the non-members of the EU almost all aspire to obtaining membership, which requires a commitment to democracy, the free market (capitalism) and a minimum standard of social policy.

The relationship between democracy, capitalism and the welfare state is, therefore, central to the study of politics. We shall explore what these terms mean and the extent they require or contradict each other. But at this stage it is worth emphasising that this combination of characteristics is historically quite rare and has by no means always been thought to be either desirable or necessary.

Democracy is a concept with a long history, but it comes as a surprise to many modern readers to find that, until the twentieth century, it was more often a term of abuse than praise. In classical

Greece, for instance, where the term originated, it was commonly understood as 'mob rule'. As described above, Ancient Greek democracy did not involve elections (officials being selected by lot) and manhood suffrage (i.e. the election of parliaments by all men – but not women) only became a common institution in the nineteenth century. Even Britain, France and the United States have only achieved universal suffrage since the end of the Second World War: university graduates had an additional vote in the UK until 1948; women only achieved the vote in France in 1945; black voters in the South were effectively disenfranchised until the implementation of the 1968 Civil Rights Act. The welfare state is a slippery term to define (see Chapter 8, p.195), but British readers may be surprised to discover that it cannot be said to have originated with the Labour victory in Britain in 1945. Many of the moves towards a welfare state in Britain were a reaction to the prior development of welfarism in Bismarck's Germany (an autocratic rather than a liberal democratic state), whilst the communist regimes of Eastern Europe claimed to have more comprehensive welfare states than any liberal democratic state. On the contrary, many US commentators have seen welfarism as the enemy of democracy.

Capitalism predated democracy in Britain, whilst in some parts of the world (e.g. Allende's Chile) the development of liberal democracy has been seen as a distinct menace to capitalism and resisted for this reason. Indeed, to use Greek political terminology, it might be argued that the natural form of government for a capitalist economy (allowing, as it does, the accumulation of large quantities of wealth in relatively few hands) is oligarchy (government by the (rich) few) rather than democracy (government by the (poor) many).

Politics between states

Already in this book, besides considering politics in many other times and places, we have looked at politics at a variety of levels within society. Thus, in considering the politics of everyday life (Chapter 1), we looked at politics in the family and in organisations such as firms; then, in relation to politics at state level, we saw that states are divided into national or state, regional and local levels. This division of state politics into various levels is something which we shall explore in more depth later on (Chapter 6). However, there is another level at which many people are already aware of politics going on, and that is the international level.

If we conceive of the world in terms of the nation-state model already described, then international politics looks much more like the politics of stateless societies than the internal politics of states. That is, there is something called international law, but there is no final authority to enforce, interpret or change it. Although the United Nations can be seen as a potential world legislature/government, it is at present based on the theory that individual states possess 'sovereignty' and are the final arbiters of what goes on within their territories. All powers of international organisations, including the United Nations, are held to depend upon the agreement of states to treaties authorising such powers.

Thus, politics at international level can be seen to depend on compromise and negotiation rather than upon authoritative decision-making by representative organs. In legal theory Monaco is as sovereign as the United States of America, and both are equally free to resort to force in the last resort to defend their national interests and to go back upon their international treaty obligations. In political practice, it is clear that smaller states, with less in the way of military and economic resources to back up their bargaining, are more dependent on the perhaps insubstantial ground of international respect for law and treaty obligations. From the point of view of the study of politics, international relations offers a particular challenge, since the processes of decision-making are often even more obscure than at national level and the consequences potentially more profound. Traditionally, historians tended to describe international relations in terms of the decisions of individual statesmen pursuing, more or less intelligently, 'the national interest', which was often related to the 'balance of power' between nations. Thus, international relations can be seen as a game, played between more or less rational players, largely of what we previously termed a 'zero-sum' variety – more power for one nation being gained at the expense of less for another, with skilful players achieving goals by forming winning coalitions.

This account can be criticised from a number of viewpoints.

First, seeing international relations as a competitive spectator sport neglects the importance consensual, non-zero-sum goals in international relations. In plain English, it is more important to ordinary citizens that everyone stays alive and continues in mutually beneficial economic and trading activities than that they belong to a state which is more powerful than the others.

This in turn relates to the question of the 'national interest'. We have seen something of the difficulty in defining a nation – e.g. can it be assumed that the English have the same interests as the Welsh? Similarly, professional politicians may experience much more satisfaction from being part of a powerful state than a simple peasant might. Again if, say, in the nineteenth century, British investors' rights in some Latin American country are safeguarded at the loss of a number of sailors' lives, does the safeguarding of one group's (relatively large) income justify the loss of several poor men's lives? The 'national interest', then, may obscure domestic conflicts of interest by wrapping them in the national flag.

In practice, to describe national policy-making in terms of individuals making choices may be a vast oversimplification, as Allison's (1987) work makes clear. In his analysis of the Cuba crisis, in which the United States was faced by a Soviet attempt to install ballistic missiles at sites in Cuba, he shows how not only the President and the Secretary of State were involved in the decision-making process, but also the perceptions of the Central Intelligence Agency (CIA), the professional military, the US representative at the UN and others. Assumptions about the motives of the other 'side' and the reactions of potential allies, and – of course – the electorate, were also seen to be crucial. Allison argues that for a full picture of the foreign policy process, decision-making must be seen as part of the processes of organisational decision-making and of political bargaining.

Politics beyond the state: international institutions

The United Nations General Assembly is in many ways an unconvincing 'world parliament' since it is based on the equal representation of giant countries (in population terms) like Brazil and Russia with mini-states like The Gambia and Luxembourg. Nor can a body which allowed dictators like 'Papa Doc' Duvalier of Haiti or General Amin of Uganda to misrepresent the populations they terrorised be seen to possess great legitimacy. As for the Security Council, the potential world 'government', at least the institution of Permanent Members (USA, China, Russia, Britain, France – each with a veto over any decision by the Council) has the merit of political realism, in that the UN cannot be expected to act effectively without great power agreement. Alas, until the 1990s, this meant virtually all effective action by the UN was stillborn. Even now, with apparently greater consensus on police actions versus Iraq and humanitarian action in the former Yugoslavia, the UN is handicapped by the lack of effective executive apparatus, whilst Europe is overrepresented, and the 'South' unrepresented amongst the Permanent Members.

However, focusing on major political decisions at the summit level of international organisations may well be a misleading guide to their importance and potential. The examples of NATO and of the European Union (EU) suggest that, when international organisations serve what is seen as a clear and necessary purpose, genuine and effective multinational co-operation is possible. Both of these are of considerable interest in that they have exercised powers which are commonly seen as fundamental activities of 'sovereign states' on a collective basis.

The EU is also of considerable interest in terms of the future direction of world politics in that it is an international organisation which has developed, to some extent, independent executive, legislative and judicial powers. Thus, although the Council of Ministers, consisting of representatives of the constituent governments (on a one minister, one state basis) retains the final executive and legislative powers within the Union and individual states have an ill-defined power to delay decisions indefinitely which they see as counter to their vital interests, on most matters individual governments can be overridden by a majority of other governments. Still more revolutionary, an independent executive authority (the Commission) exists not only to implement Council of Ministers' decisions but also to formulate a 'Community view' representing the whole of Europe. The European Court of Justice and the Commission have direct powers to intervene within European states, regardless of their individual government's views, and the directly elected European

Parliament has major budgetary and legislative powers as well as the power to sack the Commission.

Another example of the way international bodies are working effectively in the modern world can be found when one considers such obscure bodies as the International Standards Organisation (ISO) or the International Telecommunications Union (ITU). Bodies like these hammer out essential technical agreements which enable telephones across the world to operate as one vast international network; enable computer manufacturers on opposite sides of the globe to manufacture equipment which will work together: and agree on common scientific units in which new discoveries can be expressed.

Politics as a universal activity

One interesting point, then, about our brief excursion into international relations is that the more they are analysed, the less important the differences between international and domestic politics seem to be. Developing this further, it can be argued that explaining relationships between member states and the EU is very like explaining relationships between the states and the federal government in the USA. Equally, insights from domestic politics and even the politics of stateless societies can be of relevance to international politics.

To return to the theme introduced at the beginning of this chapter, the evidence presented suggests that politics in the broad sense we defined it in Chapter 1 is a more or less universal aspect of life in human societies. Strictly speaking, we have not established this – only produced evidence that politics is widespread in many human societies. For further discussion see 'Human Nature and politics' in Chapter 3. We have established, however, that centralised national governments, although a dominating feature of modern western societies, are by no means inevitable.

Recommended reading

Fortes, M. and Evans-Pritchard, E.E., 1961, *African Political Systems*, Oxford, Oxford University Press. Fascinating series of case studies of tribal politics.

Prawer, J. and Eisenstadt, S.N., 1968, 'Feudalism' in Sills, David L. (ed.), *International Encyclopaedia of Social Sciences*, New York, Macmillan, Vol. 5, 393–403. Excellent short introduction, many other useful articles in the same publication.

Eisenstadt, S.N., 1969, *The Political System of Empires: The Rise and Fall of Historical Bureaucratic Empires*, London. A classic of historical sociology – perhaps a little long for beginners.

Anderson, Benedict, 1991, *Imagined Communities: Reflections on the Origin and Spread of Nationalism*, 2nd edn, London, Verso. A highly regarded analysis of a key aspect of the modern world – nationalism.

Baylis, John and Renger, N.J., (eds), 1992, *Dilemmas of World Politics: International Issues in A Changing World*, Oxford, Oxford University Press. Gives a good idea of contemporary debates on International Relations.

Chapter 3

Ideas

Ideas and politics

This chapter explores some of the fundamental debates which, historically, have occurred about the nature of politics and of the state. Although we approach these issues here in a somewhat abstract and academic manner, it should not be forgotten that in many cases disagreements about these issues have been rooted in historical conflicts of great practical importance. Thus, it is no coincidence that many of the key English writers on such matters – for example, Hobbes [1588–1679] and Locke [1632–1704] – wrote around the time of the English Civil War when the nature of state authority was central to political events, or that major contributors to debates on the nature of revolution or nationalism (Lenin [1870–1924], Machiavelli [1469–1527]) themselves played important roles in the political events of their own times.

In the next chapter we consider how views on these issues frequently link together into more or less

consistent political worldviews or 'ideologies' and the impact these have had in shaping practical politics.

Human nature and politics

One of the major divisions in politics is about the relationship between human nature and politics. Philosophers, theologians and psychologists as well as political scientists have argued as to the inevitability of conflict and aggression amongst human beings (in this context perhaps significantly usually referred to as 'Man'). On the Right, Hobbes, de Maistre, Nietzsche [1844–1900] and others have seen conflict, violence and a struggle for dominance as intrinsic to human nature with a consequent need for a strong state to enforce peace; on the Left, the potential for consensus and co-operation among human beings has been emphasised by writers such as Thomas More [1478–1535], Locke, Rousseau [1712–88] and Tolstoy [1828–1910]. On the Right, conflict and aggression are seen as 'natural', whilst on the Left such behaviour is seen as learned.

Evidence on this key issue of 'nature versus nurture' is both plentiful and inconclusive and the reader is referred to standard texts on social psychology and anthropology for details. Summarising brutally, however, if we examine evidence from studies of genetically identical individuals it is found that they do differ in such characteristics as intelligence (and, presumably, aggressive temperament) when brought up in different families within the same society, although not so much as genetically different individuals do. Thus, there appears to be both a genetic and a social component to 'human nature' (Eysenck and Kamin (1981), Rutter and Madge (1976)). An examination of the expectations about human nature to be found in different societies shows that they do seem to differ quite radically – especially in simple or tribal societies. Thus, there are groups such as the Zuni Indians of New Mexico which place a premium on co-operation and consensus and expect and obtain a very low level of aggression from their members; whilst other groups, such as the Dobu of New Guinea, base their whole social structure on the assumption of mutual competition and aggression. Benedict suggests that both societies show a range of temperament within individuals but that

range is around a socially defined norm that differs gre[
the two (Benedict (1935)).

Many of the classical sixteenth- and seventeenth-ce[
on political theory attempted to argue the case for the r[
a state, and to obey it, from the assumed inconvenience[
inal 'state of nature' in which there was no state to mediate between individuals. Hobbes suggested that in such a state there would be a war of every man against every man and the gains in security associated with any state were thus infinitely greater than the loss of freedom involved in obeying its authorities. Early libertarians, such as Locke and Rousseau, argued against this partly by suggesting that, even without the state, men were social animals who would co-operate (although Locke concedes such co-operation might generate disputes for which an impartial arbitrator would be useful).

Is the state necessary?

As we saw in an earlier chapter, there is evidence for Locke and Rousseau's view if we understand the debate to be a literal one. Societies like the Tiv (or the Zuni or the Dobu, for that matter) do not have a centralised decision-making apparatus claiming authority over a given territorial area. Thus, the state may be desirable, but it is not, strictly speaking, necessary. However, it is difficult to envisage a modern industrial large-scale society functioning without some such mechanism. Difficult but not impossible, since a small minority – anarchists – advocates precisely this. A discussion of their view may help to illuminate the role of the modern state and lead on to its claims to our obedience.

First, it may be necessary to clarify the term 'anarchism' (see Box 6).

Our first definition represents the colloquial definition of anarchism – supported by few or no political theorists, but dreaded by conservative politicians as the consequence of illegal popular political action. Arguably it might be more correctly given as a definition of 'anarchy' rather than 'anarchism'.

Emma Goldman's [1869–1940] definition highlights the anarchists' opposing view that order need not be imposed by authority

Box 6 Definitions of 'anarchism'

Absence of government; a state of lawlessness due to the absence or inefficiency of supreme power; political disorder.

Shorter Oxford English Dictionary

The Philosophy of a new social order based on liberty unrestricted by man-made law; the theory that all forms of government rest on violence and are therefore wrong and harmful, as well as unnecessary.

Goldman (1915)

A doctrine which poses a criticism of existing society, a view of a desirable future society; and a means of passing from one to the other.

Woodcock (1975)

but should stem from free agreements between free individuals. Writers such as Tolstoy and Kropotkin [1842–1921] would argue that existing states incorporate the systematic use of violence against the population through the police and prison system (which caricature the concept of 'justice' by imprisoning the poor and defenceless) and through the armed forces (destroying the lives of millions to defend the interests of the propertied minority). Most anarchists argue that our present wasteful urban industrialised lifestyle should be replaced by a more ascetic and healthy one. Kropotkin argued that 5 hours' labour a week from everyone could yield a middle-class lifestyle for all. Autonomous communes and voluntary literary, educational, artistic and sporting associations would freely exchange goods and services on a non-profit basis (perhaps basing exchanges on Proudhon's idea of the hours of labour involved in each product or service).

As Woodcock's definition suggests, a crucial problem for anarchists is how to make the transition to the new state of affairs. Most would advocate simply withdrawing consent from current ways of doing things and practising a new libertarian lifestyle immediately. Hence, a number of Anarchists have sought to set up 'communes' independent of current states, whilst Proudhon [1809–65] advocated the setting up of an independent banking system based on labour-hours. As Howard Zim puts it:

> The anarchist sees revolutionary change as something immediate, something we must do now, where we live, where we work, It means starting this moment to do away with authoritarian relationships – between men and women, between children and parents, between one kind of worker and another kind. Such revolutionary spirit cannot be crushed like an armed uprising.
>
> Quoted in Pennock and Chapman (1978)

A minority of anarchists urge that the state machinery needs to be smashed by armed insurrection – perhaps by a worker take-over of their factories and other work-places (revolutionary syndicalism) – or they have taken to terrorist violence. Anarchist terrorism has mostly been in response to unjustified state campaigns against tiny minorities of rather theoretical anarchists. This violent tendency is well illustrated by a quotation (and title) the author could not bear to omit from this book (however marginally representative it may be of anarchism as a whole): 'In giving dynamite to the down-trodden millions of the globe, science has done its best work ... a pound of this good stuff beats a bushel of ballots all hollow' (Johann Most *Science of Revolutionary Warfare – a Manual of Instruction in the Uses and Preparation of Nitro-glycerine, Dynamite, Gun-cotton, Fulminating Mercury, Bombs, Fuses, Poisons, etc., etc.* (1885), quoted in Horowitz (1964)).

Why should I obey the state?

The example of the anarchist who declares that we should secede from the authority of the state prompts the question, debated at length by political theorists (and usually treated in texts under the heading of 'political obligation') of why we should obey the state. Of course, part of the answer to this may be merely prudential: if we do not obey the state (pay our taxes, enrol in the armed forces when required, wear clothes in public places, etc.), its agencies may detect our violation of its laws and punish them (with fine, prison sentence or incarceration in a mental institution). However, if we look for a moral justification for obedience we must look in two main directions: towards arguments based on the moral need to preserve an essential or desirable social institution and towards arguments based upon the idea of our consent to the authority of a specific form of state (probably a liberal democratic one). Conservative theorists (like Burke) have tended to emphasise the first line of argument; liberal theorists (like Locke) the second.

To the extent that the state represents a safeguard against the chaos, crime and confusion resulting from the acts of selfish and conflicting individuals, it may be seen as having a claim upon our obedience. As the institutionalisation of law it may be seen as worthy of respect and obedience. Some theologians, following St Augustine's [354–430] *City of God*, have seen the state as an institution ordained by God to discipline sinful humanity, whilst classical Greek writers such as Aristotle and Plato regarded man as a naturally social animal who should abide by the rules of the 'polity' (a community organised politically) which created the civilised conditions within which they flourished. Both schools of thought, therefore, considered obedience to the state as a normal part of the moral duty of all thinking men and women. Disobedience, therefore, is to be censured not only for the immediate harm it might do but for the example it sets to others. As the conservative point of view is that much human behaviour is habitual, a disruption of the state's subjects' habits of obedience is taken very seriously.

The democratic view stresses, instead, the duty of the good citizen to respect the products of the decision-making processes established in their name and surviving only with their consent. Even bad law should be obeyed until it can be amended by democratic processes, since the evil of undermining the democratic system is assumed to be greater than that for which the law is responsible. (However, a law enforcing genocide or slavery or other major breach of 'human rights', as discussed later in this chapter, would not come under this rubric – especially as the evil done by the law was unarguable and that done by setting an example in conscientious refusal to accept a 'democratic' enactment much less so.) Because the government reflects the interests of the majority of the community, minorities should respect its decisions whilst reserving the right to seek to reverse them. Thus, obedience to the state should reflect a rational act of choice on the part of an educated citizenry (Singer (1973)).

In terms of the classical theorists the contrast is neatly illustrated by that between Hobbes and Locke. Both used the metaphor of a legal contract adopted in a 'state of nature', but in Locke's case the establishment of a trust between the governors and the governed was envisaged as well as a contract to set up a civil society. Thus, obedience to the government remains conditional upon it carrying out its part of the compact. But in Hobbes's case the contract simply empowered a third party – the government – to enforce the peace:

> I authorize and give up my right of governing myself, to this man, or this assembly of men, on this condition, that thou give up thy right to him, and authorize all his actions in like manner . . This is the generation of the great Leviathan, or rather (to speak more reverently) of that mortal God, to which we owe under the Immortal God, our peace and defence.
>
> *Leviathan*, Ch. XVII

The nature of authority

So far, we have used the term 'authority' with some frequency without clearly defining it. In this section we attempt to clarify the concept by distinguishing it from power, by distinguishing political authority from other kinds of authority and, finally, by exploring Weber's analysis of the different types of political authority.

The definitions of power quoted in Chapter 1 Box 1 all included the idea of achieving results by a variety of means. Authority can be seen as a particular kind of power relationship in which the legitimacy (literally 'lawfulness') of the exercise of power is accepted, to some degree, by the other actors in the situation. In most political situations legitimacy implies an appeal to an established system of law, but it may take on the broader meaning of 'in accord with moral law'. Weber (Gerth and Mills (1948, Ch. X)) distinguishes between traditional authority and rational legal authority, but both of these will normally refer an appeal to an established system of law – thus, in a tribal society the customary law gives authority to chiefs, in a modern liberal democracy a rationally organised system of statute law gives authority to political and bureaucratic office holders. Both of these arrangements will be reinforced by moral doctrines – that the Gods/ancestors have bequeathed their way of life to the tribe or the sanctity of majority votes – but in stable societies, ideally, there is no conflict between moral and political obligation.

On occasion, however, rival claims to authority may conflict, particularly in societies in transition or crisis. Thus, in South Africa before the recent transition to full democracy, the authority of the King of the Zulus (traditional) on occasion conflicted with that of President Botha (rational-legal) whilst both had to defer to that of the leader of the largest popular movement – Nelson Mandela. Weber suggests the description 'charismatic' for the authority of leaders, such as Mandela at that time, who are followed because of their personal qualities rather than any legal position they may hold. Literally, this terminology derives from the Greek root 'a favour specially vouchsafed by God, especially a gift or talent' (*Shorter Oxford English Dictionary*) and emphasises, at first sight, the exceptional qualities of those exercising such authority. But, as Weber points out, such divine gifts are not always recognised – the hour brings forth the appropriate man – only in moments of crisis when normal claims to leadership are losing their authority is such authority likely to appeal. Equally, such leaders usually claim to represent new potential sources of moral authority – be they God (Mohammed), the nation (Hitler) or the people (Mandela). As the examples quoted suggest, such authority may be exercised in many different times or places for good or evil – these categories of authority were intended by Weber as morally neutral.

What is justice?

If authority is power exercised in accordance with the law, we might reasonably ask what is so special about the law? As we have seen, followers of Hobbes might be quick to assert that the alternative is violence and chaos and that almost any law is better than no law at all. Many people, however, would tend to associate law not only with order, but also with justice. For many people, law must have a moral dimension to be acceptable – or to put it another way, the 'order' enforced by the law must be of a morally defensible character. What, then, characterises such a just society? This is one of the oldest questions in political theory and one addressed directly by its first major classic text – Plato's *Republic*. To give some idea of the debates surrounding the term we shall examine not only Plato's somewhat conservative answer to this question but two later approaches: that of the nineteenth-century 'utilitarian' theorist Bentham and that of a prominent twentieth-century liberal writer, John Rawls.

Plato's answer is presented as a dialogue between his teacher Socrates and some of his friends and colleagues. One friend quotes a rival teacher, Simonides, to the effect that justice consists in giving everyone their due, which is interpreted as doing good to our friends and harm to our enemies. This is easily dismissed, since, if our enemies are good men, this would clearly be immoral. Further reformulations of this idea also seem to be logically untenable. At this point, another colleague, Thrasymachus, advances what he sees as the realistic view that justice is 'the interest of the stronger', defending this apparently paradoxical point of view by identifying justice with carrying out the law and asserting that the strongest will dominate the government of any country and rule in their own interests (a version of what we shall later describe as elite theory, which retains its supporters to this day).

Although the discussion starts on the level of individual morality (will justice lead to individual happiness and injustice to unhappiness?), Socrates argues that justice can be most clearly understood on a state level. In the ideal state there are three kinds of role to be played: the guidance of the state must be through the exercise of wisdom by the best citizens – the Guardians; the defence of the state must be in the hands of the bravest and most spirited – the Auxiliaries; whilst the the production of necessities will be carried out by the rest – the Producers. Justice resides in the harmony between the parts of society achieved by each fulfilling the role for which they are most fitted. (Similarly a just man maintains a harmony between the rational, spiritual and 'concupiscent' elements of his make-up.) Thus, Simonides' concept of justice as giving each his due is returned to, but with a clearer idea of what this entails.

This theory may be interpreted as very conservative – as supporting a hierarchical and authoritarian society in which class divisions reflect natural divisions of talent amongst the population and in which propaganda and censorship are employed (Popper (1962, Vol. 1)). There are implicit in Plato's account some more radical strands. For instance, he explicitly endorses equal educational opportunities for women and the selection of philosopher rulers on merit, not on the basis of birth.

In contrast, and more briefly, Bentham's views on the realisation of justice in the state were based on different assumptions. His sole criterion for the establishment of a just legal order was that the legislators should seek 'the greatest good of the greatest number'. Furthermore, he made the radical and democratic assumption that it was not up to philosophers to decide on the values the state should pursue and to evaluate states according to the extent to which the state embodied those values. Instead, the just state would reflect its citizen's own moral, economic and aesthetic choices. It was in this context he put forward the sometimes misrepresented thesis that 'Pushpin [read nowadays 'computer games', perhaps] is as good as Poetry'. The best way to ensure that legislators reflected the views of the inhabitants of the state, he argued, was to have them elected by universal suffrage. Justice is therefore to be found in a democratic society which respects the moral equality of the individuals composing it.

Rawls' (1971) *Theory of Justice* is the most prominent work to criticise Bentham's view which, it can be argued has dominated discussion in the nineteenth and twentieth centuries (Gorovitz (1976, 273–6)). Rawls puts forward a view of justice which deals with some of the apparent inadequacies of utilitarianism: thus it might be shown that embarrassing a few unlucky individuals on a TV show might make millions of viewers happy – thus achieving the happiness of the greatest number – but few would feel sure that this was a 'just' proceeding; nor is it easy (possible?) to compare people's subjective experience of 'utility'. His method is to consider what principles rational policy-makers would adopt if they knew a great deal about human nature and society, but had no idea of the role they themselves played in it or what goals they wished to pursue – what he calls 'a veil of ignorance'.

His conclusion is that two fundamental principles of justice would emerge: (1) each person is to have an equal right to the most extensive total system of equal basic liberties compatible with a similar system of liberty for all; (2) social and economic liberties are to be arranged so that they are both (a) to the greatest advantage of the least advantaged, and (b) attached to offices and positions open to all under conditions of fair equality of opportunity. The first principle having an absolute priority over the second. The logic of this is that if we did not know what social positions we held or what objectives we were seeking to pursue we would want to ensure that any goals could be pursued by anyone and that none would be victimised for the sake of the rest.

Rawls argues that this notion of justice accords with the common intuitions that people have on the matter and offers a logical basis for evaluating actual social orders. Gorovitz argues that :

> Such a view is plainly at odds with the rugged individualism of the unconstrained free enterprise economy, and is equally at odds with the highly controlled communist or socialist state that submerges individual's autonomy in the quest for social welfare.
>
> Gorovitz (1976, 286)

Individualism versus collectivism

In discussing concepts of power in Chapter 1, we saw that some writers tend to focus upon collective entities such as societies or classes in their analysis of politics, whilst others are more prone to focus upon the activities of individuals. Our earlier discussions in this chapter suggest that this type of difference may be more than a mere difference of focus in the method of analysis – it may also reflect a fundamental difference of values. For Bentham and Rawls, both writing in the liberal tradition (see next chapter for discussion of liberalism) the starting point for political reflection is the individual, not only because individuals can be seen as the fundamental building blocks from which societies are composed but, perhaps more importantly, because they see political arrangements as devices to be judged by the extent to which they recognise the moral equality of individuals and allow them to make decisions about their own lives in an 'autonomous' (self-governing) fashion.

Classical and medieval writers tended to see the focus of political enquiry as the creation of good societies in which, as a consequence of the wisdom of constitution makers and princes, good men would flourish. This can be seen in Plato's assumption that a just society is one in which there is a correct distribution of functions between its constituent social groups and that the just individual is the just society in microcosm. Similarly, some medieval writers fondly compared the just state to a hive of bees or colony of ants in which all did their appropriate part without a thought for the boredom and toil implicit in the ordinary 'worker' role in such societies. More recently, as we shall see in the next chapter, fascists have subordinated the good of individuals to that of the the race or nation, whilst some communists have similarly exalted the interests of party or class over that of their constituent individuals.

Rights: natural, human and legal

Like 'authority' and 'justice', 'rights' are frequently referred to in political discussion without much attempt at definition. 'Rights' are generally associated with individuals and an emphasis upon them is very much part of the broad liberal tradition dominant in modern political thought. By definition, a right may be thought of not only as an authority to act possessed by an individual but as universally possessed by individuals (in the same situation) or by individuals within a specific legal system. This is so by definition because the term 'privilege' would apply if only some individuals have power to do something in a given situation.

The doctrine that all Men ('Men' might or might not include women and children – see discussion on feminism in the next chapter) possessed 'natural' rights started to come to prominence in the seventeenth century as part of the debate, of which Hobbes and Locke were a part, on the limitations on the power of the British Crown. In the eighteenth century the revolutionary potential of these ideas was dramatically realised in the American and French revolutions. Such ideas were associated with Deism – a rational reformulation of Christian ideas – which stressed that the Creator had instituted not only natural laws which governed the motions of the planets and all other natural objects, but similar moral laws governing human relationships and had given Man the power to discover all these laws by reason. By examining how Men lived together in existing societies (and possibly outside society in a state of nature of barbarism) we can see that there are certain prerequisites for civilised co-operative living which all men should recognise. Thus, the American Declaration of Independence proclaimed inalienable and God-given rights to the life, liberty and the pursuit of happiness, whilst these were elaborated in the French Declaration of the Rights of Man.

Much of modern history could be read as the broadening of the concept of rights from a narrow legalistic application of the idea only to 'civilised' white men, to a broader concept of social and cultural rights applicable to women, non-whites and children as well (some readers may wish to add animals to the list). The concept of human rights as expressed in the United Nations Universal Declaration of human rights (1948) is thus a modern development of the earlier theory of Natural Rights. It, too, represents a moral claim to equal political treatment on behalf of those for whom it speaks.

Such natural, human or universal rights, which are largely a moral claim for equal and just treatment, should be distinguished from legal rights, which are enforceable in the courts of a specific legal system. These, in turn, can be subdivided into the rights given by any specific piece of legislation and rights which are guaranteed by the constitution.

In many systems, such as the United States, rights guaranteed by the constitution (e.g. that in the Fifth Amendment to remain silent under legal interrogation) supersede any contrary statement in ordinary legislation (see Chapter 7, pp.166–9).

Equality and needs

'Equality' in politics clearly does not mean that everyone, regardless of circumstances, should be treated equally – e.g. the blind and sighted to be equally entitled to free white sticks! 'Equality' in this sense would mean inequity (unfairness, injustice). Most commentators and the UN Universal Declaration of Human Rights endorse equality of rights and of dignity. But how far does equality of rights go?

Equality before the law is important, but in a capitalist economy this does not in itself guarantee education, health, a roof over your head or a pension in old age. (The law may merely give everyone an equal right to buy these things but not establish any sources of income to enable this to be done.) Article 25 of the Universal Declaration (1948) does envisage 'the right to security in the event of unemployment, sickness, disability, widowhood, old age or other lack of livelihood in circumstances beyond his control' and Article 26 talks of a right to a free universal system of education. Maurice Cranston (1962) and others, however, have argued against placing these 'social' rights on a par with older 'civic' rights on the grounds that they *cannot* be achieved for all in some poor countries and that such thinking encourages the idea that civic rights may be legitimately 'traded' for social rights or are also only a long-term aspiration.

'Equality before law' does imply freedom from sexual and racial discrimination. A modern issue is the legitimacy of positive discrimination in favour of disadvantaged groups such as women and ethnic minorities such as 'Untouchables' in India.

'Equal rights' are normally interpreted as to some *minimum* standard – e.g. *a* house, *a* job, etc., not that all have the same standard of housing or equal pay,

Another related but separate issue is the extent to which social policy can and should be directed toward reversing social inequalities (LeGrand (1982)). The short answer would seem to be that most of these rest much more upon the nature of the fiscal, economic and legal systems than on social policies in a narrow sense. Distinctions should also be drawn between social inequalities which are the result of *economic differences* and those which result from attempts to maintain *social distance* between different status groups. For instance, UK social class or Indian caste differences may not reflect the economic circumstances of those concerned. A British National Lottery winner might still be refused admission to a golf club on the grounds of an uncouth accent or unconventional appearance, whilst an Indian Untouchable (even if a well-paid professional) could still be rejected as a dining companion by those of Brahmin caste.

In Plato's *Republic* we saw that justice was said to be realised when each plays his/her proper part in the community according to their capacities. The more modern writers Benn and Peters (1959) paradoxically, are not so far away from this in stressing presumption in favour of equality except where *relevant differences* exist. But what differences are relevant? They suggest (a) desert, (b) property ownership, (c) need, as potentially relevant differences affecting allocation of economic resources. 'Desert' approximately equals either rewards for skill, responsibility, length of training; compensation for dirty, dangerous, etc. conditions or 'traditional relativities'. 'Property ownership' can be justified by its social utility. Both of these largely represent 'economic' or 'market'; criteria for allocation (reward by contribution) – which will be dealt with mainly in Chapter 6. This leaves 'need' to be explored here.

To say X is 'in need' means someone is short of a defined standard of provision of some goods or service. Who defines such standards and how? J. Bradshaw (1972) suggested the useful taxonomy of 'felt', 'expressed', 'normative', and 'comparative' needs.

'Felt' needs are defined as individual wants. There are many problems in using these as a basis for social policy because of their subjective nature. Do I need a Porsche? I may feel I need one badly as a result of advertising and my perceived position as a high-status university lecturer! Conversely, a senile old age pensioner may not feel he or she needs help although dying through lack of basic medical attention. Are such needs infinitely expandable? On the Right it is often claimed that the 'demand' for medical treatment may be of this nature.

'Expressed' needs comprise felt needs backed by the necessary cash resources. Among the problems in applying ideas of the market to the allocation of all social resources are the uneven and possibly unfair distribution of financial resources in a capitalist system and that some people may genuinely have greater needs than others – they may, for example, be seriously ill. (This is considered further in later chapters.)

'Normative' needs refer to professionally defined minimum standards such as nutritional minima, and the former Parker-Norris standards for council housing. The problems here include that such standards give power to different professional 'gatekeepers', e.g. housing officials in giving their assessment of how hard the applicants are trying to rehouse themselves. The standards of different doctors (and their receptionists), social workers, psychologists, etc. may well differ from gatekeeper to gatekeeper as well as from client to client. Subjective and relative social judgements are involved – adequate housing, health and education are clearly not absolutes.

'Comparative' needs involve looking at similar cases: if X and Y have similar characteristics, and Y is in receipt of a service, then X is said to be in need too. This results from a search for equality of treatment and avoids subjectivity, e.g. equality of opportunity in education, hospital waiting lists. The main problem here is that, although priorities within a service may be sorted out on this basis, there are no clear criteria to weigh different services.

The general principle to treat all equally unless justified by a relevant difference in terms of (a) social contribution made (measured by 'demand'?) or (b) need (measured by 'professional assessment') may be clear, *but* the problem of when (a) or (b) is most relevant remains.

Positive and negative freedom

One of the most frequently used and controversial words in the political vocabulary is 'freedom', (or liberty). Because it has such a good emotive ring to it (i.e. it is what Cranston (1954) calls a 'Hurrah!' word), no one can appear to be against it. Therefore philosophers and politicians redefine freedom as that of which they approve. The result is a wonderful confusion of definitions of freedom that have been produced by political philosophers, as shown in Box 7.

Box 7 Definitions of 'freedom'

consists in having of Government, and those laws by which their Life and Goods may be most their own. It is not having a share in Government.

Charles I *Speech from the Scaffold*

The assurance that every man shall be protected in doing what he believes to be his duty against the influences of authority and majorities, custom and opinion.

Lord Acton, *History of Freedom*

the mere impulse of appetite is slavery, whilst obedience to the law which we prescribe ourselves is liberty.

Rousseau, *Social Contract*

the absence of opposition.

Hobbes, *Leviathan*

the power a man has to do or forbear any particular action.

Locke, *Essay on Government*

necessity transfigured.

Hegel, *Logik*

a participation in the revelation of what-is-as-such.

Heidegger, *Existence and Being*

control over ourselves and over external nature which is founded on knowledge of natural necessity.

Engels, *Anti-Duhring*

SOURCE   From Cranston (1954), 23–4

By way of an heroic simplification which may help to get an initial grasp of the differences at stake – but which should not be mistaken as the final word on the subject – we may adopt Berlin's (1958) terminology of 'positive' and 'negative' concepts of freedom (Berlin himself went on to elaborate four concepts of freedom (1969)) The 'negative' view is that of the classic English writers that 'I am normally said to be free to the degree to which no human being interferes with my activity' (Berlin (1958), 7). The positive view is one which defines freedom as 'being one's own master' (Berlin (1958), 16). To put the matter more baldly, negative freedom is freedom *from*, whilst positive freedom is freedom *to*.

At first sight, such distinctions appear trivial and unimportant. However, one important consequence of the positive view may be that, paradoxically, it can be used to argue that, as Rousseau (1913, 15) puts it, one can be 'forced to be free'. If one is forced to obey a morally justified law which conflicts with one's immediate inclinations – 'the impulse of appetite' – then one's 'real' self is thereby said to be realised. Conversely, opponents of the 'negative' view of freedom would argue that legal freedoms of speech, assembly, equality before the law, etc. are of little benefit to Indian peasants with insufficient means to maintain themselves. Such arguments about the interpretation of 'freedom' constitute an important strand in the debate between conservatism, liberalism and socialism which we shall explore further in succeeding chapters.

Analysing political concepts

Our discussion of political ideas in this chapter has illustrated that political terms which may be taken for granted in everyday conversation or argument conceal depths of meaning and room for divergent interpretations which have lead to literally centuries of argument. In such a situation it is clear that there is a need in academic and often in everyday discussion to clarify the way in which a term is intended if it is to be understood. Plato saw philosophical enquiry as essentially about discovering the 'pure form' of each concept. Other writers, similarly, have thought of concepts as having an essential or root meaning. Most modern scholars, however, would concede that it is foolish to waste too much time attempting to establish the 'real' meaning of words which have been, and are, used in different ways even in the same society, let alone over centuries of use in a host of different ones.

Academic linguists and some contemporary philosophers tend to concentrate on the 'descriptive' definition of words, examining how they are used in common practice and perhaps offering some rules for ensuring that you are unlikely to be misunderstood by adopting an unusual or deviant use of the word. Contemporary linguists have abandoned the practice of old-style grammarians of attempting to prescribe rules for the 'correct' use of words. (Some of these rules in English were based upon misplaced attempts to transfer practices from Latin grammar into English usage.) It would be very foolish to attempt to legislate that, for instance, a word in English must always be interpreted via its Greek, Latin or German origins – language being a living and changing vehicle for communication rather than an ancient monument.

In order to communicate clearly, however, it may on occasion be useful to adopt a 'stipulative' definition and say, 'This is what I will always mean by this term'. This is frequently a legitimate and useful academic device. It may also sometimes be permissible to coin a new word for use as a technical term in order to avoid the emotive and vague commonly used one. (We earlier saw how terms such as 'political culture', 'interest articulation' and the like have been coined in this way.) The problem, as we saw earlier [Chapter 1, pp.15–16] is that such neologisms may well come to be used as imprecisely as the terms they seek to replace.

In politics, the practice of 'persuasive' definition of words is commonplace. By this, the writer or speaker tries to persuade their audience that their definition of the word in question is the superior usage. We have seen this illustrated already in this chapter (especially in our discussion of freedom). As we have seen, such attempts are more frequently intended as a device to persuade the audience about the value judgements they should make than as a technical exercise in clarifying vocabulary.

As Edelman (1977) points out, very often political debate in practice is an attempt to label your opponent's ideas with what Cranston (1954) calls a 'Boo!' word and your own with a 'Hurrah'! one. Thus, Conservatives will wish to label Labour measures as 'nationalisation' and their own as 'freedom', whilst Labour speakers now frequently denounce Thatcherite measures as sacrificing caring to 'ideology'. (In the USA doctors consistently speak of 'socialised medicine' (Boo!) rather than a National Health Service). Roy Hattersley tells the tale of how, as an apprentice Labour politician, he was once advised that, if in doubt on an issue at a party meeting, to roundly declare 'What is needed on this issue is a truly socialist policy', wait for the applause (Hurrah!), and then change the subject!

Recommended reading

Gerth, H. and Mills, C. Wright (eds), 1948, *From Max Weber: Essays In Sociology*, London, Routledge & Kegan Paul. One of the classic texts of political sociology which is more readable than some more modern writing – for authority, bureaucracy, Chinese Mandarinate, etc.

Raphael, D.D., 1990, *Problems of Political Philosophy*, 2nd edn, Basingstoke, Macmillan. Useful standard introductory text – focused on basic concepts.

Woodcock, George, 1975, *Anarchism*, Harmondsworth, Middlesex, Penguin. Raises some very fundamental questions about the state and politics.

Benn, Stanley I. and Peters, Richard S., 1959, *Social Principles and the Democratic State*, London, George Allen & Unwin. An analysis of key concepts in political theory which still repays careful reading.

Chapter 4

Movements

Right versus Left: classifying political ideas

This is a chapter about the 'isms' of politics: conservatism, liberalism, socialism, Marxism, and so on. It considers not only the general nature of these broad currents of political thinking but also gives some idea of the relationships these have had with political regimes and parties. Because this chapter covers so much ground, the ideas of individual political thinkers do not get the space they deserve. It is hoped that the reader will be inspired to examine some of these thinkers in their own words (a good starting point is a reader such as Rendell (1978) or Morgan (1992)). One of the joys of any politics degree course worth the name is the opportunity it gives for a close and critical examination of the works of individual theorists in their historical context.

It is conventional to classify political movements and thinkers as right-wing or left-wing. This apparently derives from the first French National Assembly

when the pro-monarchist conservatives sat on the right and the revolutionary republicans sat on the left of a semi-circular formation. The European and modern French parliaments adopt a similar seating pattern to this day. Such a classification can be controversial – commonly groups tend to assert they are to the left of the position that others see them in! Clearly, too, what is radical and left-wing in one context (e.g. republicanism in British Colonial North America) can become conservatism in another time or place (e.g. republicanism in the modern United States).

Generally speaking, however, the Right is seen as against political, economic and social change; the Left as in favour of it. The Right tends to be monarchist, clerical, favouring the interests of the established propertied classes, whilst the Left is identified with republicanism, anti-clericalism and the interests of the masses (workers or peasants). This picture still derives from French nineteenth-century politics.

In contemporary liberal democracies it may be helpful to supplement this picture by emphasising the existence of a large democratic 'Centre' committed to the existing constitutional system, but accepting the legitimacy of gradual social and economic change. Distant from the centre are the far Right and the far Left, being (usually) minorities who wish to drastically modify the existing constitutional and social system – the Left in an anti-capitalist, the Right in an ultra-nationalist (perhaps racist) direction.

In this chapter, we shall examine in more detail political movements, starting with what might be broadly regarded as the Right, continuing with the Left and ending with the 'Centre'.

The old Right: monarchism

Monarchism might be seen in a medieval European context as a centrist rather than a right-wing position. Certainly, conventional Catholic thought has been happy to acknowledge the legitimacy of princes. The gospel urges Christians to 'render therefore unto Caesar the things which are Caesar's' (Mathew 22: 21). The normal situation in medieval Europe was of secular government by kings or emperors who were crowned by the Pope or by archbishops authorised by him.

This was formalised in the theological and political doctrine of the 'Two Swords' – secular and clerical authority supporting each other and respecting each other's spheres of influence. In effect, there was a division of powers with, as we have seen, the Church administering areas of family and property law and having its own taxes (tithes). Whilst there was royal influence over Church appointments and churchmen often manned the royal administration, the power of the Church to place a kingdom under an interdict (preventing the faithful from taking part in the full range of religious observances) constituted in many ways a more powerful weapon than the armies of king or emperor.

It was only after the development of the modern idea of state sovereignty (e.g. as described by Bodin in his *Republic* of 1576) and especially after the assumption of leadership over the Christian Church in their countries by Protestant kings (starting with Henry VIII) that the more radical idea of the divine right of kings became established. As parliamentary forces in seventeenth-century England increasingly stressed the idea of popular sovereignty, the Stuart kings were increasingly attracted to the idea that countries could only have one sovereign and that he held authority from God not Man. In countries like France, in which republics were founded, the restoration of the power of an (executive rather than figurehead) monarchy became increasingly the trade-mark of anti-democratic and ultra-conservative forces.

In other countries which retained a monarchy, a pro-monarchist position might be combined with a more moderate stance (as in nineteenth-century Germany where Bismarck combined social reformism and nationalism in a politically powerful combination with monarchism). Paradoxically, in recent years in Spain the monarch has used his appeal to the Right to help engineer a return to constitutional democracy.

The radical Right: Nazism and fascism

In the twentieth century, however, the forces which are generally seen as furthest to the Right are not those of monarchism but those of fascism or Nazism. In many ways such movements are the furthest removed from the democratic centre since they deny the legitimacy of the idea of democracy and of universal human rights, whilst the extreme left – in the shape of communists – has generally merely claimed to be more democratic than the democrats.

Hitler's 'National Socialist' Party was, as the name suggests, not without a populist strand in that the Führer was seen as representing the true interests of the German *Volk* (people) more completely than any democratic process could do. It was also, in rhetoric at least, anti-capitalist – with capitalism seen as a Jewish conspiracy to rob the *Volk* of its birthright. The state was seen as the embodiment of the public good and clearly had the responsibility to organise the economy, the educational system and the whole of social and cultural life. A major emphasis of the movement was on the mobilisation of the German people through a single party using the modern technology of mass communication.

In practice, Nazism was dominated by the urge to power of its elite and their commitment to xenophobia, racism and nationalism. The urge to right the perceived wrong of the Versailles Treaty of 1919 and strong nationalist feelings (shared by many Germans) was elaborated into a nightmare doctrine of the right of an 'Aryan' master race to *Lebensraum* (living space) to the East and to cleanse itself of 'alien' elements such as Gypsies and Jews as well as to eliminate any mentally or physically defective specimens of their own race. The attempt to implement a state based on these doctrines resulted in the deaths of millions across the whole planet.

Hitler's views articulated in *Mein Kampf* (1969) built in many ways upon more orthodox conservative German political theorists and philosophers. Hegel [1770–1831], for instance, had stressed the importance of a strong state, its role in defining culture and the existence of a logic (or dialectic) of history which justified war by superior states upon inferior ones. Schopenhauer [1780–1860] glorified will over reason. Nietzsche [1844–1900] believed in the creation of a race of superior individuals. Views like this were combined with carefully selected 'scientific' findings about natural selection and the nature of human racial divisions to create an 'ideology' which had a powerful appeal in the politically volatile atmosphere of an economically depressed Weimar Germany. (See Chapter 5 for a discussion of 'race' and ethnicity.)

Italian fascism, by contrast, although drawing upon many of the same causes of social and political discontent and using many of the same methods to achieve power – street warfare and mass rallies, for instance – placed much less emphasis on racism. As an alternative to democracy, the appeal of the leader was combined with an attempt to create a corporatist structure of representation in which bodies such as the Church, the Army and employers' associations and even workers' syndicates could be represented. Spanish and Argentinian fascists have developed similar ideas and institutions.

With the defeat of Hitler, explicit endorsement of Nazi or fascist ideas has, on the whole, become rather unfashionable. On the extreme Right in Europe, even those who express a qualified admiration for Hitler have tended to deny that the wholesale slaughter of Jews in the Holocaust took place, rather than enthusiastically to endorse it. The Swastika is more prized as an icon for rebellious youth to embarrass parents with, than as a serious political symbol. But racist and extreme nationalist sentiments remain the mark of the extreme Right together with an anti-communist/labour rhetoric.

It is interesting that the most recent large-scale use of near-Nazi symbolism (admittedly a three, rather than a four-legged Swastika) has been by the South African AWB movement seeking to defend Apartheid in its dying days. The South African Apartheid regime could be seen as the last contemporary fascist state with an ideology based on racialism and supported by an apparatus of torture and repression. The Serbian regime in the former Yugoslavia might also be interpreted in a similar way, although here too the ideology is nominally one of nationalism rather than racialism.

Marxism

At the opposite end of the left/right political spectrum it is conventional to place the followers of Karl Marx [1818–83]. In practice, it is clear that Marxists vary enormously in their radicalism and in their beliefs. It is therefore convenient to discuss first the views of Marx and his collaborator Engels [1820–95], second, their most obviously influential disciples, Lenin and Stalin, and finally some of the other twentieth-century varieties of Marxism.

We have already seen (Chapter 1, p.20), that Marx and Engels adopt a collectivist and conflict-oriented view of politics. It is worth stressing that this is part of both a theory of history and a programme of political action. As Marx says, 'The philosophers have only *interpreted* the world differently – the point is to *change* it' (*11th Thesis on Feuerbach*, Marx and Engels (1962, Vol. II, 403)). Both the theoretical and the practical parts of their writing are impressive in their scope and depth. Marx and Engels published extensively, not only on the nature of contemporary capitalism but also on the transition from feudalism to capitalism and on ancient and oriental societies (see Marx and Engels (1962) *passim*).

In the more theoretical writings of Marx and Engels 'the dialectic of Hegel is turned upon its head' (Engels, *Feuerbach and the End of Classical German Philosophy*, Marx and Engels (1962, Vol. II, 387)) by placing contemporary (nineteenth-century) capitalism in perspective as one of several stages of history which inevitably lead on to new, higher stages. Hegel's idea of a logic of history is adopted, but instead of the ideal manifesting itself progressively through history, ideas (ideology) are seen as reflecting the underlying material 'means of production'. As Engels puts it:

> *all* past history with the exception of its primitive stages was the history of class struggles; that these warring classes of society are always the products of the modes of production and exchange – in a word, of the *economic* conditions of their time; that the economic structure of society always furnishes the real basis from which we can alone work out the ultimate explanation of the whole superstructure of juridical and political institutions as well as of the religious, philosophical, and other ideas of a given historical period.
>
> *Socialism, Utopian and Scientific*,
> Marx and Engels (1962, 134–5)

Class warfare will only cease to be the dynamic of history with the abolition of class in the future communist society (see Chapter 9 for further discusssion on the future of class divisions and the Marxist theory of history).

Much of their work was also seeking to build up a socialist movement (the International Working Men's Association) which shared their moral rejection of the exploitative nature of capitalism. As *The Communist Manifesto* shows, the theory can be impressively marshalled as rhetoric to buttress an appeal to political action. The feeling of being on the side of history, having a 'scientific' insight into social processes and being morally in the right, is a heady brew which still appeals – especially to the young and politically idealistic.

Leninism and Stalinism

In the twentieth century the most obvious heirs to Marx have been the leaders of the Soviet Union. The most ideologically creative and politically influential of these were Vladimir Illich Lenin (born V. I. Ulanov) [1870–1924] and Joseph Stalin (born Joseph Vissarionovich Djugashvili) [1879–1953], who led this successor state to the Russian Empire in their capacities as Secretaries of the Russian Social Democrat Party (Bolshevik – 'majority' – faction) and later the Communist Party of the Soviet Union.

Marx and Engels envisaged socialist revolution taking place in the most developed capitalist countries through mass action by trade unions and democratic socialist organisations. Lenin and Stalin adapted the theory to suit the needs of a conspiratorial revolutionary organisation fighting an autocratic, if ramshackle, empire in which the majority of the population were still peasants. The adoption of representative democracy would have meant the loss of power by the Bolsheviks (who, at best, were firmly supported by the relatively small group of urban workers). In order to justify permanent control of a monopoly, single-party hierarchy over the Soviet Union, the doctrines of 'the dictatorship of the proletariat' and 'democratic centralism' were developed. The party leadership were seen as representing the emergent majority – the working class – which would be the majority as industrialisation proceeded. Lenin developed Marx's concept of the dictatorship of the proletariat to mean 'the organization of the advanced guard of the oppressed as the ruling class, for the purpose of crushing the oppressors' (Lenin (1917, 225)). True democracy could only be created by eliminating the exploitative bourgeois minority. Within the party, the dominance of the leadership was defended by their greater knowledge of the 'scientific' doctrine and the prevalence of infiltrating 'counter-revolutionary' forces. Democratic centralism was defined by the 1961 Communist Party Constitution as including the election of all party organs, strict party discipline, subordination of minorities to majorities and lower organs to higher organs – in practice, unwelcome criticism from below being denounced as 'factionalism' and 'unbusinesslike' discussion if not downright treason (Schapiro (1965, 63–5)). Similarly, Russian dominance in the former empire was effectively protected by a doctrine of the existence of a new 'Soviet' nationality which superseded both 'great Russian chauvinism' and 'bourgeois (i.e. non-Russian) nationalism'.

The apparent success of the Soviet regime in building a strong industrialised state capable of defeating Nazi Germany from a previously underdeveloped peasant economy led (often directly on the basis of Soviet bayonets) to the imitation of the regime in numerous East European countries, China, the Far East and Cuba. In many cases the 'cult of personality' that developed around Stalin in the Soviet Union was imitated in relation to indigenous leaders such as Mao-Tse-Tung, Ho Chi Minh, Hoxha, and Castro. Most of these claimed, with varying degrees of justification, to have produced ideologically improved versions of Marxism of their own.

Other Marxisms

As George Orwell (1949) (1968) observed, the language employed in the totalitarian Marxist–Leninist regimes became increasingly divorced from reality with dictatorship described as democracy, enormous differences in lifestyle being characterised as equality, the repression of national movements (as in Hungary in 1956) being described as maintaining peace and freedom, and so on. Regimes which were nominally revolutionary were actually characterised by bureaucratic conservatism which was increasingly seen as inefficient as well as hypocritical.

In the interwar period, and during the Second World War, the positive role of the Leninists in opposing fascism, and the achievements of the Soviet Union in terms of apparent economic growth and positive welfare measures, together with a degree of direct financial subsidy to sympathetic West European parties and unions, meant that European socialists tended to identify with 'communism'. The major socialist movements in such countries as France and Italy remained aligned with Moscow and continued to describe themselves as communist even through most of the cold war period. Intellectuals such as Jean-Paul Sartre in France continued to describe themselves as communists despite increasing problems of conscience in identifying with regimes which ruthlessly persecuted their own dissenting intellectuals.

However, increasingly, such Western Marxists began to take independent intellectual stands apart from the rather stultifying orthodoxy of Marxist–Leninism as well as distancing themselves from the Soviet regime. In particular, the idea of rigid economic determinism in history came in for re-evaluation, perhaps most notably in Italy, where Gramsci (1969) stressed the humanistic strands in Marx's early writings and the role of ideology in influencing the functioning of the modern state.

The British writer Ralph Miliband (1969) stressed the role of the state in exercising a semi-autonomous role in history. Whilst continuing to take a pessimistic view of the likelihood of a capitalist economic system 'primarily geared to the private purposes of those who own and control its material resources' satisfying the needs of ordinary people (Miliband (1969, 268)), he concedes that 'the British political system does incorporate a number of democratic features which makes it possible for "ordinary people" to make themselves heard'. The system of 'capitalist democracy' is one of competition between capital and labour with a strong bias in favour of the former. There is 'permanent and fundamental contradiction or tension between the promise of popular power enshrined in universal suffrage, and the curbing or denying of that promise in practice' (Miliband (1984, 1)). Miliband is pessimistic about the potential of social democrats to empower ordinary people whilst regarding orthodox communists as too authoritarian. In practice, he appears to anticipate a great danger of a drift from capitalist democracy to 'capitalist authoritarianism' (Miliband (1984, 154)).

A perhaps more radical break with Stalinism is represented by a number of minor Marxist groups who were influenced by the writings of Leon Trotsky (born Lev Davidovich Bronstein) [1879–1940]. Trotsky had been a major colleague of Lenin's in the revolutionary period – acting as military Chief of Staff during the revolution and actually espousing the possibility of an independent Russian revolution before the Bolshevik Party in the pre-revolutionary era. After his expulsion by Stalin from the USSR, and before his assassination on Stalin's orders in Mexico in 1940, Trotsky denounced the way in which Communist Party rule had created a new class of exploiters in the Soviet Union – the party 'Apparatchiks' (Trotsky (1937)). This theme was elaborated by other critics such as Milovan Djilas (1966) who aligned himself with the revisionist Yugoslav regime. Under Tito the Yugoslavs attempted to develop a more humane and participative version of communism in which work-place democracy and multinational participation played a greater role than in the USSR.

The events in Paris of 1968 are a vivid illustration of the diversity of the modern Left (Seale and McConville (1968)). A student protest against the Gaullist government's somewhat inept attempts to ban politics from university campuses mushroomed into larger demands for university reform, the end of the Vietnam war and finally the replacement of the Gaullist regime by a true 'participative' democracy. The occupation of factories by strikers, the erection of barricades in Paris and a general strike were felt to lay the ground for a revolution by the student-led Trotskyist and Maoist 'groupuscules' who led many of the protests. The orthodox Communist Party, however, was more concerned to preserve its control over the bulk of the trade union movement and its parliamentary electability than to identify itself with immediate and radical political and social change.

Totalitarianism and radicalism

After our discussions of communism and fascism, we can now return to the concept of 'totalitarianism' in more detail. In Chapter 2 we saw that Crick (1993) defined totalitarianism largely in terms of its all-encompassing role in contrast to modern republican (or liberal democratic) regimes which leave a much greater area to private initiative and control.

Other writers (e.g. Arendt (1967), Friedrich (1964)) have stressed not only the scope of the activities of the totalitarian state but the similarity of the methods employed by them to control the population. The totalitarian state is seen as one which employs modern technology and techniques of organisation to enforce total control over the lives of the population of a large modern industrialised state. Thus, both Nazi Germany and the Stalinist Soviet Union employed a single mass party to generate and enforce enthusiasm on the part of the population. Modern communication methods such as newspapers, cinema and radio were monopolised by the regime and used to propagate a 'cult of personality' around the leader. The use of 'the Terror' – the employment of torture, and the mass extermination of whole segments of the population, is also seen as characteristic of such regimes – although historic dictatorships have also used such methods this has not usually been on such a vast scale nor so systematically. Certainly, from a liberal perspective, the fact that the ostensible purposes of these regimes differed – establishing a classless or a racially pure society – seems less significant than the horrific reality of their excesses.

Critics of such an approach to the analysis of modern states have variously argued that it seeks to tar all progressive socialist regimes with the Hitler/Stalin brush; that the post-Stalin Soviet Union was a conservative bureaucratic society rather than one based on terror; or even that the concept 'totalitarian' control is better applied to the activities of modern capitalism in creating a consumer society. Thus Marcuse argues that in modern automated consumer societies:

> the productive apparatus tends to become totalitarian to the extent which it determines not only socially needed occupations skills and attitudes but also individual needs and aspirations . . . Technology serves to institute new, more effective, and more pleasant forms of social control.
>
> Marcuse (1964, 13)

Another slippery political term is 'radical'. The author is happy to quote the *Shorter Oxford English Dictionary* on this. Generally, in adjectival use, radical means going to the root, origin or foundation. Politically, in English it refers to 'an advocate of "radical reform"; one who holds the most advanced views of political reform on democratic lines and thus belongs to the extreme section of the [English] Liberal party (1802)'. In France, radicals are particularly identified with anti-clericalism and pro-republicanism. More generally, though, in politics, one might use radicalism to characterise a style of politics which frequently returns to one set of theoretical first principles in seeking solutions to all sorts of problems and oppose it to pragmatism which emphasises the practical consequences of a decision rather than its theoretical roots. (Pragmatism can be a formal philosophical doctrine associated with the name of the American writer John Dewey [1859–1952] viz., the whole meaning of a conception is seen in its practical consequences.) A radical, then, might tend in a number of different directions but always to an extreme degree.

Radicals in politics were once, as we have seen, mainly extreme democrats, more recently the term has often been applied to far-Left socialists, but increasingly it has been on other dimensions that radicalism can be measured. Islamic fundamentalists, radical feminists, Greenpeace, even Thatcherite Conservatives in Britain could all be described as 'radicals', but the principles to which they appeal are very different from each other and from earlier generations of political activists. The similarity that these theorists share is a tendency to solve all sorts of different problems from their own rather limited repertoire of concepts. Everything comes down to the Koran, patriarchal domination, ecological crisis or the market, as the case may be. We shall discuss several of these radical approaches in the next few sections.

Radical theism

> When Adam delved and Eve span,
> Who was then the gentleman?

> (John Ball)

John Ball, the priest who led the peasants' revolt in 1381, was one of many popular leaders who placed a more radical interpretation on the bible than did official Church leaders. The radical possibilities of the Gospel message that the poor would inherit the earth and the Protestant stress on the sovereignty of the individual conscience have strongly influenced the left of the British political tradition. The Diggers and Levellers in the civil war period threw doubt not only upon the position of the established Church, but upon the existing basis of property and political representation (Greenleaf (1983, 351)).

In the New World, in colonies such as seventeenth-century Massachusetts and Connecticut, membership of the dominant Christian sect was virtually the same as citizenship (Morison and Commager (1962, Vol. I, 57–65)). Similarly, in such continental cities as Calvin's Geneva the processes of government and the interpretation of God's word were virtually indistinguishable (Tawney (1938, 132)). At a later stage in American history (1847) the Mormon leader Brigham Young led his people out of the United states to found Salt Lake City where they could practise their own religion (including polygamy) in accordance with Young's interpretation of the Book of Mormon (Morison and Commager (1962, Vol. I, 590–3)).

Thus it is clear that Christian fundamentalism can be a considerable political force – as it remains to this day in the United States, where the backing of the Evangelicals may have proved decisive in securing a Reagan victory in 1988. 'Fundamentalism' – a literal approach to the interpretation of the Bible – is, strictly speaking, of course, a purely theological doctrine and not equivalent to a belief in the political supremacy of the Church. Some fundamentalists would endorse a strict separation of secular and religious matters, but where they are in a majority this distinction has often ceased to be of practical importance. None the less, it is Islamic fundamentalism which appears in many ways the most dynamic political-religious movement in the late twentieth century.

Islamic fundamentalism

Islamic 'fundamentalism' is something of a misnomer since virtually all Muslims take the same sort of literal approach to the status and interpretation of the Qur'ān that Protestant Evangelicals take to the Bible. What is under discussion here is the increasingly high profile which religion is taking in the countries of the South. Because of a historic legacy deriving from a European conflict with Islam during the Crusades and as a part of colonialism, there is a tendency in the West to identify Islamic 'fundamentalism' with intolerance, fanaticism, terrorism and the like (Said (1987)). There is, in fact, little evidence for such an identification – Islamic doctrine being explicitly a tolerant one in relation to 'The People of the Book' – Jews and Christians. As recent events in Bosnia suggest, the intolerance as between Muslims and Christians has often been the other way around.

What is clear is the attraction of Islam in the South as a sophisticated and 'civilised' religion which permits polygamy and is not identified, as is Christianity, with the former colonial powers (Gbadamosi (1978)). Hence, in areas such as southern Nigeria, where tribal religions formerly predominated, Islam is growing much faster than Christianity, whilst in areas which have been historically Muslim, such as Egypt, the reassertion of Islamic identity is a part of the rejection of a temporary colonial inheritance.

The search for a suitable anti-colonial ideology led in many places to an enthusiasm for Marxist-style (single-party) socialism, but this proved, in many cases (e.g. Ghana) to be a short-lived and unedifying experiment. The apparent failure of Marxist-Leninism in the Soviet Union and Eastern Europe has further reduced its attractiveness in the South (as well as removing the doctrine's major sponsor). Thus, Islam now appears in these countries as the only major alternative to capitalism and democracy.

Islam has the great advantage of offering not only a religious doctrine but a social and cultural tradition separate from, and equal or in many respects superior to, that of Christian Europe. Centuries of theological and artistic achievement can be drawn upon. Pilgrims making the journey to Mecca (usually by jet airliner rather than camel train) will be greeted by the spectacle of vast assemblies of the faithful from all over the world with whom to exchange experiences. The doctrine of Islam has always been one not only of common religious observance but the assertion of a social and political unity of all the faithful – the *ummat* (Islamic community). Hence, the Qur'ānic verse 'This your nation is a single nation, and I am your Lord so worship me'. (Surah 21: verse 92, quoted in Algar (1980)).

The political appeal of Islam can be seen in the way in which pragmatic politicians, like Saddam Hussein in Iraq, have turned to it as a way of generating political support. The Ayatollah Khomeini, in Iran, was immensely effective in denouncing the Shah as a catspaw of the American Satan in allowing alcohol, Coca-Cola and mini-skirts and discouraging polygamy and hashish. He described Islamic government as the government of the 'oppressed upon earth' in a reference to the Qur'ānic verse, 'And we wish to show favour to those who have been oppressed upon earth, and to make them leaders and inheritors' (Surah 28: verse 5. quoted in Algar (1980)).

The difficulties in applying Islam to contemporary political problems and structures are, however, considerable. Perhaps the major difficulty being its strict incompatibility with ideas with which it is often, in practice, confused. Thus, in the Middle East, nationalism, pan-Arabism and Islam are often identified – yet Syrian or Egyptian nationalism may conflict with a sense of Arab identity; whilst many Muslims are Iranian (Persian), African, Indian or Indonesian rather than Arab. In opposition to Western influences such distinctions may not matter very much, but in constructing alternative political institutions or alliances they do.

Whilst the Qur'ānic tradition does have some positive statements to make on economic matters – the immorality of interest payments, the duty to make payments to the poor (*zakat*) – these have proved difficult to institutionalise in a modern (i.e. capitalist) economic context. Similarly, the Qur'ān makes it clear that the *ummat* should be ruled by those faithful to its religious prescriptions, be united and that rulers should listen to the voice of the community – but no concrete political and religious institutions are laid down. The two major Islamic traditions – the Shi'ite and the Sunni differed early on on the succession to the caliphate (political leadership) (see Fischer (1980)). The Shi'ites also give greater emphasis to the importance of religious scholars and the Iranian constitution gives them a formal role greater than that found elsewhere. The relationship between the strongly developed traditions of Qur'ānic law and the modern state, and the role of electoral institutions, are thus matters of considerable debate within Islamic countries.

The conclusion must be that so far Islam has proved a useful weapon of opposition to Western influences, but much less effective in constructing an alternative model of political and economic management, or in uniting the faithful politically.

Ecology as political radicalism

Although as early as the beginning of the nineteenth century Wordsworth was opposing the coming of the steam train to the Lake District as fatal to its character and Blake was denouncing the 'dark Satanic mills' of the Industrial Revolution, the conservation of the natural environment has not become a major element in practical politics until relatively recently (although conservationism did figure quite largely in the nineteenth-century US progressive movement). Only in recent years have ecology or green parties been represented in European legislatures and presented a comprehensive political programme – although, of course, pressure groups have pressed environmental causes such as rural planning, National Parks and smoke and noise abatement.

Governments have been involved with environmental issues from almost the earliest times. In England royal forests like the New Forest were protected for a variety of reasons including recreation (hunting), as an economic and strategic resource (timber for the navy) and are now increasingly seen as threatened habitats to be protected for the sake of the rare species within them as well. In the United States the 'unsettled' lands of the West were viewed as federal property to be allocated in the public interest.

The green movement is unusual, however, in deriving an overall coherent philosophy from a scientific discipline. Ecology is the science which studies the relationship between organisms and their physical environment. As scientific study has proceeded, the multiple interdependences between the different organic species on the planet and the crucial impact of climatic and geological influences have become clear to us in a way which was not obvious to earlier generations, despite their closer relationship to natural influences inherent in a more agrarian economy.

With the development of an industrial urban civilisation dependent upon the consumption of fossil fuels, and our own increasing knowledge, it has become clear that the environment is being moulded in potentially dangerous ways by human beings as never before. The Rio Earth Summit of June 1992 found political leaders from all over the globe discussing seriously the depletion of world resources (especially non-renewable energy sources), the phenomenon of global warming, the dangers of chemical, biological and radiation pollution in the atmosphere and oceans, and the destruction of animal and plant species through the destruction of valuable habitats such as the rain forest. Non-governmental groups at the same summit stressed the human population explosion and the maldistribution of resources between North and South as contributing to what they regard as a single problem resulting essentially from uncontrolled industrial growth.

The various wings of the green movement are inclined to unite in seeing these problems as the dominant political agenda for humanity in the late twentieth and early twenty-first centuries. Resources are being used up at an exponential (ever-increasing) rate, whilst the healthy complexity of the ecology of the planet is being continually reduced by commercial agriculture and industrial pollution. Thus, virtually all issues, from human reproduction through patterns of industrial investment and domestic consumption to tourism, can be viewed in an ecological light.

Divisions within the movement can be observed, particularly between what one might call the romantics and the scientists. On the 'romantic' side, the stress is on back-to-nature ideas such as homeopathy, vegetarianism, naturism and developing folk-music-playing rural communities. On the 'scientific' side the stress is on projections of economic and ecological disaster if present trends in industrialisation and consumption continue. A different division has also been observed between what is sometimes called the 'light anthropocentric' and the 'deep ecology' wings (Vincent (1992, 217)). The former stress the practical problems for human beings and may concentrate on individual problems pragmatically; the latter call for a total change of attitude by humans to recognise the intrinsic value of all other species.

An interesting example of the 'deep ecology' approach is James Lovelock's (1979) 'Gaia' hypothesis. This sees the earth as a single self-regulating organism. He stresses that living things created the atmosphere, the fertility of the soil, the temperature of the atmosphere, the oxygen we breathe, etc. and are, in turn, crucially dependent upon these things. It would seem to be a matter of some debate whether, despite the scientific terminology, this is a scientific, moral or spiritual doctrine. One implication of this would seem to be that, if necessary, Gaia will wipe out any species – including humanity – which seeks to upset the natural harmony of the eco-sphere!

As a political doctrine for intellectuals, 'ecologism' has great advantages: it has something to say on almost every issue, is opposed to many contemporary orthodoxies (especially the desirability of economic growth), has a variety of esoteric insights to offer and has appealing emotional undertones. In this sense, then, 'ecologism' can be seen as a rather radical and oppositional doctrine. On the other hand, in asserting the rights of succeeding generations against the present, there are echoes of the conservative sentiments expressed by Burke: 'I attest the retiring, I attest the advancing generations, between which, as a link in the great chain of eternal order we stand' (quoted in Sabine (1951, 519)). On the level of practical politics, greens can identify themselves with a variety of appealing local movements, especially of the NIMBY (*not in my back yard*) variety. There may, however, be major problems in educating large electorates in the need for measures which run directly counter to the consumerist trends of the times and in achieving the necessary international co-ordination to attain green objectives. (There is a discussion of the likely future influence of environmental factors in Chapter 9.)

Feminism as political radicalism

A consciousness of the need for political action to secure equal rights for women is scarcely new. As we saw in an earlier chapter, Plato envisaged women participating on an equal basis in government in Classical times. As early as 1792 Mary Wollstonecraft was arguing the case for female emancipation (Wollstonecraft (1985)). By the beginning of the twentieth century women had achieved the franchise in some American states and the Women's Suffrage movement had become a major political issue in Britain with radicals prepared to use violence against property and even suicide as a political weapon. Despite achieving universal suffrage in virtually all Western democracies, feminism remains a live political issue for many and the overwhelming passion of a few.

The vote has not brought equality of pay, status or opportunity for women. Attitudes to this fact may be roughly summarised in Box 8.

Box 8   Attitudes to gender differences

	Radical feminist	*Moderate*	*Conservative*
Problem	**Patriarchy** – government by men. Domination and **exploitation** of women by older men. Ideology dominates many women's thought as well as social institutions and socialization.	**Under-representation of women; sexual discrimination**.	**None** – apparent inequalities reflect *different* role women play in society. Caring for others, beauty, gentleness more important than power etc.
Causes	**Sexist power structure** – Rowbotham: sexual division of labour; Firestone: male control of female reproduction; Marxist: see Engels, reserve army of labour.	**Prejudice – ignorance** – tradition socialisation.	**Biology** – evolution or God has given females genetic tendency to passivity, caring, conscientious disposition.

Box 8   continued

	Radical feminist	*Moderate*	*Conservative*
Solution	**Revolution** – Marxist, personal or lesbian? Society must be remade: assumptions re family, carers, careers, politics, etc. reversed.	**Integration** – women to play full part in existing society.	**Apartheid** – women to remain separate but equal.
Action	**Women's liberation** – remove male structures of domination and ideology; Personal: take control of own life; Marxist: as part of proletarian revolution.	**Female participation; education; piece-meal legal action** – use legal rights to full, e.g. political nominations, educational opportunities.	**Legal action inappropriate** – safeguard family values.

'Radical' feminists have tended to see feminism as an all-embracing matter which should determine attitudes to a wide variety of issues – including the nature of work authority structures and careers, education, taxation and personal relationships. The nature of Western society has been warped by the aggressive and acquisitive elderly males of the species dominating and exploiting the young and the female.

Possibly as a result of media overreaction and misrepresentation of the views of a minority of radical feminists (customarily caricatured as bra-burning lesbians in the tabloid press), many people of moderate views would now hesitate to describe themselves as 'feminists'. However, moderates are now found endorsing what most people of the older generation of feminists would have regarded as a feminist stand. Thus, they take for granted the desirability of equal political rights for women, freedom to pursue any career without discrimination and equal pay for equal work.

Even amongst conservatives on the issue, few can be found to argue for the inferiority of women – in many cases the ostensibly flattering line is taken that women have quite rightly preferred not to get involved in male power games and should not compromise their essential nature by doing so (compare comments on racial apartheid in Chapter 5).

Radical feminists would argue that their more moderate sisters mistake the size of the problem in asserting equal status in a male-dominated society. Their analysis of the problem and suggested strategy and tactics, vary greatly from one group to another.

Thus, Marxist feminists tend to follow Engels in seeing the exploitation of women as being part of the capitalist phenomenon of a 'reserve army of labour'. Capitalists exploit an undertrained and underpaid and often part-time female work-force in order to keep the more organised and militant male work-force in order, allowing women to come somewhere near to their true potential only in the absence of men at the war-front. True emancipation can only come with the triumph of a proletarian revolution which will wipe away these repressive mechanisms (together with the bourgeois view of the family as male property). Other writers are less convinced that male domination is associated with capitalism pointing to the recurrence of a sexual division of labour in many non-capitalist societies (Rowbotham (1972)) and the power accruing to males until recently from their control of female reproduction (Firestone (1971)).

Most radical feminists have taken a line similar to the anarchists (indeed, Emma Goldman (1915) is a pioneer in both movements) in advocating that revolution must begin in the private lives of those who are convinced of its desirability. 'The personal is the political' is the slogan of many radical feminists, who argue that the centralised and authoritarian imposition of a way of life is a male style of politics. A tiny minority go one step further and argue that males will never voluntarily give up their power – no ruling class does – so that only in separatist lesbian communities can women achieve equality and freedom.

Although, to some extent, feminist ideas can be seen as an extension of liberal ideas on the rights of all to self-development, and some feminists have been influenced by Marxist doctrines about exploitation and ideology, the mainstream of the women's movement has been very much a series of autonomous self-help groups responding to the personal and political situations of their members.

The end of ideology?

It will be apparent to most readers that the predominant political style in modern European and North American democracies is what we have called 'pragmatic' rather than 'radical'. Democratic politicians in general seem slow to relate their policy stands to explicit general principles and appear to be content to manage existing societies rather than to try to fundamentally change them. Few contemporary Presidents, Prime Ministers or Cabinet Ministers would be happy to be labelled as Marxists, fascists, or as radical feminists or ecologists (or radical anything else) but tend to cling to the electorally safe centre ground of politics.

Such tendencies have been described as 'The End of Ideology' (Bell (1960)), but this may be a somewhat confusing description. One should distinguish between the somewhat cavalier approach to ideas which is typical of most practical politicians and the absence of any ideas. Similarly, a period of international confrontation between Marxist-Leninist and liberal democratic/capitalist systems may be drawing to an end, but this does not mean that new 'ideological' confrontations (for instance on religion, gender and ecology) may not occur.

A key factor here is the interpretation given to the concept of 'ideology'. One school of thought led by Karl Popper (1962) interprets 'ideology' as a way of political thinking typical of totalitarian movements. To Popper, an ideology is an all-encompassing and closed system of thought. Not only does such a system have something to say about virtually all political social and moral issues, but it is virtually impossible to disprove because there is always an explanation, within the terms of the ideology, for any apparent deviation from its predictions. Thus, for some (perhaps crude) Marxists, the revolution is always 'imminent' – but when it fails to come it is because the revolution was betrayed by its leaders, objective social conditions were misinterpreted or capitalism found new outlets for its surpluses. To give a simpler example of a closed system of thought; believers in magic will always point to examples when spells have worked – but if they 'fail' it is not because magic is nonsense but because the particular magician concerned was incompetent or a stronger magician invoked a counter-spell.

For Popper, then, ideological thinking should be opposed to scientific theorising which always produces *falsifiable* hypotheses. A scientific approach to social matters consists in developing piecemeal explanations about how things work and testing them out, not in having a grand theory which explains everything. The validity of scientific propositions (which are falsifiable) can be agreed upon by any two persons of good will in the light of the current evidence and are subject to modification in the light of new evidence. To make political judgments, however, people must also employ judgments about values which are specific to them and cannot be resolved by looking at evidence. Political innovation therefore depends upon building consensus about values between the people concerned as well as correctly interpreting cause and effect. Consequently, rather than building some grand Utopia on the basis of first principles, social change should proceed by means of 'piecemeal social engineering'.

From this point of view, the political doctrines of the centre – democratic socialism, liberalism and conservatism – are all non-ideological since they accept the need to base social policy upon as scientific as possible a review of its effects, and upon the value-judgements of the members of the community affected.

However, it is quite common to use the word 'ideology' in a much looser way to mean any more or less cohesive set of political principles. In this sense liberalism, socialism and conservatism can also be described as 'ideologies'. Marxists, as we have seen, tend to use the word to suggest the dominant ideas of a society which they see as reflecting its means of production. Thus, from many points of view, liberalism (in the broad sense described below) may fairly be described as the ideology of the capitalist era. As with many political terms, no definitive use of the concept can be prescribed – McClellan

(1986) notes twenty-seven different interpretations of the concept – what is important is that the sense in which it is used is clearly understood. Box 9 summarises three major views.

Box 9   Ideology as a political concept

Popper   an all-encompassing and closed system of thought (the opposite of scientific thinking);

Broad Sense   any more or less coherent set of political principles;

Marxist   the dominant ideas of a society seen as reflecting its means of production.

Liberalism

Liberalism may be understood in a broad or in a narrower sense. In the broad sense, one can argue that liberal ideas of individualism and constitutionalism form the basis of a constitutional consensus shared by most of the mainstream parties in the states of the European Union, the United States and many other 'liberal democracies'. In the narrower sense, liberalism is a doctrine professed by a number of democratic parties distinguished from more conservative/Christian democratic parties on the right and socialist parties on the left – the Liberal International being a formal expression of this and including the US (mainly New York) Liberal Party and the UK Liberal Democrats. An intermediate use of the term is common in the United States, where people on the left of the two main parties are frequently described as liberals with the expectation that they favour such causes as internationalism, civil rights and increased government intervention and spending for social welfare (many of these ideas being similar to those of the British Liberal Democrats).

A helpful simplification may be to distinguish three phases in the development of liberal ideas. The earliest phase is the establishment of the idea of constitutional government based upon individual rights. The United States' Constitution is a good expression of this. It incorporates ideas such as government being based on the consent of the governed, the constitution as a government of laws not of men, and the entrenchment of individual rights in the constitution. These are all a systematic expression of the American colonies' inheritance of the British parliamentary constitutional tradition and the Founding Fathers explicitly referred to the writings of Locke and to Montesquieu's [1688–1755] interpretation of the British Constitution (the Separation of Powers) (see Chapter 7, p.158).

In the second phase, nineteenth-century liberal writers like Bentham and the Millses developed the democratic implications of earlier statements and the experiences of earlier generations. The link with capitalism was also made explicit in a defence of doctrines of free trade and the desirability of a minimal state, building upon the writings of economists such as Adam Smith [1723–90] and Ricardo [1772–1823]. In England and on the Continent, liberals increasingly were seen as the party of the new modernising manufacturing elite opposed to the more conservative, if not 'feudal', landed gentry. In both Europe and North America liberals increasingly were the party of political reform and universal suffrage.

A third phase in the development of liberalism was marked in philosophical terms by the writings of the English Idealists (see Milne (1962)), including F.H. Bradley, Bernard Bosanquet, Josiah Royce (an American writer with some similar ideas) and most notably T.H. Green [1836–82] and Leonard Hobhouse [1864-1929]. The theme of much of idealist writing was a development of a theme evident in the writings of John Stuart Mill (1910) that the state exists so as to guarantee a system of rights which will enable individuals to pursue their moral development. As Green puts it, 'The state presupposes rights and rights of individuals. It is a form which society takes to maintain them.' (Green (1941, 144)). 'Only through the possession of rights can the power of the individual freely to make a common good of his own have reality given to it' (Green (1941, 45)). These rights include the right to private property, but these must be exercised in such a way as not to prevent others exercising them too. The state may thus intervene to regulate property and other rights in the interests of the development of a common sense of citizenship by all. The state cannot cannot directly promote 'habits of true citizenship' but it should actively concern itself with 'the removal of obstacles' (Green (1941, 208, 209)). He explicitly endorses state intervention to enable the mass of the population to enjoy reasonable standards of health, housing and access to property rights (Green (1941, 209)).

Hobhouse (1964 – originally published in 1911) gives a more explicit statement of political liberalism, identifying liberalism with civil, fiscal, personal, social, economic, domestic, local, racial, national, international and political liberty (Hobhouse (1964, Ch.II). He then goes on to make the further clear assertion that 'full liberty implies full equality' and to assert the correctness of distinguishing in terms of taxation between earned and unearned income and between acquired and inherited wealth (Hobhouse (1964, Ch. VIII)).

The third phase of liberalism is associated in Britain in the twentieth century with the political careers, speeches and writings of Lloyd George, John Maynard Keynes and Lord Beveridge. Lloyd George, as Chancellor of the Exchequer in the Liberal government before the First World War, can be seen as the practical inaugurator of social liberalism with his introduction of both old age pensions and death duties – that is, both state welfare schemes and progressive taxation. Beveridge in his Second World War Coalition government White Paper put forward a blueprint for the modern welfare state in which state-organised 'insurance' schemes and taxation would protect all citizens from the four giants of Ignorance, Want, Sloth and Disease. Keynes, as an economist and administrator, successfully argued the need for government intervention to ensure the efficient working of a capitalist economy. In the United States the inter-war Roosevelt New Deal administration adopted rather pragmatically a similar interventionist approach to the economy and welfare which has influenced the liberal Left ever since. Continental European liberal and radical parties have not all adopted this third phase of liberalism – indeed, left-wing Christian democrat movements like the former French MRP (Mouvement Republicain Populaire) may be seen as in some respects having much more in common with the British Liberal Democrats than their nominal allies in the Liberal International.

Conservatism

It can be argued that conservatism is more of an attitude than a doctrine. In every society many, often a majority, have been happy to conserve the existing values and institutions of that society. Naturally, the more prosperous and successful members of any given society are, the more likely to identify with its core values and institutions than poor and less successful citizens. Conservatives in a military dictatorship in the South are likely to be committed to radically different institutions and values to those in democratic industrial Britain or the United States.

Some components of a basic conservative attitude might, however, be suggested. A pessimism about human nature is often to be discerned (see previous chapter) with an associated stress on the need for domestic 'law and order' measures and strong armed forces to repel international threats. The need to support existing spiritual as well as secular authority will also be evident. Nationalism and support for 'family values' will usually also be found.

In the aftermath of the French revolution Edmund Burke [1729–97] sought to articulate a suspicion of rationalist egalitarianism and to praise instead the strength of the genius of the national constitution:

> We are afraid to put men to live and trade each on his own private stock of reason; because we suspect this stock in each man is so small, and that the individual would do better to avail themselves of the general bank and capital of nations and ages.
>
> Burke (1907 Vol. IV, 95)

Rather than a contract between individuals – like a trading agreement – the state is instituted as a partnership between the generations, 'between those who are living and those who are dead', to be approached with reverence.

Many of the themes presented somewhat rhetorically and unsystematically by Burke were expounded in a more philosophical, systematic and perhaps less intelligible way by nineteenth-century German idealists such as Hegel, to whom we have already referred.

In Britain the Conservative Party has supported both the Throne and the established Church. In the United States the symbols of continuity are now the national and state constitutions (interpreted to stress the limitations on government), the flag, prayers in schools and the like. Historically, conservatives in both countries have tended to be suspicious of grand theories of government and pragmatic in their pursuit of political support. Those on the Left have been attacked as pedlars of disunity and conflict, with trade unionism regarded with distaste – in America its links to socialism and 'hence' to the Soviet Union making it doubly unacceptable in recent years. British conservatives, however, were much influenced by Disraeli's [1804–81] doctrine, popularised in his novel *Sybil* and in his political practice as Prime Minister (1868 and 1874–80), that the idea of 'One Nation' should be preserved through a direct appeal to the interests of the working classes on the part of benevolent Tory governments. In the nineteenth century the Conservative Party was still led by a mainly aristocratic leadership who combined ideas of *noblesse oblige* with an inclination to 'dish the Whigs' by adopting popular social measures. The Liberals were often reluctant, because of their ideological commitment to *laissez-faire* (and the support of the new urban bourgeoisie), to take such measures.

Traditional conservative suspicion of grand theory may be epitomised by reference to the work of Michael Oakeshott:

> To some people 'government' appears as a vast reservoir of power which inspires them to dream of what use may be made of it. They have favourite projects of various dimensions, which they sincerely believe are for the benefit of mankind ... They are, thus disposed to recognise government as an instrument of passion; the art of politics is to inflame and direct desire ... Now the disposition of the Conservative in respect of politics reflects a quite different view ... to inject into activities of already too passionate men an ingredient of moderation; to restrain, to deflate, to pacify and to reconcile; not to stoke the fires of desire but to damp them down.
>
> Oakeshott (1962, 191–2)

In a well-known and rather striking image Michael Oakeshott further describes the politics as to:

> sail a bottomless and boundless sea; there is neither harbour for shelter nor floor for anchorage, neither starting-place nor appointed destination. The enterprise is to keep afloat on an even keel; the sea is both friend and enemy; and the seamanship consists in using the resources of a traditional manner of behaviour in order to make a friend of every hostile occasion.
>
> Oakeshott (1962, 127)

Thatcherism as political radicalism

It is somewhat paradoxical that, as the twentieth century has progressed, traditional conservatism in England has been somewhat eclipsed by a variety of neo-liberalism within the Conservative Party. Although the Conservative Party continues to attract some traditional 'one-nation' pragmatic supporters, an increasing number of MPs have become committed to the idea that the political and economic system requires radical reform to allow market forces to achieve and efficient and effective allocation of resources. The doctrine, which has become identified as 'Thatcherism', may have originated in the United States with such thinkers as Hayek (1979) and Milton Friedman (Friedman and Friedman (1980)). It was preached by Ronald Reagan in his Republican presidential campaigns, but its most sustained practical influence has been on Margaret Thatcher's Conservative administration from 1979.

The doctrine is discussed and evaluated at greater length in subsequent chapters (especially Chapter 6), but the point which is striking in this context is the extent to which the Thatcherites have – in distinction to usual British Conservative pragmatism – insisted on applying one theoretical analysis to a wide variety of policy areas. The extent of their opposition to the growth of the 'nanny state' and their insistence on the introduction of market mechanisms and privatisation, not only to social welfare areas but even to prisons, the Post Office and the armed forces, is remarkable.

'Thatcherism' can be seen as a variety of liberalism in its insistence on the importance of the free market, its individualism and support for electoral democracy on a national level. However, it retains support for the Crown, 'traditional family values' and a suspicion of internationalism (i.e. a lukewarm attitude to European Union political integration) from the conservative tradition.

Christian democracy

In recent years whilst what the British might call 'Thatcherite' political attitudes have been strong in the United States, the strongest organised force on the political right has been Christian fundamentalism with its emphasis on the so-called 'moral majority' issues of abortion, pornography and the like.

In Continental Europe, of course, the moderate centre-right position held by the Conservatives in Britain is occupied in many countries by the Christian democrats, whose enthusiasm for capitalism is balanced by electoral links to the countryside and by the Church's belief in co-operation and compassion in social affairs. In a number of countries, links with the trade union movement reinforce Christian democrat claims to a centrist rather than conservative/right-wing classification (Michael Smart in Smith (1989, 380)). Twentieth-century Catholic encyclicals on social matters have, for instance, stressed the moral dignity of labour and the legitimacy of involving the representatives of labour in decision-making in the work-place. They also endorse the idea of democratic decentralisation or subsidiarity (see Chapter 6).

The strongest Christian democratic parties seem to be in those Catholic countries where the Church has adopted something of a self-denying ordinance, allowing practical politicians room for manoeuvre. For simplicity, Protestant democratic parties have been omitted – but they are important in Holland and of influence in Switzerland and the Nordic countries. The CDU in Germany does include Protestants but attracts more support from Catholics (Dalton (1988, Ch. 8)). Thus, Christian democracy has been defined as

> a movement of those who aim to solve – with the aid of Christian principles and 'democratic' techniques – that range

of temporal problems which the Church has repeatedly and solemnly declared to lie within the 'supreme' competence of lay society, and outside direct ecclesiastical control.

> Fogarty (1957, 6), quoted in Smith (1989, 54)

More specifically, Irving discerns three basic principles in contemporary European Christian Democracy:

'Christian Principles' (in the sense of a broad commitment to basic human rights, particularly those of the individual); 'democracy' (in the sense of a clear cut commitment to liberal democracy) and 'integration' (in the dual sense of a commitment to class reconciliation through the concept of the broad-based *Volkspartei* and to transnational reconciliation through the strong Christian Democratic commitment to European integration).

> Irving (1979, xvii)

As Irving argues (1979, xxi), Christian democracy shares conservative values of individualism, respect for property values, anti-communism and dislike of excessive state intervention. However, unlike British Thatcherites, Christian democrats have favoured 'concertation' – consultation between government, industry, the trade unions and other interest groups. Couple this with an enthusiasm for Europe, and the similarities with the Heath wing of the modern UK Conservative Party are evident. (Edward Heath [Prime Minister 1970–74] is well known for his enthusiasm for European integration and, despite some more market-oriented policies early in his prime-ministerial period, he has tended to endorse more liberal stances on social issues and a willingness to consult and negotiate with interest groups.)

Socialism and social democracy

Last but not least in our review of 'isms', we come to socialism. We have already seen that both Marxists and many anarchists regard themselves as socialists – possibly as the only real socialists. Millions of people, however, remain committed to socialism without regarding themselves as disciples of Marx or opponents of the very concept of a state. Nor, as we have seen, does being influenced by Marxist ideas necessarily mean an admiration for the Soviet Union. For many Socialists the doctrine is the opposite of totalitarianism – it is a commitment to values of equality and justice for all. An interesting survey of British Labour MPs showed the book which had most influenced their political thinking was George Orwell's *1984* – a novel satirising the Stalinist approach to politics (Orwell (1949)). In a recent Fabian pamphlet Tony Blair writes of two socialist traditions: a Marxist economic determinist and collectivist tradition and another 'based on the belief that socialism is a set of values or beliefs – sometimes called ethical socialism' (Blair (1994, 2)). These values he defines as 'social justice, the equal worth of each citizen, equality of opportunity, community (1994, 4). This latter tradition he sees as predominant in 'European social democracy' and appropriate to the contemporary Labour Party.

Historically, it does seem that a strain of indigenous radicalism often associated with the non-conformist churches and stretching back to John Ball is more important than Marxism in the British socialist tradition. The non-conformist churches trained many Labour speakers in the skills of oratory and social organisation. Apparently, Tony Blair is a member of a formal Christian socialist group (*Guardian* (1994)). Certainly more important than Marxism has been the influence of a strong trade union and co-operative movement, both of which in England pre-date both Marx and the Labour Party. The Labour Party originated early in this century as The Labour Representation Committee to represent organised labour in Parliament. Only in 1918 did the LRC become the Labour Party, allow individual members and adopt a socialist statement of objectives in Clause 4 of its constitution – apparently in an attempt to appeal for middle-class intellectual support (McKibbin (1983, 97)).

Clause 4 of the Labour Party's 1918 Constitution stated that the objective of the party was:

> to secure for the workers by hand or by brain the full fruit of their industry and the most equitable distribution thereof that may be possible upon the basis of common ownership of the

means of production, distribution and exchange, and the best obtainable system of popular administration and control of each industry or service.

There have been many subsequent attempts to drop this statement by Labour leaders because it is interpreted as identifying the party too closely with the idea of nationalisation – even though the phrases 'common ownership' and 'best obtainable . . .' were surely meant to allow for at least cooperative and municipal ownership and possibly a more flexible interpretation still. For many years labourism might have been defined in terms of a Fabian strategy to bring about the collective management of the economy through a reliance on the power of the collective might of the organised working class. As George Bernard Shaw put it in *Fabian Tract 13* (1891), socialism was a doctrine of 'gradualist Collectivism brought about by a strategy of resolute constitutionalism'. The 'revisionists' who have wished to drop Clause 4 have argued that socialism is to be found more in a commitment to egalitarian and libertarian values than in specific measures to achieve these at any particular time. In Tony Blair's words, 'the old-style collectivism of several decades' age' is no longer radicalism but 'the neo-conservatism of the left' (Blair (1994, 7)). A similar debate has taken place within many continental European socialist (and former communist) parties – all the sharper in those cases where the party has been explicitly Marxist in the past.

Most writers on socialism have agreed that it is, in some sense, about a commitment to equality, but there has been little consensus about the nature of that commitment (Vincent (1992, 101–4)). Generally speaking, however, democratic socialists have agreed on emphasising equality of rights for all; in rejecting the legitimacy of extremist coercive and violent tactics, given the presence of a liberal democratic state with opportunities for peaceful and constitutional change; and in rejecting the unfairnesses of unregulated capitalist economics. The range of opinions within these parameters has been and remains a very large one. The new version of the Labour Party's Clause 4 is sufficiently broad to encompass many versions of 'democratic socialism' – and might also be acceptable to many Christian democrats, liberals and conservatives – but would exclude even a democratic version of a fully planned economy (see Box 10).

Box 10   The Labour party's new clause 4 (1995)

1. The Labour Party is a democratic socialist party. It believes that by the strength of our common endeavour, we achieve more than we achieve alone so as to create for each of us the means to realise our true potential and for all of us a community in which power, wealth and opportunity are in the hands of the many not the few, where the rights we enjoy reflect the duties we owe, and where we live together, freely, in a spirit of solidarity, tolerance and respect.

2. To these ends we work for:

• a dynamic economy, serving the public interest, in which the enterprise of the market and the rigour of competition are joined with the forces of partnership and co-operation to produce the wealth the nation needs and the opportunity for all to work and prosper, with a thriving private sector and high quality public services, where those undertakings essential to the common good are either owned by the public or accountable to them;

• a just society, which judges its strength by the condition of the weak as much as the strong, provides security against fear, and justice at work; which nurtures families, promotes equality of opportunity and delivers people from the tyranny of poverty, prejudice and the abuse of power.

• an open democracy, in which government is held to account by the people; decisions are taken as far as practicable by the communities they affect; and where fundamental human rights are guaranteed.

Box 10   continued

• a healthy environment, which we protect, enhance and hold in trust for future generations.

3. Labour is committed to the defence and security of the British people, and to co-operating in European institutions, the United Nations, the Commonwealth and other international bodies to secure peace, freedom, democracy, economic security and environmental protection for all.

4. Labour will work in pursuit of these aims with trade unions, co-operative societies and other affiliated organisations, and also with voluntary organisations, consumer groups and other representative bodies.

5. On the basis of these principles, Labour seeks the trust of the people to govern.

Conclusion

As we have seen, the 'Left'/'Right' distinction is a shaky one indeed. It conflates a number of different distinctions in attitudes: to the *degree* of change from the *status quo* – if in favour or against change from the present situation (which in turn is affected by which *status quo* one is considering!); to the *direction* of change – if in favour or against capitalism, clericalism or some other key political value; and to the *method* of change – constitutional or revolutionary.

In terms of the conventional distinction, fascism and communism may be seen as occupying opposite extremes, with liberal democrats at the centre, but from a 'centre' point of view, constitutional individualism constitutes one alternative whilst totalitarian collectivism (whether of the 'Right' or the 'Left') is the opposite extreme. Some anarchists might go one stage further seeing non-violent individualistic anarchism as the real Left, with liberal democrats back in the centre (classified according to the degree of force they are prepared to apply in the interests of 'society'), with Leninists and fascists as

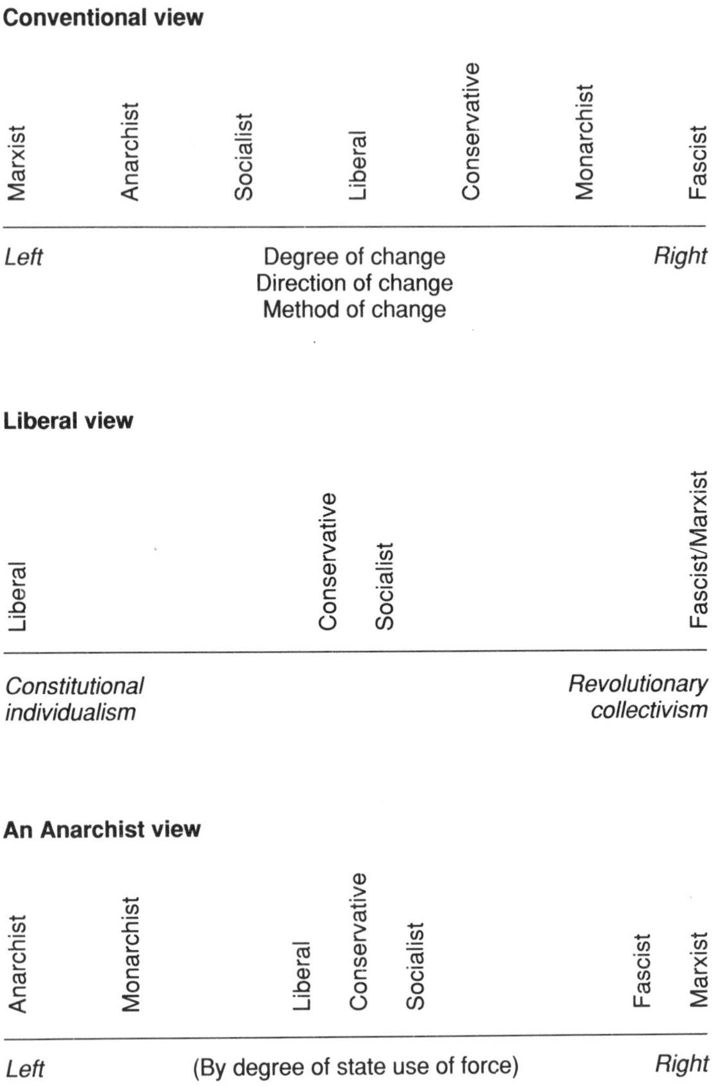

Conventional view

Marxist	Anarchist	Socialist	Liberal	Conservative	Monarchist	Fascist

Left   Degree of change   *Right*
Direction of change
Method of change

Liberal view

Liberal	Conservative	Socialist	Fascist/Marxist

*Constitutional
individualism*

*Revolutionary
collectivism*

An Anarchist view

Anarchist	Monarchist	Liberal	Conservative	Socialist	Fascist	Marxist

Left   (By degree of state use of force)   *Right*

FIGURE 4.1 Classifying political movements

the extreme Right, since both are prepared to mould individuals to a blueprint by force (see Figure 4.1).

The values around which political activity is conceived of as being polarised may well be changing as the twenty-first century approaches: those relating to class receding and controversies relating to gender, race, international inequalities and ecology becoming more important.

The possibility of a consolidation of the centre streams of thought also seems very likely to the author; the differences between revisionist democratic socialism, social liberalism, Christian democracy and pragmatic conservatism are surely small compared with the gulf which separates them from some of their unconstitutional radical and authoritarian alternatives.

Recommended reading

Eccleshall, Robert *et al.*, 1994, *Political Ideologies: an Introduction*, 2nd edn, London, Routledge. Useful standard introductory text – focused on the various isms.

Morgan, Michael L. (ed.), 1992, *Classics of Moral and Political Theory*, Indianopolis, Hackett. Reader including the standard texts and commentary.

or Rendell, Michael J., 1978, *Introduction to Political Thought*, London, Sidgwick & Jackson. Reader including the standard texts and commentary, more accessible for beginners than the above but unfortunately out of print.

de Crespigny, Anthony and Minogue, Kenneth (eds), 1976, *Contemporary Political Philosophers*, London, Methuen. Useful collection of essays on some key recent political theorists.

Jansen, J.H., 1979, *Militant Islam*, London, Pan. A little dated but a very readable and sensible introduction to the topic.

Bryson, Valerie, 1992, *Feminist Political Theory: An Introduction*, London, Macmillan. Useful introduction to a key issue in contemporary debate.

Plamenatz, John [revised Plamenatz, M.E. and Wokler, Robert], 1992, *Man and Society*, 2nd edn, London, Longman, 3 Volumes. Standard British text on the history of political thought concentrating on classic writers such as Machiavelli, Hobbes, Rousseau, Bentham and Marx.

Chapter 5

Issues

What are the issues in politics?

In an earlier chapter we considered whether the divisions between human beings and their tendency to conflict and aggression required a state and concluded that whilst not indispensable, a mechanism for the resolution of disputes was certainly required. In this chapter we return to the question from a rather different angle – to consider the nature of such disputes more precisely. In the twenty-first century, which will shortly be upon us, these divisions remain great enough to make our survival as a species – certainly living in civilised communities – problematic. The threat of nuclear destruction remains, although superpower confrontation may have waned. Individuals and groups remain in aggressive confrontation divided by lines of ideology, nationalism, 'race', wealth and poverty, and sexual identity. We first consider the nature of these divisions and then go on to consider how such differences can be managed.

Such divisions can be seen from many perspectives, but it may help to see them in four main ways: the struggle for power; the management of public policy; the conflict of ideas; and the clash of social interests. The same political conflict may often be helpfully seen in the light of all four perspectives, rather than exclusively in terms of one of them.

The state and the struggle for power

The establishment of state machinery seems inevitably to bring with it the establishment not only of a hierarchy of power (which occurs by definition – power is being centralised in the hands of a few – even if they hold it in trust for others), but also a hierarchy of prestige and of economic resources. In most societies (one possible exception is the Zuni indians of New Mexico (Benedict (1935)) this seems then to produce conflicts between politicians to achieve the political offices with most prestige and power. This struggle for power – which may involve anything from open and honourable oratorical competition before the electorate to corruption, blackmail and murder – is what some people think of as 'politics', and may give rise to cynicism and even despair about the political process. Such activities are often described as 'Machiavellian' even by people who have never read *The Prince* (1961), which does indeed describe many ruthless manoeuvres to achieve and maintain power. (e.g. Section VIII: 'Those Who Come To Power By Crime'). An account of politics without a consideration of such matters cannot be regarded as realistic – and many textbooks on politics still fail in this respect.

However, most political situations require politicians to generate support by acquiring allies wedded to them by more than a cynical desire to share the fruits of office. Public support has to be acquired by appealing to broader ideas or interests at least apparently shared by the politician and his 'constituency' ('constituency' includes the support of, say, the Church for a royal minister in a kingdom or the support of the army for a third world minister – not just the electorate). The ideas of the public good to which politicians appeal in this way may indeed be served by the most cynical of politicians. Thus, it matters little whether Lincoln, in freeing American slaves in the Civil War, did so out of a conviction that they were morally entitled to be liberated or because he saw it as expedient in order to ensure a Northern victory – the cause of freedom was still advanced. (He appears to have been wedded, in fact, to the cause of US unity above that of Abolition or, probably, his own self-interest). Machiavelli [1469–1527], indeed has often been interpreted not as a political cynic but as a nationalist prepared to use whatever means were available. His book ends in an 'Exhortation to liberate Italy from the barbarians' (Machiavelli (1961)).

Given the opaque nature of human motivation, it would be an insubstantial ground for a study of politics to base it mainly upon some theory of the motivation of politicians. Their struggle for power is evident, their motives may be pure or selfish – but most probably are a mixture of virtue, selfishness and a desire for recognition. It can be argued that more important for us are the conditions which allow politicians to succeed or fail rather than the motivations which drive them. The existence of positions of power to which new blood must inevitably succeed (if only as a result of the death of an hereditary monarch) ensures that some 'struggle for power' must take place. In the language of the functionalists, political recruitment must take place to political roles within the system. What is interesting is what impact the way this is done has on the policy outputs of the system.

The inter-state struggle for power

Just as the creation of a state can be seen to make some sort of struggle for power among politicians inevitable, so the existence of a number of states in an international arena makes likely a competition for power amongst 'statesmen' (as politicians in their international role are more likely to be called). As we saw in Chapter 2, there has been a tendency to see relationships amongst states as a ('zero-sum') competition for prestige and influence. Politicians often seek domestic prestige by seeking to appear important international statesmen, which may take the relatively harmless form of holding 'summits' or appearing as the successful arbiter of some dispute between third parties, but which can consist in acquiring extra colonial territories (nineteenth-century version) or commissioning the ballistic missile chastisement of a third world transgressor (USA in the 1990s version).

The costs and dangers of international diplomatic forays will vary dramatically with the stability of the international system. In ancient times the cost of foreign adventures for a Roman or Chinese Emperor (or a general with ambitions to the post) seemed relatively small given the overwhelming preponderance of power on one side against the divided states surrounding it. In the 1990s the case may be the same for an American President. More dangerous, clearly, was the 'bi-polar' world of the cold war in which a rough equivalence of power between the Soviet Bloc and the US-led NATO alliance gave the world the appearance of a chess-board upon which a dangerous game was being played. Luckily, players on both sides appreciated that neither had the three-to-one military superiority which strategists deem necessary for a successful attack (or they were deterred by the prospect of nuclear 'overkill').

Historical precedents (1914 and 1939 especially) suggest that still more dangerous than either of these situations is the 'balance of power' situation, in which a larger number of more or less evenly balanced 'powers' exist in a state of some uncertainty regarding alliances and relative strengths. It may then become easy for even a rational 'player' of the international 'game' to miscalculate the consequences of a proposed move (e.g. an ultimatum to a minor player to give up some territory; a proposal to base missiles near to a competitor). If some of the 'players' are not in fact rational – or do not recognise the rules of the game – then the situation is the more dangerous (see Wright and Walt (1986), *Review of International Studies* (1989)).

Without attempting a more sophisticated analysis of the variety of international situations which are possible, the built-in (or 'structural') instabilities of inter-state relationships based upon a number of independent armed states is evident. If independence can only be guaranteed by alliances with other states and/or strong military forces, the incentive exists to continually build up one's own armed forces and to expand the web of alliances of which one is a member – and perhaps to 'destabilise' opposing alliances/states. Yet each increment in one state's forces will only provoke a similar response on the other side; every change in the structure of alliances prompts a recalculation of the balance of advantage – which may be miscalculated – and further attempts at subversion on the other side. The situation is therefore likely to increase in danger as the years go by – 'arms races' are an in-built feature of such a system.

Lasswell (in Huntington (1962a)) has pointed out an additional problem of such situations (primarily in the context of the cold war) in his 'garrison state' hypothesis. Such confrontations may occur without any aggressive intent on either side – each side being merely preoccupied with maintaining their own security. However, as confrontation proceeds 'the military definition of reality' comes to predominate. The other side is increasingly seen as the Enemy, diplomacy is confounded with intelligence and subversion, cultural contacts are seen as part of a propaganda war, academic institutions are seen as strategic resources, industrial discontent is seen as subversion, and so on. This is clearly a threat to domestic democratic institutions where they exist, although it should not be thought that the dominance of the military necessarily leads to aggression, since professional soldiers are well aware of the hazards and destructiveness of modern warfare (Huntington (1957)).

Ideas and practical politics

Perceptive readers may have been struck by the fact that although much has been said so far in this chapter of relevance to the cold war no mention has been made of concepts such as communism, capitalism and the like. What, then, is the relevance of the sorts of concepts and ideas discussed in the previous two chapters to the real world of political conflict (and compromise)? The relationship seems to be a highly complex one.

Only for a tiny minority can it be said that there is no real distinction – that political activity is the attempt to implement some coherent and comprehensive political doctrine (an 'ideology'). Such an approach is now largely confined to tiny radical fringe parties such as the Socialist Workers' Party in Britain – what the French term 'groupuscules' – and seems out of joint with the predominant pragmatism of the times.

For ordinary voters, much research on voting behaviour suggests that they are more concerned with the record of the current government in securing (or not) economic prosperity, than with the implementation of any abstract programmes of social justice. In most countries, certainly in Britain, the electorate has had little or no political education at school, and the 'tabloid' mass media provide political information in pre-digested 'sound-bite' form rather than in a coherent and structured way. That is not to say, however, that formal political theories have not influenced ordinary voters. Keynes (1936, Book 6, Ch. 24) wrote 'Practical men who believe themselves to be quite exempt from any intellectual influences, are usually the slaves of some defunct economist'. A similar observation can surely be made of the 'practical' voter. The ordinary voter in Britain is doubtless the unknowing heir to the Natural Right theorists such as Locke, whom we have discussed earlier, in that without any acquaintanceship with their works, many of their concepts are taken for granted as 'common sense'.

For all practical politicians, political ideas constitute a major part of their stock-in-trade. As Edelman (1977) argues, words are potent weapons in the business of building alliances, marking points of conflict, buying votes at least expense and confusing issues which might divide. Regardless of politicians' own views, they must be sensitive to the nuances of the abstract terms in which they present the issues. To what extent abstract ideas of democracy, freedom, socialism or liberalism determine the objectives of individual politicians or governments is much more difficult to establish. Some, no doubt, retain their initial enthusiasm for grand programmes of change – Mrs Thatcher's approach was sufficiently 'ideological' to justify the coining of the term 'Thatcherism', whilst leaders such as Kwame Nkrumah of Ghana, Enver Hoxha of Albania and Colonel Gadahfi of Libya have all made claims to fame as ideologists as well as statesmen. However, historical studies of even such strong leaders as Churchill, de Gaulle and Kennedy seem to suggest that the practical necessity to compromise in order to retain office and influence, and the impact of unforeseen events, often sway the most determined and strong-minded of leaders. Certainly, a major category of writing by socialist intellectuals comes into the category of 'how we were betrayed by our parliamentary leaders' (Michels (1915)).

Managing public policy – for whom?

If political issues are to extend to more than who should rule, but are not normally dictated by an ideological agenda, where do they come from? Observation suggests that politicians in power spend much of their time on routine 'housekeeping' functions (managing the public service including its welfare and defence operations, raising and spending taxes), reacting to unexpected emergencies such as war, epidemics, famine and floods and reacting to problems raised by press and public. In short, we are reminded of Deutsch's (1963) analogy of government as the steering mechanism for society or Oakeshott's (1962) metaphor of statesmanship as steering a ship at sea to an unknown destination.

To the non-political ordinary citizen it often appears obvious that what the government/politicians should concentrate on is finding sensible solutions to whatever problems occur without excessive concentration on party/ideological considerations. This idea of 'rational policy-making' also has its disciples in the academic sphere as we shall see in Chapter 8. In practice, many middle-of-the-road politicians (e.g. 'one nation' Conservatives in Britain, much of the Labour Right, most Republicans and Democrats in the USA) and a great many civil servants share a similar orientation to public life.

Our discussion of Bachrach and Baratz's (1970) work earlier suggests one difficulty with such an approach – who defines what is a problem? A related difficulty raises similar issues – what is an acceptable 'solution'? Bachrach and Baratz, writing in a US context, stress the domination of WASPs (White Anglo-Saxon Protestants) in setting the agenda of US politics. In Britain we could perhaps go further and suggest that the 'chattering classes' who dominate politics, the media, academic and professional life and the civil service are still predominantly London-resident public school/Oxford or Cambridge Arts graduates and the like. What such people see as urgent problems are not necessarily the same as what ordinary people, who left school at the minimum leaving age, are employed in manual jobs (or are unemployed) and live in Lancashire or Scotland, would place in the same category.

Similarly, the 'same' problem may be understood in radically different terms from different perspectives. Thus, the existence of increasing numbers of young unmarried mothers can be seen primarily as a symptom of Britain's moral decline, as a serious threat to the social security budget, as a consequence of the failure of sex education, as a symptom of the emergence of a deprived underclass on Britain's former council estates; or it may not be regarded as a problem at all, but merely a consequence of changing individual moral choices or indeed as a welcome sign of inevitable progress toward the extinction of the bourgeois/patriarchial family.

Hence, too, a 'solution' is an equally contentious matter. In our example, does this mean no more premarital sex; fathers supporting financially all their biological children; no more 'unprotected' premarital sex; full employment and community renewal in deprived areas; or abandoning the expectation that all children are brought up in two-parent families? The terminology of 'problem' and 'solution', as de Jouvenal (1963) points out, may also be introducing a misleading mathematical analogy – that reasoning will lead us to a unique resolution of a defined problem. One might more sensibly speak of managing a situation.

Further consideration of this 'problem' will make clear another vital point about the nature of political conflict. We can see that the same problem has been seen through different ideological spectacles in the example (moral majority, 'Thatcherite', liberal, socialist, feminist), but it is also clear that different perspectives are to some extent a question of from whose eyes we are looking (the moralising detached observer, the taxpayer, a sympathetic outsider, the mothers, fathers or children concerned, fellow residents of stigmatised estates, etc.). In short, political conflicts are as much about the *interests* of groups of people as they are about power struggles, ideas or social management.

As we shall see in more detail in Chapter 7, almost any group of people – from Flat Earthers to the owners of Pit Bull Terriers – can combine to press a political policy issue, but it will be enlightening to consider which groups people most usually consider themselves to belong to from the point of view of pressing their political interests. In short, we turn to the important question of political identity.

Political identity

One important clue to the way people identify themselves politically is to consider the names of some typical political parties:

UK	Conservative, Liberal, Labour, Scottish National (SNP)
USA	Democratic, Republican
Continental Europe	Christian Democrat, Communist, Peasant, Socialist, Radical
Asia	Jan Sangh, Malaysian Chinese Association (MCA), Congress Party of India
S. Africa	Inkatha
Mexico	Institutional Revolutionary Party (PRI)

A few of these names may be interpreted as referring in the most general way to a temperamental approach to politics: Conservative (wishing to hold on to what we have – favouring little or gradual change); Radical (seeking root and branch reform); Revolutionary (seeking the total overthrow of the existing order). Conventionally, people's political attitudes are seen as lying on a Right/Left spectrum of this sort and in some two-party systems the division between the two major parties has been explained by some commentators in these, 'temperamental' terms (e.g. Conservative/Liberal in nineteenth-century Britain and Republican/Democrat in the USA).

More of the names refer to the general sets of political ideas which we have already considered – liberal, socialist, communist, conservative.

What is striking, however, is the number of names which refer specifically to sectional groups within a state's population: national (SNP, Inkatha ('Spear of the [Zulu] Nation)); ethnic/racial (MCA); religious (Christian Democrat, Jan Sangh (Hindu)) or class/occupation (Labour, Peasant). Indeed, if we look behind the official name of political parties we find that they frequently are, in fact, mainly or exclusively supported by one such group: for instance, the Republican Party of India was formerly called the Scheduled Castes Federation (i.e. the 'untouchables'), whilst the former grandly titled Nigerian National Democratic Party was, in fact, confined to a faction of the

Yoruba peoples of western Nigeria. Conversely, some parties, like the Congress Party of India and the PRI, seek to unite virtually everyone in the state in the cause of nationalism.

Many studies of voting behaviour reinforce this picture of voters identifying with political parties (however abstractly described) largely as an expression of national, ethnic/racial, religious or class loyalties (this being as true in the United States and the UK as in India or South Africa). Parties are seen as fighting for the interests of 'our' group, so that 'we' benefit from their success. Nor is this behaviour limited to the voting arena; much cabinet building, voting in legislatures and arguing about federal principles and social justice seems explicable in the same terms (Enloe (1986)).

At one level such behaviour is unsurprising – human beings are clearly social animals loyal to the in-group and suspicious, at least, of out-groups (see Sherif *et al.* (1966), a classic study of boys at a summer camp). The problem, as Tajfel and Turner (1979) point out, is that in building a positive sense of 'social identity', in-groups often resort to 'stereotyping' out-groups. That is, all members of the out-group are perceived as having a standard set of (inferior) qualities to one's own. But, as students of politics, we may wish to consider why the pattern of such loyalties varies from place to place. The functionalist concepts of political socialisation and political culture may help to describe and explain these differences, but the explanation they offer is only a partial one, as we shall see.

Political socialisation and political culture

The short answer to why people identify themselves in different ways is to point to the formative political experiences which have moulded them – to the processes of 'political socialisation'. In short they have learnt who they are. The term 'socialisation' does seem preferable to the perhaps more familiar term 'education' because it stresses the broader and informal influences at work. In particular, home influences have been demonstrated to be much more important than school or college education. The mass media are also an important source of political information and attitudes. It is also probable that influences in early adulthood, when habits of voting or other forms of political participation are established, can be important – this would include influences from workmates or comrades-in-arms and key political events at this time. In fact, political generations sharing common experiences and attitudes may exist – thus all those who grew up in immediate post-war Britain share experiences of austerity – e.g. sweet-rationing! – followed by the onset of television and the 'Never Had It So Good' era ('Never Had It So Good' being the Conservative slogan in the 1959 general election). In short, people tend to absorb the political values and ideas of the key face-to-face social groups to which they belong, as illustrated in Box 11.

Box 11   Political socialisation

Definitions

the personal and social origins of political outlooks.
                                    Dawson *et al.* (1977, 1)

is the process of induction into political culture. Its end product is a set of attitudes, cognitions, value standards and feelings – toward the political system, its various roles, and role incumbents. It also includes knowledge of, values affecting, and feelings toward the inputs of demands and claims into the system, and its authoritative output.
                        Almond in Almond and Coleman (1960, 26–58)

Typical research findings

(a) Attitudes to President   % Agreeing in school grade

	2	4	6	8	10	12
'President cares a lot' (1961)	75	56	46	43		
(1974)	79	65	32	28	22	16

SOURCES   Hershey and Hill (1975); Easton and Dennis (1969); Hess and Torney (1967)

Box 11   continued

(b) Most popularly used sources of information about foreign people

Nationality	N. American	Bantu (sic)	Brazilian	Turkish
6 year olds	TV movies (parents)	parents	parents (contact)	parents friends
10 year olds	TV movies books courses texts magazines	parents contact teachers	movies magazines contact	books texts courses magazines

SOURCE   Lambert and Klineberg (1967)

A number of fascinating studies have documented the considerable differences between countries and social groups as to their perceptions and level of knowledge of politics and their attitudes towards political power and institutions. Some of these differences in 'political culture' are summarised in Box 12 and clearly are important in understanding differences between political systems in different countries.

So one explanation as to why people identify politically with distinct social groups is that they have been socialised into diverse political cultures in which different lines of social division are important. However, this does not explain why political cultures vary in this way. For this, we have to look at the history and social structures of the specific countries concerned. It can be argued that the concepts of culture and socialisation have merely assisted us somewhat in the systematic description of the problem, rather than solving it.

Box 12   Political culture

Definition

The mental and intellectual environment in which poli-tics is shaped, interpreted and judged. The knowledge, beliefs, values and attitudes of individuals and soci-eties towards government and politics.

Pye and Verba (1965)

Typical research findings

	% Agreeing				
	USA	UK	Germany	Italy	Mexico
Participation/parochialism 'National govt. has great effect on daily life'	41	33	38	23	7
Trust/distrust 'Most people can be trusted'	55	49	19	7	30
Hierarchy-acceptance/resentment 'Expect equal consideration from bureaucracy'	48	59	53	35	14
Can affect an unjust law	75	62	38	28	38
Liberty-toleration/coercion Against cross-party marriage	4	12+		58*	
Loyalty Most proud of govt./ pol. insts.	85	46	7	3	30

Key   + = Conservative/Labour * = Christian Democrat/Communist
SOURCE   Almond and Verba (1963)

Types of political culture

Parochial/Subject/Participant individuals
Homogeneous/Fragmented/Dual cultures

Localism, nationalism and ethnicity

One sort of division which seems to be almost universal in larger political systems is what Allardt and Littunen (1964) and others have termed vertical lines of division – those between localities, regions and, in some cases, national areas within states. It can be argued that, other things being equal, the nearer people live together, and hence the more communication and, probably, economic and social interdependence there is between them, the more they are likely to perceive themselves as having interests in common. Hence, people in the village of Haworth may see themselves first as Haworth residents, then perhaps as people from the Bradford area or West Riding, almost certainly as Yorkshire folk, as English, as British, and possibly as Europeans too. Political (or sporting!) divisions may arise between the interests of Yorkshire and Lancashire without either ceasing to feel loyalty to England. Divisions between England and Scotland may not preclude common action in Europe, and so on. Similarly, a resident of Harlem may also feel themselves to be a citizen of New York City and New York State as well as of the United States. Clearly, the influence of geographical nearness will be influenced by a host of other factors which may affect the strength of local or regional loyalties. For example: how mobile is the population (if a resident of Haworth is commuting daily to Bradford and was born in nearby Keighley, then the West Riding identity may be more important to them than to someone born in Lancashire); how socially and linguistically divided are the geographical communities (a Gaelic-speaking Scot may feel a greater separation from England than an English-speaking one); what is the nature of the economy (a self-sufficient peasant agricultural community for example, will feel much stronger local ties than a university-based one).

As the Scottish/English dimension also suggests, the influence of historical conquests and of migration is a major factor in these sorts of divisions. Scots have, of course, historically moved (many would say been driven) both southwards into England and across the sea to Northern Ireland and the United States. Here, they and their descendants may retain, to a lesser or greater extent, a Scottish identity which may cut across their 'residential' identity. In New York, of course, almost everyone has such a secondary identity, being Puerto-Rican, Jewish, Irish or African-Americans. In Bradford a substantial minority of inhabitants are of Bangladeshi and Pakistani origin. Many African states resemble a jigsaw in which an untidy pattern of migration and conquest by its original inhabitants has been framed by the artificial straight lines of the European-imposed colonial boundaries.

These secondary or 'ethnic' identities may be of greater or lesser social and political importance depending upon a similar variety of factors to those influencing localism. Major factors include the arithmetic balance between communities and their relative economic and political power. Thus, a small group occupying an unimportant but useful economic role (e.g. Chinese or Indians running take-aways and restaurants) in an otherwise undivided community may be almost invisible, whereas a similar sized group which owns a large part of the land upon which the majority community lives and farms (e.g. a European group in a post-colonial country) may be extremely visible and vulnerable to political pressure. Another factor may be the degree of linguistic, cultural and religious differences between groups – the greater the differences the less easy it may be for the groups to communicate, integrate and negotiate.

Racial and ethnic integration

An important psychological and political factor seems to be the 'racial' identity of the ethnic groups concerned. By 'racial' is meant the existence of real or assumed visible physical differences – particularly in skin colour – between the groups. Such differences are socially rather than biologically defined – existing human communities being virtually all extremely mixed genetically and not according to the biological definition of 'race'. For instance, most US 'blacks' would be regarded as whites in tropical Africa; most South African 'whites' probably have some 'black' ancestry. In essence, this often means a division between 'whites' and 'non-whites'. (As E.M. Forster (1972) pointed out, literally it would be more accurate and perhaps desirably deflating to refer to this as pinko-grey and non-pinko-grey).

The importance of the distinction between black and white

'races' seems to link quite clearly with our inheritance from the period of European imperialism in which a racial justification was advanced for both slavery and colonialism. For instance, British imperial prosperity was for long founded on the triangular trade, by means of which arms, metal tools and trinkets were exported to West Africa, where they were exchanged for slaves who were transported to the Caribbean or American colonies to be used in growing tobacco, spices and cotton. These valuable commodities, in turn, could then be transported back to Liverpool, Bristol or London. Each leg of the journey was enormously profitable, but the subjection of negro slaves and the conquest of the Caribbean and North America had to be justified in terms of the superiority of white Christian civilisation over the alleged barbarity of the 'natives'. As the European powers, and later the United States, continued their competitive acquisition of much of the globe, their success in subduing less well-armed and aggressive societies was, in turn, held to be an indication of this alleged superiority.

This historical legacy of racism has been accentuated by a web of cultural and literary symbolism – with black the colour of evil, white the symbol of innocence – and racist pseudo-scientific findings about the inherited lower intelligence of 'non-Aryan' races.

The importance of racism is dramatically illustrated if we consider the history of ethnic relations in US cities. Waves of ethnic groups – Irish, Russian, Italian, Jewish, Puerto Rican – have arrived successively in many American cities to go through similar processes of accommodation, integration and assimilation. At first, such groups have been accommodated in the worst city-centre slums, in multiple-occupation 'tenements'. They have taken the worst-paid, lowest status jobs and usually formed isolated groups, seeking help from already established members of their own community. Very often, first- and even second-generation immigrants sought to maintain their own cultural, religious and linguistic traditions and planned to return to their country of origin on retirement.

However, such groups have consistently gradually assimilated to the American 'way of life'. First, they have become politically organised – even if through corrupt 'bosses' and trade unions – their votes and bargaining power being sought first by others, then by members of their own community. Next, second- and third-generation immigrants have sought acceptance in the wider American society by Anglicising names, obtaining college educations, moving out into the affluent suburbs. Integration has gradually occurred partly on the basis of the new immigrant group accepting American values and citizenship (tolerance, democracy and affluence having often attracted the group in the first place), but also on the basis of America accepting a rich kaleidoscope of cultural traditions and religious beliefs within society. The power of many 'immigrant' groups has been comfortably accepted in many respects – consider the giant St Patrick's Day parade every year in New York and the political power of the Kennedy family. Whilst Catholicism was, at first, regarded as a badge of inferior immigrant status (and as late as the 1920s Al Smith's candidacy for the presidency may have been defeated by a Protestant backlash) it is now just one more fully acceptable 'denomination' of Christianity (Jones (1960)).

In contrast to this, the African-American group was one of the first to arrive in what is now the United States (indeed, the original constitution envisaged banning the further importation of slaves after 1808) but has been the last to achieve anything near equal status with the WASP majority. For many years blacks were mainly detained as slaves on Southern rural farms and plantations. But even after Emancipation in 1865 they remained the victims of massive social and political discrimination. Although they long ago lost their specific African languages and cultures, have contributed greatly to distinctive American culture and interbred extensively with the white population, it was only with the Civil Rights Act of 1965 that they can be said to have achieved anything like full and effective citizenship.

Dominance, assimilation and social pluralism

As far as both ethnic and racial relations are concerned, three main alternative social and political patterns seem possible. First, a relationship of (usually racial) social and political dominance – the South African term of 'Apartheid' being appropriate. The most complete expression of this being where one group is enslaved by the other. In more recent years, however, such a frank state of affairs has seemed unacceptably bad public relations in a world in which the rhetoric, at least, of democracy predominates. Therefore, the language of equality and nationalism usually prevails. In America the official doctrine of 'separate but equal' prevailed between the landmark Supreme Court rulings of *Plessey v. Ferguson* (1896) and *Brown v. The Board of Education of Topeka* (1954) (see Chapter 7, p.167, until it was conceded that such a doctrine was a contradiction in terms. In Africa, white dominance in South Africa was justified by the creation of 'Homelands' in which blacks were accorded the trappings of sovereignty – millions of blacks being declared aliens in the land of their birth. In contemporary Europe there is a similar tendency to declare immigrant 'guest workers' of unsuitable ethnic origin to be non-citizens without rights. Similarly, in Malaysia, 'Malays' (those who speak Malay, practise Islam and conform to Malay customs) have a special status in citizenship and land law as opposed to others, in effect those of Chinese and Indian origin (Suffian and Lee *et al.* (1978, 94)).

An alternative approach to the management of ethnic and racial differences is an assimilationist one, in which members of 'minority' communities are granted equality and rights to the extent to which they adopt the way of life of the 'dominant' group. Thus, as we have seen, French colonial policy was based on the doctrine of the equality of all civilised men – civilisation being equated largely with French education, language and loyalty! In effect, US citizenship policy has had some elements of this, with a requirement for fluency in English, knowledge of the constitution and the swearing of allegiance. In Britain, a number of Conservative politicians have also demanded that immigrants should learn to play cricket (or, if they already do so, cheer England at test matches) and respect the Christian inheritance of their new homeland.

Another model for achieving the integration of different ethnic or racial groups in one society is the pluralist one which, to a large extent, has predominated in the USA. In European terms one might call it the Swiss model – in which separate groups respect each others' linguistic, religious and cultural inheritances. Whilst a degree of convergence may take place in terms of values and political habits, there is no requirement that one group's values be seen as the orthodoxy for the society as a whole. Clearly, tolerance and negotiated compromises must mark such a society if it is to endure.

A distinction should be drawn between social and political pluralism. What we have been describing is a model of social pluralism in an ethnically or racially mixed society. Politically, this may be accompanied by explicit provision for the participation of different social groups in government, as in Switzerland, where the linguistically and religiously distinct cantons are guaranteed participation in the federal cabinet (a similar arrangement has been attempted less happily in the Lebanon). The same result may be achieved more informally, as in the Netherlands, where separate religious and political traditions are accommodated by having separate radio stations and schools; or in the United States where ethnic representation is accomplished through a flexible party and interest group system and a decentralised constitution.

Political pluralism, however, is a broader concept, which fits well with social pluralism in the sense we have used it. But it is broader in that it suggests *any* group is free to pursue its interests in the political system and stands a realistic chance of exercising influence. A more sophisticated treatment of this concept requires us to consider other sorts of policy issues in addition to those we have so far dealt with.

Elites, classes and political pluralism

We have already discussed the concept of 'vertical' lines of division within society – meaning that geographical communities may come into conflict. It is clear that 'horizontal' divisions also frequently divide societies, so that within virtually every geographical community there are to be found rich and poor, the powerful and the powerless, those with prestige and those without. As Pareto (1976) puts it, for every desirable unevenly distributed social quality, there exists an 'elite' who possess that quality in abundance – economic, political social, sporting, even 'sex appeal'. There is also, of course, a usually more numerous, 'mass' who suffer from a relative lack of that quality.

As C. Wright Mills (1956) argues, the existence of elites is hardly in dispute as far as modern industrial societies are concerned.

What is more controversial is the political significance of this observation and the causes of these differences. Simplifying somewhat, we can say that historically three main models have been used in discussing this issue: elite theorists, who see the main political division as being between the holders of political power and the rest; Marxists, who see political and social divisions as reflecting economic divisions – classes as the fundamental political entities; and pluralists, who regard the divisions between elites and masses as only one of a series of non-coincidental lines of division within society.

This argument can be formulated in an alternative fashion: is there a single ruling group in modern industrial societies? If so, what are its characteristics – is this 'class rule'?

This being a big question – perhaps *the* big question – in politics, it is worth considering carefully, and the reader would be foolish to accept a conclusion from the author without investigating the mass of evidence which has been accumulated about different societies in more depth. Rather than seeking a definitive conclusion now, it may be more useful to offer some guidelines on evaluating the sort of evidence which has been put forward.

At this point it is worth re-stressing a point made in Chapter 1: a number of the writers on all sides in this debate are long on theoretical propositions, suppositions and rhetoric, and short on evidence. Also, evidence that a proposition applies in one or two places and times does not constitute proof that it is universal.

It is striking that writers supporting different models, tend to discuss different types of evidence. Thus elite theorists such as Pareto (1976), Mosca (1939), Michels (1915) and Mills (1956), focus on *who rules*. They often lay great stress on alleged universal traits of human nature (e.g. the desire for power, status and wealth) and their consequences for politics. They then demonstrate the existence of hierarchies of power, wealth and status in many societies. The strategies which individuals adopt to achieve such positions are often considered with realism (if not cynicism). It is shown that ruling elites tend to share a privileged lifestyle. (Michels's famous observation that two deputies, one of whom is a socialist and one of whom is not, have more in common than two socialists one of whom is a deputy and the other is not is fairly typical.) Mills is interesting in seeking to demonstrate in some detail the social, economic and educational interrelationships and common lifestyle of a number of 'separate' US elites – the businessmen, the military and top federal government appointees. (He is also unusual amongst 'elite' theorists in disliking the elite influence he portrays.) Similarly, in Britain a whole literature exists analysing such interrelationships within the British 'Establishment' (e.g. Thomas (1959)), who tend to have attended the same schools, universities and clubs.

Marxist evidence has often concentrated on *in whose interests* decisions are taken. Thus, on the basis that the proof of the pudding is in the eating, the distribution of income and of wealth in capitalist societies is shown to be still grossly uneven, despite decades of 'progressive' taxation and the welfare state. Similarly, the educational and health opportunities of the working classes can be demonstrated to be much less than those of the upper classes. The argument is that the apparent opportunities for political participation by workers in a democracy are negated by continued bourgeois control of social structures such as the educational system, the mass media, and the state apparatus as well as control of the economy.

Pluralist writers have tended to concentrate on *how political decisions are made*. Analysts such as Dahl (1961) and most mainstream writers on British and American politics have stressed that any group of citizens is free to influence politicians in competitive party systems, and that the latter must listen to groups outside of the 'power elite' if they are to remain in office. Numerous case studies have examined how actual political decisions have been taken and found that the same narrow group of professional politicians has not always taken decisions, but that, for instance, doctors' professional associations strongly influence decisions on health policy, neighbourhood action groups can influence planning decisions, and so on.

To some extent, therefore, it can be argued that the findings of these different groups of writers are actually complementary rather than as conflicting as they often claim or imply. We can simultaneously accept the ideas that people in different elite groups do have a great deal of interaction and a substantially common lifestyle; that politicians are often unscrupulous in search of their personal objectives; that political change in democracy does not necessarily result in social and economic equality and is conditioned by cultural and ideological assumptions which reflect the power of existing dominant minorities; and that competitive party systems enable, but do not ensure, that groups of like-minded people can influence the policy process. More sophisticated versions of each model do often concede many of these points.

And yet, important differences of perspective do remain. In the end, readers will need to make a personal judgement about the relative importance of the issues discussed and the strength of the empirical findings. Are the similarities between the members of the 'power elite' so great that the ideological and policy differences they profess pale into insignificance? Does the welfare state represent a triumph for popular mass influence or is it merely a device to cloak the continuing injustice of the capitalist economic system? Does the machinery of pressure groups and elections have a real effect on the policy process? These are real and fascinating issues on which both one's own value-judgements and a greater knowledge of how actual political systems work must have an influence.

Conclusion

In this chapter we have seen political issues as arising from a number of different conflicts. These can be summarised in a slightly different way from that presented so far as is shown in Box 13.

We shall return to a number of these themes in later parts of the book – for instance, 'distributive' issues are considered at more length in Chapters 6 (Mechanisms) and 8 (Policy-Making); 'process' issues in Chapter 7 (Democracy); and 'redistributive' issues in the final chapter (Futures). But, in relation to all of them, the remarks we made earlier about political 'problems' and political 'solutions' can be applied. That is, the person who defines what the problem is, will also tend to define what is regarded as an acceptable solution. With so many divisions between the different sections of humanity, it is unlikely that lasting 'solutions' can be found to major problems which will be acceptable to all the parties affected. This is doubly so if we consider the tendencies to change in political systems covered at more length in the final chapter. In the author's view, then, a

---

Box 13   Major political divisions

Who are we?

identity issues – nationalism, race, ethnicity, class, gender, religion

What do we do?

distributive issues – how to deliver state services, regulate the economy

How do we do it?

process issues - conservatism\radicalism, constitutional

Who benefits?

redistributive issues – rich v. poor (people, regions, states)

SOURCE   After Rose (1969)

---

pluralist approach to the management of political differences is both desirable and almost inevitable: groups must learn to tolerate and negotiate with those who have very different perspectives upon the issues which arise.

Recommended reading

Bottomore, T.B., 1993, *Elites and Society*, 2nd edn, London, Routledge. Excellent theoretical introduction to some of the basic concepts of political sociology.

Dawson, Richard E. and Prewitt, Kenneth, *et al.*, 1977, *Political Socialization*, Boston, Little Brown. Gives a good idea of the US functionalist approach.

Enlow, Cynthia, 1986, *Ethnic Conflict and Political Development: An*

Analytic Study, Collier-Macmillan. A wide-ranging US study of the impact of racial and similar conflicts.

Smith, Anthony, 1991, *National Identity*, Harmondsworth, Middlesex, Penguin. Useful study by a leading British scholar in the area of nationalism.

Solomos, John, 1993, *Race and Racism in Britain*, 2nd edn, Basingstoke, Macmillan. A more policy- and UK-oriented view.

Welch, Stephen, 1993, *The Concept of Political Culture*, Basingstoke, Macmillan. More advanced and critical treatment than Dawson.

Chapter 6

Mechanisms

When should the state decide?

We have seen in earlier chapters that philosophers have debated interminably and without reaching agreement how human beings should live together, and that, within existing societies, rival cultural, religious and other groups seek to foster their own way of life.

Many classical and medieval thinkers such as Plato or Aquinas tended to assume that once a rational moral decision had been taken as to what constituted the good life, then of course the state should adopt and promote that life. In modern multicultural societies, the opposite assumption may be made: that individuals and groups should be free to pursue their own vision of the good life – no consensus on such issues being possible.

In this chapter we consider the extent to which social decisions are, and should be, made by the state authorities. Further, we examine another question, less discussed by classical theorists: if a state authority

should take a decision, which level or kind of state authority that should be.

The case for individual freedom

The case for allowing individuals to have the greatest possible degree of freedom in making decisions which affect their lives has been powerfully made in the classic liberal texts such as John Stuart Mill's (1910) essay *On Liberty*. Essentially, this has been argued from within the Protestant tradition of stress on the value of individual moral conscience and from a scientific and rationalist standpoint of valuing the search for truth through experimentation and free enquiry. Only unconstrained decisions are seen as having moral value, and truth will emerge from trying out contesting theories. Thus, a state which forces citizens to do the 'right' thing and censors alternative ideas is not promoting human virtue but merely mechanical obedience. Hence, even statesmen within a society with a clear consensus on the nature of good and evil would be wrong not to allow individuals to learn for themselves. Moreover, most liberals would subscribe to the view that there is no uncontested source of moral judgments and that a greater understanding of morality can only emerge if people cannot only argue, but also practise, rival moral codes (or rival interpretations of the moral code).

Thus, it is argued from that, at the very least, there should always be a presumption in favour of the individual's freedom to decide their own fate, and that good reason must be shown for overriding individual, by collective, judgement.

The case for the market

A less moralistic but allied line of argument derives from the utilitarians and the early liberal economists. If the state is seeking to promote (following Bentham) 'the greatest happiness of the greatest number', it should not lose sight of the fact that only individuals can judge their own happiness.

With only a finite amount of real resources, a centralised deployment of resources by the state will result in waste. The argument of the early economists (since enthusiastically endorsed by fashionable neo-liberal conservative commentators such as Milton Friedman (Friedman and Friedman (1980), and Hayek (1979)) is that if we each have an equal amount of real resources with which to achieve satisfaction, some will achieve more satisfaction from buying fishing rods or fashionable clothes, others from the purchase of fast cars or the consumption of malt whisky. For the state to allocate everyone equal amounts of fishing equipment, cars, clothes and whisky, and proceed on the assumption that all citizens want the same, will lead to dissatisfaction and waste. Thus, fishing enthusiasts may find that the concrete they wanted to be used to dam a river has been used to construct a bridge over it to somewhere they did not wish to go; fashion enthusiasts may find themselves allocated rayon pants when they aspired to a woollen kilt (or whatever is fashionable at the time); sporting motorists may be issued with Trabant motor cars incapable of reaching the speeds they wish to attain; tee-totallers may throw away in disgust an allocation of malt whisky which their neighbours would savour with relish. The state cannot achieve the level of information and efficiency required to satisfy individual consumer needs.

This account of a fully centralised planned economy could be dismissed as an exaggerated fantasy, but an examination of the experience of the Soviet economy suggests it is not so far from the truth (Fainsod (1963), Nove (1980)). Whilst, in the Soviet model in the Stalinist era, consumers were paid in money and could dispose of their incomes largely as they pleased, the goods available in the shops were determined by the operation of a somewhat arbitrary national plan and prices bore little relationship to the cost of production. Since managers were rewarded for over-fulfilling their plan quotas rather than making profits, despite the fact that they might well not have official access to the necessary raw materials, they might resort to such expedients as making all their shoes in small sizes so as to minimise the use of raw materials. That large-footed customers could not obtain shoes and the shops were congested with unsold small sizes would be of no significance. Conversely, housing was rented and cheap – but there was no incentive to build more housing and gross overcrowding resulted.

The argument is, therefore, that a free market economy enables individuals to allocate resources in such a way as to maximise everyone's satisfaction. Not only does the introduction of a market economy in which all are free to spend their money income as they please enable a painless 'swap' of the whisky ration for fishing tackle, but factories manufacturing rayon pants when such items are out of fashion will go out of business to be replaced by weavers of kilts (or whatever is currently in demand). Further, the sports car enthusiast may give up leisure to earn extra resources in (say) overtime payments in order to secure a faster car than almost anybody else, whilst the keen fisherman or fisherwoman may decide to live simply in a remote area on the proceeds of only part-time employment. As Adam Smith described, the 'invisible hand' of the market balances supply and demand to the satisfaction of all in the market-place.

The limits of individualism

Even the most enthusiastic proponent of individual freedom is, however, likely to accept that there are limits on what individuals can be allowed to do. Most clearly this is the case where my freedom to do as I please unhindered comes directly into conflict with your wish to do as you please. Thus, we cannot both be free to drive on whatever side of the road we please without disastrous consequences! I cannot logically both be free to take any property I like, and to be secure in my right to any property I have.

Thus, most liberals (if not all anarchists), have accepted the need for the state to guarantee minimum levels of freedom by enforcing rights of life, liberty and property for all individuals. The argument here is that the state has not only the resources to enforce its judgement but also is impartial in making them. Private individuals will naturally differ as to who is encroaching upon the rights of whom in case of conflict – no one should be judge in their own case. The state is seen as offering a just resolution of such disputes and as a source of general rules upon which such disputes can be resolved.

Many (traditional) conservative thinkers (e.g. FitzJames Stephens (1873)), however, would go much further in questioning the case for freedom made by Mill and others. They see the individualistic picture of moral development painted by the liberals as theoretical and misleading. Individuals are seen as absorbing the traditional moral values of their family and community, as a result of example and a disciplined upbringing. To allow individuals to flout the moral standards of the community is thus an affront to justice and, by influencing others against authority, is liable to cause widespread harm. Thus, pornography, for instance, can be seen in terms of a major threat to family values rather than a minor abuse of the freedom of expression.

On the Left, too, there is also emphasis on the need for social support – but in making social innovation. Whilst some of the values implicit in the existing community may be rejected, there is often stress on the need to build a new consensus on values in the rebuilt community which will overcome the inherited evils of the past. Whether in the (voluntary) shared communal values of the Israeli kibbutz or the totalitarian and imposed shared life of Chinese communes or Soviet collective farms there is a common belief in the power and need for social conformity.

Problems of market decision-making

The undoubted advantages of decentralised yet subtly co-operative decision-making through the market mechanism may need little emphasis in an era in which the inadequacies of centralised economic planning have been demonstrated by the collapse of the Soviet Union's economy and the increasing abandonment of the system in China. With its superior productivity and response to consumer demand, the market mechanism might appear to have justified itself. Yet the inadequacies of raw capitalism seem hardly less than those of raw centralised planning.

In terms of the justification we have so far considered – the market as a device to achieve the satisfaction of consumer demand – capitalism seems at best a doubtful device when viewed in practice rather than in terms of abstract theoretical economic models. If the theoretical assumption is made of an equal distribution of resources to everyone at the outset, then, in the short term, the market mechanism seems to be a fair device for decision-making. However, the engine of capitalism remains the profit motive – which is no more than each individual seeking to maximise the returns to their efforts – an apparently unexceptionable idea. The problem being that the accumulation of profit over time into the hands of successful businessmen ('entrepreneurs' in economic jargon) leads to a grossly unfair distribution of resources. This is particularly the case when wealth is inherited – the result being an arbitrary distribution of purchasing power and consumer satisfaction. In many cases, the distribution of wealth is the consequence of obscure historical events in periods when the market system hardly functioned (e.g. English aristocrats who continue to own a totally disproportionate share of the land or, for that matter, the superior share of the earth's resources owned by the current generation of North Americans).

Further distortions in the market mechanism, familiar to all economists, include the absence in many industries and places of the 'perfect competition' assumed in the model of the market mechanism explained by Adam Smith and usually assumed by its political proponents. That is, for consumers to obtain the goods that will maximise their satisfaction in return for their expenditure, it is necessary for them to have full knowledge of the goods and prices available and for new entrepreneurs to be able to enter the market freely whenever exceptional profits are being made in an industry. The number of producers is assumed to be so large they cannot affect the market price. Instead, markets are almost always 'imperfect' in that consumers are misled by advertising, new competition faces considerable barriers to entry into the market and governments may subsidise domestic producers and tax or impede foreign competition .

The case for government intervention in markets

Thus, a good case can be made, even by liberals, for extensive state intervention in actual economies. Even nineteenth-century liberals were anxious for the government to make provision so that in economic matters the state ensured that the currency was sound, that fair bargains were made (for example the UK Sale of Goods Act required that goods be of 'merchantable' quality – i.e. reasonably fit for the use intended) and that monopolies should be prohibited. In the home of capitalism, the United States, there is a strong tradition of public intervention to ensure that markets are not monopolised by unfair trade agreements between producers. Thus, intervention by the state to attempt to maintain and restore competition would seem desirable, even if the logic of the market is endorsed.

One development of the argument that efficient allocation of resources only takes place where competition, in fact, exists, is to advocate a special role for the state in those industries which constitute 'natural monopolies'. Thus, in the case of 'public utilities ' – like gas, water and electricity, telephones and possibly cable television – where one provider normally sets up a local pipe or cable network which it would be impracticable and possibly socially disruptive for a second provider to attempt to duplicate, it is argued that the state should protect consumers from the levying of monopoly profits. In Britain this was formerly done by setting up local or national government undertakings to do the job. In the United States, and more recently in British 'privatised' industries, a state regulator has been substituted for the operation of normal competitive forces. The regulator is supported by special legislation which often limits the profits the utilities can make or the prices they can levy.

From the point of view that the market mechanism is a device to optimise the distribution of resources amongst individuals, it might also be argued, as radical liberals do, that action by the state to ensure that all citizens have a minimum purchasing power is also justified. Thus, Lord Beveridge in the 1940s, argued for a National Insurance scheme which helped lay the foundations of the modern welfare state. More recently, even some right-wing, but market-oriented conservatives ('neo-liberals' as we termed them earlier) have argued for a 'negative income tax' with similar effect. Conversely, on the same logic, measures to reduce large fortunes such as taxes on capital and, especially, inheritance/gift taxes can be justified. Such an approach has proved more controversial since it strikes at the interests of powerful elites and has been held to undermine the incentive of the profit motive upon which the capitalist market system depends.

Another point which remains controversial is the extent to which the government needs to intervene in a market economy in order to maintain overall economic stability and encourage financial growth. Nineteenth- and early twentieth-century economists tended to assume that a financially sound (i.e. on the gold standard) and competitive economy would be in a state of at least long-term equilibrium (perhaps affected by temporary fluctuations in the form of 'trade cycles'). The experience of the inter-war economic depression convinced John Maynard Keynes (1936), and the majority of economists in the immediate post-war period who were influenced by him, that full employment, financial stability and economic growth could not be achieved by automatic monetary mechanisms but must be achieved by managing the government's finances so as to boost investment and expenditure in periods of recession, and curb inflation by higher taxes and interest rates and reduction in government expenditure in periods of over-expansion.

Experience of 'stop/go' economic management and excessive inflation in the 1960 and 1970s brought back into fashion (especially on the Right) a modern version of the classic theory, with writers such as Milton Friedman influencing the conservative governments of (for instance) Mrs Thatcher and President Ronald Reagan in favour of policies stressing the need to maintain the value of money and eschewing (in theory at least) excessive government borrowing to finance economic recovery.

Many socialist and nationalist thinkers, would, of course, go much further in urging the inadequacy of the market mechanism in responding to social needs. They would argue that the government needs to plan the development of the national economy so that vital economic resources are not pre-empted by foreigners or neglected by capitalists who are pre-occupied with short-term profit at the expense of long-term benefits to the community. We have already briefly discussed the Soviet model of a completely planned economy, but countries such as France and Japan have a long tradition of national governmental involvement in a predominantly 'capitalist' economy through discussion with leading industrialists and manipulation of the banking and taxation systems so as to protect strategic political objectives.

Public goods

The classical economists also accepted that the operation of the market was not an appropriate way of allocating resources for some goods

– especially those for which it was difficult or inefficient to share out the benefits resulting from their production to specific individuals. Therefore, specific individuals might not be prepared voluntarily to spend enough on these goods, even though the whole community would suffer from lack of expenditure on them. These 'public goods' have usually been considered to include the provision of a system of justice and public safety (including prisons, fire-brigades and policing); public health measures, such as inoculation of people against infectious diseases, provision of roads, bridges and footpaths; and defence and foreign affairs. Thus, it seems sensible for everyone to pay on a fair basis (whether this means equally or in some kind of proportion to means might be debated) for, for instance, policing and justice, rather than wait for crimes to be committed and then raise the cost of the judicial process from those concerned. In any case, in this example, most people would be unhappy to see a murder investigation abandoned because the victim's family could not afford the large-scale investigation – the community having an interest in the deterrent effects of prosecuting all crimes. Similarly, individuals could be charged for the use of public highways and bridges – but this 'toll' system was largely dropped after the nineteenth century because, amongst other things, such a collection mechanism is very expensive compared with taxation, potential users are deterred from making use of facilities which have already been paid for; and highway providers are put in a local monopoly situation. In the twenty-first century, however, the ease with which electronic road pricing technology can be applied, the wish to discourage use of roads on energy/ecology grounds and the greater likelihood of alternative transport may lead to a return to the older pattern!

Private and public costs and benefits

Another factor which may raise the desirability of state intervention in the market – and one which raises some very topical issues – is a consideration of the impact of private decisions on public costs and benefits (and, indeed, vice versa). The classic case is that of a factory profitably (for the entrepreneurs concerned) producing some perfectly innocuous product, but from dangerous ingredients which are perhaps the product of an ugly open-cast mining process, cause industrial illnesses amongst its work-force and spread toxic residues from its chimneys. The costs to the community in ill-health and a worsened environment may well exceed the benefits to consumers and share-holders. There is surely a good case for government intervention, either by way of direct regulations against unsafe working practices and the imposition of planning controls or by implementing the 'polluter pays' principle by taxing any anti-social aspects of the activity at a rate reflecting the costs it imposes on the rest of the community.

A perhaps more difficult case of a similar sort of problem (but this time, considering social cost/private benefit as opposed to private benefit/social cost in the previous example) is in an area such as education, where government expenditure on private individuals gives a benefit to the person concerned. Where all citizens receive similar benefits in early life and pay taxes to finance this at a later stage, then no great inequity would seem to occur. However, where a limited proportion of citizens receive more education (say at nursery or higher stages) and subsequently are seen to greatly benefit thereby (e.g. with increased salaries in later life), then it is not surprising that demands may come from less privileged taxpayers for some additional contri-bution by those benefiting. (Further discussion of education policy is to be found in Chapter 8, pp.201–2).

Problems of government intervention

By way of counter-balance to this long list of reasons for the govern-ment to intervene, it is worth briefly signposting some general objec-tions to any expansion in the role of the state. These have generally been associated with the neo-liberal Right. Two major objections may be discerned. One is the fiscal and administrative burden of continu-ally expanding the 'nanny state' for one apparently minor good reason after another. The result, it is alleged, will be that ordinary citizens' discretionary expenditure will be largely taken away by the resulting burden of taxes, whilst businessmen are handicapped at every turn by petty bureaucracy. The health of the economy will be submerged by the rising tide of public expenditure. The second major argument is allied to this: the assumption is made in many of these arguments that 'the state' can make more rational decisions than the market but, in practice, this means that decisions will be made by remote bureaucrats who are motivated not by the 'public interest' but by the desire to expand and defend their own empires (Tullock (1962)).

Whilst not accepting these criticisms unquestioningly and entirely, clearly the case for state intervention is very much dependent upon the quality of decision-making which is achieved in the public sector and whether the economic resources devoted to this seem in proportion to the benefits achieved (i.e. can the public sector deliver 'value for money'?) – an issue explored further in Chapter 8.

Voluntary organisation

So far, we have examined this question largely as if there were only two alternative modes of social action – decisions either are taken by individuals through the market mechanism or they are taken by 'the state'. This is, however, clearly an oversimplification.

In the first place, it has to be emphasised that much 'individual' decision-making is not market-oriented, but reflects patterns of social co-operation which are more altruistic than the sort of bargaining for individual advantage which is normally associated with the market. People not only seek their own satisfaction but that of their family, their neighbours, various community groupings with which they identify (e.g. ethnic groups, churches, nations) and they may sacrifice immediate self-interest to causes as varied as vegetarianism, racial purity or world government.

The idea that market decision-making is a form of individual choice is also an oversimplification. Individuals are generally confronted with alternatives which are the results of social processes over which they have little control. Many consumers, unlike an affluent minority in highly industrialised countries, have little 'discretionary income' with which to exercise choice – 'consumer sovereignty' may seem like a shallow joke to many in India, Africa and China, and of limited relevance to those living on social security benefits in the West. Discretion on the supply side of the economy seems still less real for the many individuals with limited marketable skills, little or no capital and few employment opportunities.

Social co-operation on a voluntary basis, especially between relatives and neighbours, is clearly an older and more basic form of human behaviour than market behaviour. As we have seen, there have been, perhaps Utopian, attempts to set up local communities on such a basis right up to the present day. As we shall see when we look at social policy, the importance of family ties and behaviour is still difficult to underestimate even in modern communities in which work, leisure and spiritual activities, which were previously family-based, are now carried on outside the family home.

In the present context, however, it is vital to consider the role of voluntary sector organisations in carrying out activities which might otherwise be the subject of market or government determination. Churches are an interesting example of voluntary organisations, since, as we have seen, in earlier times they have frequently had a legal monopoly on matters which are now seen as predominantly concerns of the state or the individual. For members of these bodies, their decisions may retain a greater legitimacy than those of the state. Churches retain a commitment to charitable works and to influencing government policy on 'moral' issues, from contraception to aid to the third world.

More generally, a whole range of voluntary organisations carry out co-operative activities which enable their members to achieve satisfaction with little reference to either the market or state sector of the economy. Examples of this include leisure groups such as football clubs or ramblers groups, educational groups, such as the play school and Franco-British University of the Third Age movements, economic activities such as providing food or clothing may take place via allotment and knitting societies, and some of the oldest voluntary groups provide welfare services to their members (friendly societies, the Freemasons, alumni associations). The British Royal National Lifeboat Institution is an interesting example of the provision of what might be expected to be a public good (a free public emergency sea rescue service).

Most voluntary organisations, however, do relate to the state in one or both of two ways. First, they may provide services to the community in collaboration with the government – and increasingly often as contractors to it. Thus, in Britain the Women's Royal Voluntary

Service often deliver 'Meals on Wheels' to social service departments' clients; National Health Service hospitals are supported by Leagues of Friends who may raise additional funds for specialist equipment, visit lonely patients, or drive outpatients to the hospital; the National Society for Prevention of Cruelty to Children has special legal powers in its work of protecting children, and Citizens Advice Bureaux, staffed by volunteers, are usually financed by local councils.

Second, many voluntary organisations lobby the state to pass legislation or spend money on causes helpful to their client group. Thus, the Royal Society for Prevention of Cruelty to Animals is the major source of legislation in the United Kingdom after the government. Veterans' groups and the National Rifle Association are very influential on US legislation. Some bodies, such as the National Viewers and Listeners' Association in Britain may do little other than lobby various public authorities.

A recent British report (Knight (1993)) has advocated that these two kinds of voluntary associations be formally separated, with only service organisations receiving charitable status and tax exemptions. This seems to neglect the frequent interdependence of the two roles. Service provision often leads to useful expertise in an area which the government needs to listen to. Thus, Oxfam and Médecins Sans Frontières can speak from extensive experience of development work in third world countries when lobbying governments for more official aid, or the National Association of Citizens' Advice Bureaux gives useful and detailed information on the effectiveness of social legislation by collecting information on the patterns of problems reported by its voluntary advisers.

The choice of social decision-making mechanisms

In political arguments the choice of social decision-making mechanisms is often debated in terms of simple dichotomies (see Box 14).

The approach we have adopted here suggests, rather, a more pragmatic approach where it is appropriate to consider the issue, the time and the place before deciding upon which way social decisions should be resolved. In addition to a pure market or state system, it is clear that a mixed system in which the market is regulated and

---

Box 14   Choice of social decision-making mechanism

From the Right

Individual freedom = Consumer sovereignty = Good
versus State decision-making = Bureaucracy = Bad

From the Left

Capitalism = Exploitation = Bad
versus Welfare state = Democracy = Good.

---

adjusted by the state (the so-called 'social market') is often a viable alternative to consider. Nor should the role of voluntary co-operation through family and neighbourhood networks or more formal organisations be neglected.

In deciding the appropriate role of the state, an important consideration should be how far it is likely to reach a more rational decision than the market; how far it can effectively involve ordinary citizens in the decision-making process – so they do not regard its decisions as remote and 'bureaucratic' – and whether the increased costs of such decision-making seem justified by any improvement in its quality. It seems appropriate, therefore, to consider and assess the governmental process in more detail than we have done so far. This we shall do in succeeding chapters.

Which state should decide? – subsidiarity

One obvious way to minimise the degree to which state decision-making is seen as remote and bureaucratic is, of course, to try to keep the state concerned as small and consequently as unbureaucratic as possible. We thus return to the second part of the question we introduced at the beginning of this chapter – if a state authority *should* take a decision, which level or kind of state authority that should be?

In the *Social Contract* (1913) Jean Jacques Rousseau suggested that giant nation-states could only really be free once every few years at general election time. He compared all such arrangements unfavourably with his native Geneva, in which the citizens could be intimately involved in the sovereign government of their own community. Similarly, as we have seen, anarchists advocate dividing the whole world into a network of voluntary self-governing communities.

The disadvantages of a multitude of small-scale states may include an increased likelihood of inter-state violence (though at least such states would probably lack the capacity to go nuclear!), a failure to express larger senses of national or regional identity, and possibly a lack of capacity for large-scale investment necessary for complex transport systems, advanced health, education and research facilities (manned exploration of outer space, for example, would be unlikely in the absence of 'super-states' like the USA and EU). There might also be considerable problems in maintaining a system of international trade and finance.

In practice, therefore, most of the world is arranged, as we saw in Chapter 2, so that there exist a series of levels of government over any given territorial area. In the United States, for instance, many people live in a city with a municipal government, which may well be part of a larger county; they all reside in a State, as well as being subject to the government of the United States. Similarly, in the United Kingdom many people are subject to two different layers of local government, the UK government and, effectively, a European 'government' – the European Union.

The actual distribution of governmental powers between layers of government is somewhat haphazard in practice, with historical influences being very important. In the UK we have seen that the idea of the sovereignty of the national parliament has contributed to a strong concentration of power at the national level. In the United States and in Switzerland, in contrast, many of the component states or cantons preceded the federal governments and retain exceptionally strong powers. However, the trend in most parts of the world, however unpalatable it may be, has been towards a greater concentration of powers at the highest level of government.

Many factors have contributed to this trend toward centralisation. One simple factor is that the central government will normally be the biggest government in the state and therefore contain the greatest concentration of expertise. The doctrine of national state sovereignty not only lends legitimacy to central government decision-makers but also ensures that they are expected to co-ordinate relations with other states and control the major organisations capable of physical coercion (not only the armed forces but probably also some sort of internal riot squad). A major factor in most systems is that the highest level of government usually controls the most effective taxing mechanisms – particularly income tax. Clearly, too, in many areas of government, as in business, 'economies of scale' mean that large, often computerised, operations can be more efficient than smaller ones.

Opposed to these centralising tendencies are not only the democratic considerations to which we have referred above and upon which we will elaborate in the next chapter, but also the need to deliver policy effectively to citizens where they live. As circumstances will vary from local district to local district, a 'top-down' central solution to a centrally conceived problem may translate into an inappropriate response to local problems (see Chapter 8).

A sensible general principle to resolve the question of which level to allocate government powers to, is the principle of 'subsidiarity' recently incorporated in the Maastricht Treaty on the future of the European Union (see Box 15).

Box 15   The principle of subsidiarity

Advocates that political decisions should always be made at the lowest possible level of government.

The advantages of better democratic control and the greater flexibility of response to local circumstances create a presumption in favour of the lower level. In contemporary British circumstances it would appear, however, that the Major government has been prone to interpret this principle somewhat selectively, in that there does not appear to have been the same emphasis on leaving to local government the maximum decision-making power as the central UK government has asserted in its relations with Europe (see Duff (1993)).

It is interesting to observe that the principle of subsidiarity has been strongly endorsed in twentieth-century papal encyclicals. Thus Leo XIII in *Quadragesimo Ano* (1941) wrote 'It is an injustice, a grave evil and a disturbance of right order for a large and higher organization to arrogate to itself functions which can be performed efficiently by smaller and lower bodies'. Subsidiarity is therefore a principle which fits easily with the Christian democratic parties of Europe.

Federalism, devolution, decentralisation

Two further related aspects of the division of powers between levels of government are worth exploration. First, who divides the powers between levels of government? Second, what are relationships between levels when they are both concerned with an issue? This is summarised in Box 16

Box 16   Relations between levels of government

In principle a **'federal'** system is one in which the allocation of powers is independent of either level of government in question. Each has its defined sphere of influence, this normally being laid down in a written constitution and interpreted independently (probably by the courts in case of dispute).

In a system of **'devolution'** a higher level of government creates and gives powers to a lower (elected) level of government to exercise.

In a system of **'decentralisation'** subordinate local administrative agencies are created by a central government and may be given some discretion to interpret central policy and consult local opinion.

On the face of things, therefore, one might expect the lower levels of government in a federal system to act independently of the upper layers; the lower levels in a devolved system to negotiate a local interpretation of national policies within a framework of national statutory guidance; whilst in decentralised systems the local bureaucrats would merely interpret national policies according to local circumstances.

In practice, in all systems some measure of co-ordination, co-operation and negotiation between levels seems to emerge. Thus, American writers on contemporary US federalism have tended to use the term 'co-operative federalism' to indicate the extent to which state authorities have tended to co-operate with federal policy initiatives, partly in order to obtain access to large subsidies from the federal budget. Conversely, realistic analysis of the way government bureaucracies work suggests that even career national bureaucrats have to be motivated to implement central policies. At its most extreme, a part of a central bureaucracy may be so much under the influence of a local 'Mafia' that national policies conflicting with local interests may be ignored, as in Italy (Banfield and Banfield (1967)) or, conversely, as in the Soviet Union, nominally independent state authorities may be under the almost total political control of a centralised political party (Schapiro (1965)). The European Union is a classic example of the 'fuzzy' sorts of relationships which can emerge between levels of government. We shall deal in more detail with its nature and likely evolution in our final chapter.

Recommended reading

Coates, David, (ed.), *The Question of UK Decline*, Hemel Hempstead, Harvester Wheatsheaf. Stimulating collection of views from across the political and academic spectrum on the reality and causes of UK economic political and social decline.

Friedman, Milton and Friedman, Rose, 1980, *Free To Choose*, Harmondsworth, Middlesex, Penguin. A popular exposition of the fashionable market-oriented view of the relationship between government and the economy.

Mill, John Stuart, (ed. A.D. Lindsay), 1910, *On Liberty, Representative Government, Utilitarianism*, London, Dent. 'On Liberty' is the basic liberal text on individualism and freedom. It is also lucid and readable.

Stevens, Joe B. 1993, *The Economics of Collective Choice*, Oxford, Westview. A more challenging and academic treatment of attempts to apply market-oriented models to understanding society.

Zimmerman, Joseph F. 1992, *Contemporary American Federalism: The Growth of National Power*, Leicester, Leicester University Press. For an overview of recent developments relating to the division of power amongst different levels of government in the home of federalism.

Chapter 7

Democracy

How can government be democratic?

As we established in Chapter 2, it is by no means inevitable that the government of a state should be 'democratic'. The establishment of authoritarian, fascist, military, theocratic or traditionalist regimes cannot be dismissed as impossible anachronisms, even at the end of the twentieth century. However, for the purposes of this discussion, it is convenient to assume the desirability of popular government – what President Lincoln described in the Gettysburg Address as 'government of the People, by the People – and for the People' and to ask, instead, what purposes such government may be thought to serve and how these can best be realised.

Lincoln's memorable definition may suggest three key elements of democracy – that it is 'of' the people, not only in the sense of being 'over' all the people but that it derives its legitimacy from their commitment to it (government by consent); that it is

151

'by' the people in the sense that they participate extensively in governmental processes; and 'for' the people in that it seeks to realise the common welfare and safeguard the rights of individuals.

These principles would be widely accepted not only in the liberal democracies of Western Europe, North America and Australasia, but even in communist countries and single-party nationalist regimes in the 'South'. Much controversy remains, however, about the interpretation of these principles and their relative weight where they conflict. Thus, liberal democracies stress the safeguarding of individual rights and the idea of the rule of law. Communist regimes stress popular participation and the pursuit of the interests of the common man. Populist nationalist leaders stress their legitimacy as leaders by consent of the people and as interpreters of the national destiny (MacPherson (1966)).

Participation and direct democracy

The oldest recorded form of democracy, as we briefly discussed earlier, is that of the Greek city-states. Important decisions being taken by all the citizens (i.e. excluding foreigners, women and slaves – most of the population!) in a popular assembly by majority vote. Government officials ('magistrates') were chosen on a temporary basis by lot. It is worth remarking that Aristotle regarded this as a poor form of government because popular decisions were unrestrained by any legal protection of (rich) minorities. It is also worth considering whether, for instance, the lynching of even an obviously guilty person by the majority of the population in a small community can properly be regarded as 'democratic'. None the less, because the majority of citizens had to be convinced if the community were to act, it seems a very high standard of information and debate was often obtained alongside great commitment and loyalty to state.

It is often thought that such direct democracies are no longer possible with the increased complexity and scale of human societies. However, decision-making by the majority of citizens is still practised in Switzerland and in several states of the United States where, on the initiative of a fixed proportion of the electorate or a minimum number of voters, a referendum must be held on any issue, the result having the status of a constitutional amendment. Again, where decisions are made in this way there is commonly a very widespread popular debate on all the issues raised.

Such a situation should perhaps be distinguished from the much more common constitutional device of allowing or requiring the government to call a popular vote on particular issues. The problem being that such a referendum on specific issues may easily be converted into a 'plebiscite' – a vote of confidence in the government proposing the vote. Strong populist leaders such as France's General de Gaulle or Russia's President Yeltsin have often used such a device to strengthen themselves against parliamentary opponents.

In fact, the size of modern democracies is no longer a barrier to the exercise of this sort of popular democracy, since the existence of relatively easy and swift forms of mass communication and the possibility of electronic polling through the telephone or other networks means that 'teledemocracy' is now a possibility (Arterton (1987), Saward (1993)). In any case, it is still possible to exercise this form of control in small communities on a local level (e.g. British and New England parish meetings).

The idea of involving as many citizens as possible in the governmental process remains an important element in the concept of democracy, helping to support the maintenance of the local government system and the jury in Anglo-American democracies. The former USSR attempted to support its 'democratic' credentials by the election of large numbers of citizens to Soviets (councils), electoral commissions, factory and collective farm councils and the like.

Choosing rulers

In modern liberal democracies, however, democracy is often thought of primarily in terms of the opportunity for citizens to freely choose their rulers at periodic intervals, rather than to make governmental decisions for themselves.

There seems little doubt that forcing rival groups of potential rulers to compete for popular votes is an important element in ensuring that modern democracies do maintain some responsiveness to the interests and desires of their electorates. For lack of this simple device, many third world and communist regimes do seem to have lost contact with their constituencies and consequently collapsed.

Free elections seem to be a prerequisite of democracy – something which cannot be dispensed with – and an institution which is more difficult to implement than those who take it for granted might suspect (Mckenzie (1958)). A secret ballot, freedom from blatant election bribery and corruption, parties free to campaign anywhere in the country, and a reasonably unbiased electoral system seem simple and obvious devices in those countries which have achieved them. However, experiences in Eastern Europe and Africa, Asia and Latin America in recent years have shown how difficult such conditions are to achieve.

More subtle factors, however, can be seen to affect the effectiveness and responsiveness of democracies. In particular, the extent to which the political parties and constitutional arrangements offer a real choice to the electorate (in this respect the USA might be thought to be less 'democratic' than Britain) and the extent to which the educational and economic condition of the mass of the electorate makes effective political participation by them a real possibility (e.g. many rural Latin American electorates seem to have been cynically manipulated by a small urban elite (Andreski (1966)).

Electoral systems

Many discussions of liberal democracy place great emphasis on the range of electoral systems used and the assessment of the merits of each. In particular, the merits of 'proportional representation' versus 'first-past-the-post' systems have often been debated at length. Fascinating though the topic may be to many political scientists and armchair reformers, it seems of much less fundamental importance than many of the less discussed issues involved in achieving free elections which we have just considered.

In fact, few electoral systems are either based simply on a single-member constituency 'first-past-the post' system like Britain's or on a national constituency divided proportionally between the parties like Israel's. Many single-member constituency systems incorporate ways of ensuring (or increasing the likelihood of) a majority at constituency level. Thus, France has a second ballot in any constituency in which no candidate gains an overall majority; the USA has a preliminary 'primary' election within each of the two major parties so only two serious candidates are likely to emerge for the election proper; whilst in Australia voters record preferences for candidates in order so that the votes of the weaker candidates can be transferred until one candidate obtains a majority. Most 'proportional' systems have area or regional (rather than national) constituencies, several combine single-member constituencies with a national 'pooling system' (e.g. Germany). Almost all have a minimum quota of votes to obtain seats in the legislature.

It is worth echoing the conclusion of Rae's excellent (1967) study that all existing electoral systems are less than perfectly proportional (even Israel has a minimum vote quota for a party to be represented in parliament) and that the major factor affecting proportionality is the size of the constituency employed. To achieve perfect proportionality between seats allocated in parliament and votes for each national party, a single national constituency would have to be employed. However, the cost of this might well be thought too high in terms of breaking the links between individual voters and specific representatives and the power it would give to national party organisations in determining candidates' places on the national list.

Relatively less proportional systems, like Britain's, may be defended as yielding strong or stable government. In recent years the author's personal feeling, however, is that 'strong' government has come to mean unrepresentative and unresponsive government in Britain. Certainly, however, the viability of the executive produced by the system must be weighed in assessing such systems, alongside the links to constituencies and the proportionality of the legislature. To some degree the assessment of electoral systems must depend upon current political circumstances and the political preferences of the assessor.

In the abstract, the preferred solution might be to achieve rough proportionality and a specific link between each voter and an elected representative with area constituencies (perhaps of four or five members) elected by single transferable vote. This is the Irish system, also favoured by the British Liberal Democrats. However, it is worth stressing that a major consideration in 'electoral engineering' should be the political credibility of the system with the electorate as a whole. A simple long-established system which is widely accepted should only be sacrificed for an overwhelming advantage. An incomprehensible and complicated system seen as unnecessarily favouring the political forces which recently initiated it would be a poor exchange for such a system even if it was technically superior in the sense of being more proportional.

The electoral system is at the heart of the credibility (legitimacy) of modern democracies, so that it is important to try to establish as broad a consensus as possible about the system employed. Situations (such as has occurred in post-war France (Campbell (1965)) in which major changes of government bring about a consequent change in the electoral system are liable to breed cynicism and apathy on the part of the electorate.

Forms of representative democracy

In addition to the issue of how governments are elected, another key issue in considering the workings of modern democracies is the nature of those governments and the mechanisms for enforcing responsibility of governments to the people. The complex relationships between the elected legislature, the government, electorate and the judiciary are summarised briefly in Box 17 and explored in more detail in succeeding sections.

Presidential versus parliamentary government

The two major types of liberal democratic constitution to be found in the world today are the parliamentary and presidential systems. The major features of these are outlined in Box 18 (p.159) which is based on the work of Verney (1959). Parliamentary systems are found, not only in Britain and the many Commonwealth countries which have retained the 'Westminster model' (for the problems of this in Nigeria see Tansey and Kermode (1967/8)), but in most West European states as well (Smith (1989. Chs 5,7,8,), Derbyshire and Derbyshire (1991, Table 11, p.55)) classified 43 states as having parliamentary

Box 17   Forms of representative democracy

Presidential

Directly elected head of state and government, independent legislature and judiciary

e.g. USA, Latin America

Parliamentary

Head of state appoints head of government responsible to legislature.

e.g. UK, Sweden, Italy

Hybrid

Directly elected head of state appoints head of government responsible to legislature.

e.g. France, Russia

Consociational

Minorities have constitutional right to representation in government.

e.g. Switzerland, South Africa

One-party

One party legally controls government.

e.g. Soviet Union, Tanzania

---

executives, 26 of which were Commonwealth members. Presidential systems, in this sense, are those like the United States of America, with a directly elected executive president, and are the most common form of constitutional government, with 53 states classified as limited parliamentary executives by the Derbyshires. They are found chiefly in the Americas (21) and Africa (15) (Tables 13 and 14, p.60–1).

The main differences between the systems may be expressed in terms of the separation and balance of powers. Following Montesquieu's interpretation of the eighteenth-century UK constitution, presidential systems not only divide the powers of government into legislative (law making), executive (law enforcing) and judicial (law interpreting) institutions, but seek to separate these in terms of personnel and balance them against each other. Democratic government is seen in terms of a refusal to concentrate potentially tyrannical power so that it cannot be used to take away individual rights. Federalism is seen as a further expression of the same approach. In parliamentary systems the main expression of democracy is seen in the enforcement of the responsibility of the executive to the people through parliament – in practice the independence of the judiciary is accepted but the executive and legislative powers work in concert as a result of the government's legislative majority.

'Hybrid' systems

Not all systems, however, fit easily into either of the above constitutional moulds. The Derbyshires found six states with what they described as 'dual executives' and we describe here as 'hybrid' systems. For instance, both contemporary (1994) France and Russia have adopted some features of each model with a directly elected president with strong powers who appoints a prime minister to head the administration who is also responsible to parliament. In both cases, it seems that the drafters of the constitution anticipated a strong leader (de Gaulle, Yeltsin) faced by a scattering of weak parties. The problem with this system is that the electorate may not elect a legislature sympathetic to the political ideas of the president. If, as has happened in France, legislative elections take place after an interval, and a new and different coalition of political forces is clearly in the ascendant, then the president must decide whether to 'cohabit' with the opposition forces – compromising on policy and government personnel – or to confront the opposition and cause a constitutional crisis.

Box 18   Parliamentary *versus* presidential systems

	Parliamentary	**Presidential**
Assembly	'Parliament'	Assembly only
Executive	Separate heads of state and government	Popularly elected President
Head of government	Appointed by head of state	Also head of state
Appointment of government	Head of government appoints ministry	President appoints departmental heads
Responsibility	Government collectively responsible to assembly	President responsible to people
Personnel	Ministers usually parliamentarians	Executive/legislative separation
Dissolution of Assembly	Head of state on advice of head of government	Not possible

SOURCE   Verney (1959)

Consociational democracy

Possibly a more radical institutional reinterpretation of democracy can be seen in what is sometimes called 'consociational' democracy. In all liberal democratic systems a legitimate role is allotted to minority (opposition) political forces outside of the government. In Britain this is institutionalised in the term 'Leader of Her Majesty's Opposition'. In consociational democracy the attempt is made to ensure that all significant minorities, as well as the majority, are actually represented in government. The best-known and most successful example of this is Switzerland, where the government (the Federal Council) must be composed of representatives of all the major parties in parliament in proportion to their strength.

Such an arrangement seems particularly suited to societies which are deeply divided on national, linguistic or religious lines, in which important groups may be in a permanent minority. Thus, in Switzerland, French, German and Italian speakers, Protestants and Catholics, are all automatically represented in the government. Less successful attempts at similar arrangements in other divided societies include the Lebanon and abortive attempts at 'power sharing' in Northern Ireland. The latest attempt to use such a device can be seen in South Africa's 1994 constitution in which both the majority black (ANC) and the minority white (Nationalist) populations have been virtually guaranteed a role in government, at least during a transitional period.

'Convention'-style constitutions: one-party democracy

Verney discusses a third major type of democratic constitution in addition to the parliamentary and presidential models; what he terms the 'convention' style constitution modelled on the revolutionary French Assembly of 1789. The French constitutional tradition emphasised the legitimacy of the sovereign national assembly based on the popular vote. The Assembly could not be dissolved and exercised detailed control over the personnel of government drawn from its ranks. Some modern French constitutions (especially the Third Republic from 1870 to 1940) could be described in these terms, and on the letter of the constitutional instruments, the Soviet constitution and many former Eastern Bloc constitutions influenced by it, also appeared to be based on this model.

It would be more realistic to describe Soviet-style democracy as one-party democracy, however, since the legal predominance of the assembly was clearly only a fiction which scarcely masked the monopoly of the Communist Party over both government, legislature and every other social and political institution within the state. Only one party-sponsored candidate was presented in each constituency and all resolutions of parliament were passed unanimously on the initiative of the government/party. The party, in turn, was controlled from the top through the device of 'democratic centralism', so that a claim to democracy could only be justified by an appeal to the top party members' superior grasp of 'scientific' socialism which enabled them to discern and represent the interests of the working masses more certainly than the workers themselves. It is perhaps surprising that such an unlikely doctrine could be taken seriously for so long, not only in the Soviet Union itself – where scepticism could prove fatal in the literal sense – but even amongst intelligent commentators in the West.

Another version of one-party democracy has been put forward in a number of post-colonial regimes. Here, a virtually all-encompassing political coalition has been created to fight for independence – often centred upon some 'charismatic' popular leader. Not unnaturally the national(ist) party obtains an overwhelming victory at the independence general election. Opposition to the national leader seems like treason. The national party now has a monopoly of the considerable patronage dispensed by the new state. In such circumstances it is not surprising for virtually all opposition to the party to disappear. Indeed, a similar state of affairs occurred in the United States after its national revolution (Lipset (1979)). In many newly independent states ethnic and racial antagonisms both constitute a serious threat to the continued integrity of the state and the natural basis for any multiparty democratic system. In such circumstances, the single-party regime may be made a legal as well as a political fact – the Soviet example serving as additional justification for such a move, particularly since communist regimes professed 'anti-imperialist' rhetoric appealed to nationalist leaders fighting the imperial/colonialist powers.

The reality of such one-party regimes has differed greatly. In many – such as Nkrumah's Ghana – Marxist rhetoric about the importance of the party masked the reality of its virtual absorption by the government machine (Dowse (1969)). In a few states – such as Tanzania – interesting experiments were attempted to combine the legitimacy and strength of a single national party with opportunities for popular participation and choice through contested primary elections.

The three arms of government

It may be helpful to clarify some of the terminology relating to political institutions which we have been employing in this chapter. In particular some further discussion of each of three arms of government – executive, legislative and judicial – seems desirable .

The executive

The executive not only enforces the laws, but also proposes changes in them to the legislature and conducts foreign relations. In the broad sense, it includes the head of state, the political members of the government and the civil servants who staff the offices of state.

Different systems differ greatly in how roles are distributed amongst the executive. As we have seen, formal head of state duties such as convening and dissolving the legislature, receiving distinguished visitors, presenting honours and decorations, signing legislation into law, opening new buildings and the like may be reserved to a hereditary sovereign or a semi-retired distinguished 'statesman'. Such kings, queens, presidents or governors customarily lead uneventful (if comfortable) lives, but in times of crisis may have to arbitrate on which leading politician is most likely to command a parliamentary majority if the current prime minister loses the confidence of the legislature.

The number of political posts (that is, jobs to which politicians are appointed by the head of government) in the national executive may vary from something like 5,000 posts in the United States to only about 200 in Britain (excluding appointments to 'quangos'). Clearly, the smaller the number of 'political' posts, the more top civil service jobs are likely to have a policy content. Virtually all systems have a large civil service of permanent state employees recruited on 'merit' (normally via special competitive examinations or on the basis of professional or academic qualifications). Their role will vary from country to country. The British Civil Service is relatively unusual in its degree of unity, with a stress on 'generalist' administrators who may move from department to department. In France and the United States, for instance, there is a greater tendency to recruit say agronomists for the Agriculture Department, accountants for the Audit Department and so on.

It is also usual for modern executives to have some rule-making powers – 'delegated legislation' in the UK, 'decrees' in some continental European systems. These would normally cover detailed technical matters like the construction and use regulations for motor vehicles or the approving of by-laws by local authorities. As well as introducing regular legislation, the executive often has a veto on legislation through a requirement that the head of state must sign legislation.

The legislature

Legislatures in virtually all systems not only have a large formal role in making laws, but also have powers to investigate and, to some degree, control or influence the executive. A major element in this is usually the need for annual financial revenues and expenditures to be approved.

All legislatures work through a committee system – the more effective the legislature, the stronger and more complex this tends to be. They usually also work through some variant of the UK system of three 'readings' of proposed legislation ('Bills') in full session, and a committee stage. In many legislatures, but not usually in Westminster-style parliaments, the committee stage of the process is the most significant and takes place before the main debates in permanent specialised committees.

Most legislatures are bicameral – they have two 'houses' – but in almost all, the 'lower' house (popularly elected by universal suffrage in geographical constituencies) is the one which has ultimate power and to which (in parliamentary systems) the government is responsible. In federal systems the upper house represents the constituent states, in many other systems it is indirectly elected via panels of local government councillors – but other strange variants are to be found (e.g. the UK House of Lords, university representatives, arbitrary division of elected representatives into two houses, etc.).

The United States is unusual in that, if anything, the upper house – the Senate, consisting of two Senators from each of the fifty states – is the most important chamber. In practice, the crucial decisions on legislation occur in bargaining between a joint committee of both houses and the President – who can threaten to use his veto.

The judiciary

As was stated earlier, all liberal democracies endorse the principle of an independent judiciary but vary as to the degree of power judges may exercise in constitutional matters. There are three main traditions in this respect:

> *British judges* are formally amongst the least powerful in being limited by the prerogative powers of the Crown, the doctrine of the sovereignty of Parliament and the lack of an enforceable declaration of rights as well as a tradition of deference to the executive in such matters as official secrecy and executive discretion. Despite this, it should be conceded that they have usually been sturdily independent within their defined limits and usually seek to interpret legislation as respecting the traditional rights of 'Englishmen'.

> *US judges*, however, are in a much stronger position in that they have established their powers of 'judicial review' of legislative and executive action (see pp.166–7) in the light of the Constitution which includes a Bill of Rights for individuals.

> *In the continental (Napoleonic) tradition* administrative courts in practice today often independently exercise a degree of control over executive action without parallel in Britain. Separate constitutional courts to review the constitutionality of laws or government decrees are also to be found in a number of states.

Constitutions and constitutionalism

So far we have considered the different forms of constitutional arrangements to be found in representative democracies – parliamentary, presidential, etc., – hardly mentioning the word 'constitution'. However, constitutionalism is so central to modern democratic politics that further analysis of the term is a necessity in a work such as this.

K.C. Wheare (1951) makes it clear that there are two main senses of the word: first, the fundamental political institutions of a country (something any country with a reasonably settled system of government can be said to have); second, a written document which usually defines these and the rights of the citizens of the state. Clearly, the United Kingdom does not have the latter – although there are various legal documents such as the Magna Carta, the Bill of Rights and so on, which are seen as helping to define its constitutional arrangements. The so-called 'unwritten' constitution is one of the distinctive features of the British political tradition, since only a few other democracies such as Israel and New Zealand are in the same position.

As Wheare and others (e.g. Bogdanor (1988)) have shown, liberal democratic constitutions usually have a variety of political functions to perform: first, they perform a symbolic and legitimising role in asserting and demonstrating the democratic credentials of the political system concerned; second, they are usually intended to protect and conserve the fundamental political institutions they define and to establish how they may be legitimately changed; third, they are intended to protect the fundamental rights of individual citizens.

More generally, from a broadly conservative and liberal perspective, it may be said that constitutional government means the 'government of laws, not of men' and that constitutions exist to limit the power of the government of the day in the interests of democracy and individual rights. Conversely, some socialist and radical interpretations would lay greater stress on the idea that constitutions empower democratic governments to change society to achieve a more just social order.

Where written constitutions exist, they often mark a revolutionary change in the political system, so that they may be originally written in circumstances which emphasise a radical interpretation of constitutions, but as they persist the emphasis may change to a conservative and legalistic interpretation of them. Britain's 'unwritten' constitution is usually defended as fulfilling the purposes of written constitutions more effectively than do these, more recent, documents. This has become a matter for considerable debate in Britain in recent years, however.

The symbolic role of the constitutional document is often of considerable importance. The United States Constitution, for instance, is treated with some reverence and the first act of each President is to take an oath or affirmation that 'I will faithfully execute the Office of President of the United States, and will to the best of my ability, preserve, protect and defend the Constitution of the United States'. Similarly, the French Declaration of the Rights of Man has a similar key role in French political culture.

It is often argued that Britain is unusual in embodying much of its constitution in 'conventions' – generally accepted rules which are not part of the law but whose breach may rapidly involve the breach thereof. These are seen as a more flexible way of expressing the constitution than a written legal document. It is worth pointing out that conventions are, in fact, found in any mature constitutional system – for instance, in the USA, conventions surrounding the operation of the Electoral College have effectively transformed what the founders intended as an indirect election of the President into a national popular vote.

Rights and constitutions

Most written constitutions, as we have seen, incorporate some sort of declaration of the rights of citizens of the country concerned. However, there is an important distinction to be drawn between a mere declaration which is intended as a guide to politicians – and perhaps for judges to consider in their interpretation of laws – and a *justiciable* bill of rights which is seen as a binding part of the constitution, superior in status to ordinary law and superseding it in case of conflict. A declaration may be of some symbolic political usefulness but a bill of rights is clearly more likely to be directly useful to ordinary citizens who consider their rights have been taken away or abused by the executive or legislature.

In the United States there is a long history of judicial use of the federal constitution to declare invalid both acts of the President and even federal legislation ('judicial review'). The main parts of the Constitution which have been used in this way are the first ten Amendments to the Constitution (which include the rights to free speech and assembly as well as, more controversially, rights against self-incrimination and the right to bear arms) and the Civil War Amendments against slavery and racial discrimination. These clauses are still more frequently invoked against state and local authorities. There are many examples of brave decisions by the Supreme Court to defend individual rights (say, to free speech) in this way, but also of decisions by the Court to prevent progressive social measures being implemented in the name of property rights. The political and social climate of the times has clearly influenced Court decisions on many occasions. As for instance in 1896 (*Plessey v. Ferguson*) when it declared that 'separate but equal' facilities for negroes on a railway train were constitutional, and again in 1954 (*Brown v. Board of Education of Topeka*) when it declared that separate educational facilities for negroes could not, in fact, be equal (see Chapter 5, p.124). In brief, a bill of rights takes power away from elected politicians (and bureaucrats!) and transfers it to lawyers and may not always have the positive outcome its (often left-wing) British proponents anticipate.

Dicey and other traditionalist British constitutionalists have preferred to rest their hopes for the protection of individual rights on a widespread attachment by all Britons to their ancient common law rights reaffirmed in historical documents such as Magna Carta and the Bill of Rights, but not legally entrenched by them against later legislation. Asserting the responsibility of the executive to the popularly elected Commons for all its actions is seen as a major guarantee of rights for the individual. MPs have traditionally been prepared to defend the rights of their constituents of any party by interrogating ministers on their behalf in the Commons. Similarly, such features of the common law as the right to trial by jury, the right to silence in court and under police interrogation, the Writ (now Judicial Order) of Habeas Corpus ('produce the body'), have been seen as superior protection for individuals to either American constitutional guarantees or continental systems of special administrative courts.

Britain does not have its own detailed declaration of rights (the Bill of Rights is a more limited document than its name might suggest), but it is a signatory to both the UN and European Declarations on Human Rights. The European document does have a Commission and Court to interpret it, and it may be significant that the British government has been the subject of more actions than any other signatory (perhaps because of the relative lack of legal remedies within the UK). As a conventional international organisation, however, the European Court of Human Rights (which is not a part of the European Union machinery) cannot enforce its judgments in Britain but must rely upon shaming the British government and legislature into action if it finds against UK authorities.

One Scandinavian institution which has been adopted more recently in Britain to help defend individual rights against administrative error or invasion is a Parliamentary Commissioner for Administration (the 'Ombudsman') who can independently investigate actions by government departments in cases of apparent 'maladministration'. (Similar Ombudsmen have since been introduced in Britain for the health service, local government, banking, insurance and building societies.) This innovation was originally opposed as a breach of British parliamentary traditions but this objection was overcome by having the Ombudsman report to a Parliamentary Committee. The major limitations on the British parliamentary Ombudsman are that his jurisdiction is limited to errors of administration by a department for which a minister is responsible (e.g. an 'unfair' piece of delegated legislation would be outside of his jurisdiction) and that the Ombudsman can only recommend remedial action to the minister (although this is usually effective under the searchlight of parliamentary publicity). In Sweden, where the Ombudsman originated, he has much stronger powers to insist on remedies and operates within a tradition of open government in which all government documents are open to inspection.

As briefly indicated earlier, in much of continental Europe the tradition stretching back to administrative reforms introduced by Napoleon is for there to be a separate set of administrative courts. Whilst these were, no doubt, intended originally to be more sympathetic to the executive than ordinary local courts, they have now developed a sturdy judicial independence combined with considerable administrative expertise. In France, for instance, top graduates of the Ecole National d'Administration (ENA) aspire to become members of the Council of State which is the superior administrative court (the ENA being perhaps the most prestigious postgraduate-level educational institution in the country).

How democratic constitutions work in practice

Democratic constitutional arrangements can operate in a number of different ways in practice depending upon the use the government makes of the constitutional powers it has. Most democratic systems give numerous opportunities for the government to consult and listen to the electorate – the extent to which the government does so, and with which parts of the electorate, makes an enormous difference to the overall nature of the system. Three alternative ways of working such a system which will be outlined here are pluralism, corporatism and centralisation. We will also relate these accounts of how the constitution is being worked to the more general political theories of power introduced in Chapter 5 (pluralism, elite theories, and – to some extent – Marxism).

Pluralism

In a politically pluralist system the legitimacy of a host of social and political interest groups is recognised. All have an equal chance to be involved in an open political process by which social decisions are reached through a process of widespread discussion, negotiation and compromise, particularly amongst those groups most affected by the decisions concerned. In the last resort, where conflicts cannot be resolved into a consensus, the interests of the groups commanding majority support in the population as a whole will predominate, but strong feelings by groups most affected may count for more than weaker preferences by more numerous less affected groups. Substantial efforts will be made to facilitate tolerant compromises whereby different (for instance) religious, national or regional groups may adopt different solutions to the same problems.

Public compromises between groups may often be struck in

such systems in negotiations between different political parties within a governmental coalition (continental Europe), or in legislative bargaining or in compromises between the legislature and the executive (e.g. the USA). In the UK, a well-known constitutional authority, Sir Ivor Jennings (1957) has suggested that it is a convention of the constitution that representatives of interests affected by a bill to be laid before Parliament should be consulted by the executive whilst it is being drafted, as well as being given the opportunity to table amendments to bills as they go through the Commons and Lords.

Where different levels of government exist (e.g. European, British and local or federal, state and local) the pluralist principle is that of 'subsidiarity', as discussed at the end of the last chapter. In the Netherlands, such principles have become firmly entrenched with, on one interpretation, contemporary central government coalition governments being reduced to largely setting the procedural rules for local policy-making communities (Frissen (1994)).

What I have been describing here is pluralism as a political ideal as advocated by such writers as Sir Ernest Barker (1961).

Corporatism

It has been suggested that pluralism is too optimistic a description of policy-making in many contemporary 'liberal democracies', and the alternative description of 'corporatism' was often thought to be appropriate in 1970s Britain. It is clear that much policy-making in Britain is made behind closed doors – in Whitehall rather than at Westminster. This does not necessarily mean that no consultation takes place – an extensive network of official committees and unofficial contacts with representatives from professional, academic, managerial, trade union, and other bodies does exist. It is customary, as Jennings (1957) indicated, to sound these out on policy proposals. Similarly, much policy-making in Brussels is made in closed negotiations between governmental delegations and by obscure discussions between the Commission and those interest groups organised on a European basis. In the United States, Congress is open to representations from any of the thousands of interest groups which exist in the country, but only a relatively select group of interests have effective and permanent relationships with the key policy-making committees in their areas – often contributing heavily to the election expenses of key committee chairmen and exercising a virtual veto on key executive appointments in what Cater (1965) calls the 'sub-government' relating to their policy area.

'Corporatism' indicates that the consultation tends to be some-what selective, with established bodies like the Confederation of British Industry, the American Medical Association, and the French CGT (Confederation General du Travail – the main trades union confederation) being regularly consulted whilst grass-roots opinion is held to be virtually represented by these. Producer and metropolitan groups, perhaps inevitably, tend to be much more strongly represented than consumer and provincial interests. These somewhat cosy arrange-ments were reinforced by what some writers have called 'co-optation', whereby the favoured interest groups were even involved in admin-istering the policies evolved, and were expected to sell them to their members. Some hostile critics have described such a system as 'fascism with a human face' (Pahl and Winkler (1975)) and suggested that all sorts of 'feather-bedding' of special interests resulted.

This description of liberal democracy as a corporatist system is, of course, a variety of what we earlier described as elite theory.

Centralisation

In Britain, Mrs Thatcher and the far Right of the Conservative Party have been especially hostile to the idea of 'corporatism' and denounced the growth of quangos which accompanied the increase of such policies. Rather than fascism, they saw these developments as the institutionalisation of a 'nanny socialist state'. Their view was that too many decisions were being taken by vested interests (including the trade unions) behind closed doors at the expense of the citizen – when citizens (in their role as consumers) could take these decisions through the market. Hence, the need was seen for a radical reshaping and trimming of the state – requiring strong central political leadership to enforce budgetary control and attain efficiency through market forces.

Partly for these reasons, there has been much less emphasis

within British government in recent years on consultation, compromise and negotiation. Instead, the emphasis has been on the need for the government, having had its programme approved at the polls, to impress the electorate with its decisive implementation of a radical programme. Policies (such as the Criminal Justice Act, 1994) are being pushed through against, or without the advice of, the professional groups most concerned.

Traditional British emphasis on the autonomy of local government has also been considerably undermined by a new stricter insistence on central financial control, the compulsory putting out to tender of many local services, taking schools out of local government control and other similar measures.

Of course, a more hostile interpretation of these same developments is that the Conservative Party has become more open in its advocacy of a straight capitalist system with its over-riding of the interests of ordinary people in the interests of the capitalist 'bourgeoisie'- what Miliband (1984) would describe as a slide from 'capitalist democracy' towards 'capitalist authoritarianism'. The trappings of democratic institutions can be combined with limitations which make them ineffective:

> trade unions might be allowed in such a regime providing they do not organise strikes. Parties might operate providing they were not subversive. Political activity might be possible, providing permission had been obtained for it. Newspapers would be allowed providing they did not foment 'class hatred' or 'spread disaffection'. . . . There would be censorship, but on a limited basis; on the other hand, self-censorship would be unlimited.
>
> Miliband (1984, 154)

Such developments do not, however, seem typical of trends in liberal democracies generally – despite a widespread tendency towards the adoption of Thatcherite economic policies such as privatisation and monetarism, the predominant political style in Western Europe remains one of 'concertation' (see Chapter 4, p.99) as epitomised in the Social Chapter of the Maastricht Treaty.

Political communication

So far in this chapter we have considered democratic government in terms of the extent of popular participation in government, the extent to which the people can influence the choice of governors and the form which democratic institutions might take. Arguably more important than any of these, however, is the responsiveness of government to people's views and interests and even its capacity to leave well alone (to respect their rights).

In Chapter 1 we saw that Easton (1979) and many other writers view a political system as a mechanism for authoritative decision-making linked by 'inputs' and 'outputs' to its environment. In this very simple model of politics two of the four elements (i.e. 50 per cent) consists of communication.

The responsiveness of governments involves, clearly, both governments receiving an accurate picture of the electorate's needs and the electorate having a clear picture of the government's activities. Communication between the government and the electorate and the government's monitoring of the objective effects of its policies and gathering information about policy alternatives are clearly central to a successful democratic system.

Even a very simple model of communication suggests some important variables. Who are the senders and recipients of the information? What quantity of information flows? Are they one-way (simplex) or two-way (duplex)? Are messages accurately encoded and decoded? Does 'noise' interfere with accurate reception? Does information overload prevent essential information being distinguished? In the space available, only some of these points are followed up here.

In terms of the three models of how the constitution might work introduced earlier (centralisation, corporatism and pluralism), we can see that they involve different patterns of communication.

In a centralised pattern, most communication can consist of the government and the opposition broadcasting their views to the voters. At lengthy intervals the voters take a measured view of performance over the last four or five years and send back a simple message of acceptance or rejection at the polls (i.e. two simplex flows of information)!

In the corporatist model, these flows are supplemented by additional duplex flows of information between the government and selected corporate organisations in which the government seeks to improve the quality of policy-making by obtaining specialist advice, and negotiates some concessions with some of those most affected in return for assistance in implementing policies smoothly. The leadership of these organisations may, in turn, communicate with their members in a similar duplex flow or alternately, attempt to 'virtually' represent them by assuming a knowledge of their interests and views, taking a renewal of subscriptions as agreement to their interpretation of their members' interests.

In the pluralist model communication flows are most complicated and diffuse. There must be widespread knowledge, not only of the government actions but also of its intentions so that these can be influenced before they are finalised. Elaborate duplex information flows connect not only the government and interest groups but also enable interest groups and political parties to negotiate compromises amongst each other in order to better influence events. The government needs a good knowledge of public opinion if it is to reflect a public consensus.

We shall elaborate upon these models somewhat and consider which seems nearest to current practice by looking in more detail at the activities of some of the political institutions which are usually thought of as playing a key role in political communication: political parties, pressure or interest groups and the mass media.

Political parties

Political parties may be thought of as social groups which seek to wholly or partially take over the government of a country, usually by contesting elections. Thus, they seek to take power for their leading members, either for its own sake (the psychological, social and economic rewards of office), on behalf of some social group (e.g. labour, farmers, Protestants) or with some ideological objective in mind (e.g. national independence, socialism). We have seen that the names of parties are often a bad guide to their objectives; it is also worth stressing that most – probably all – parties are coalitions of people with different objectives in mind.

In most Liberal Democratic countries, the main obvious communication function of political parties is to contest elections – selecting candidates in constituencies, canvassing and organising voters, composing and delivering election addresses in constituencies and running local poster and national media campaigns. By offering voters candidates with commitments to certain policies (especially as identified by the national leadership), they make national elections a choice by electors of rival governments as well as the selection of legislators.

To understand such parties it is necessary to distinguish between the role of the voluntary membership in the constituencies (even the most active of which do little more than pay their subscriptions, attend the odd social event and perhaps occasionally act as 'tellers' at polling stations or deliver leaflets in their street); the activists who run constituency parties, act as local councillors and attend conferences or conventions; professionals who are employed by the local or national parties; and parliamentarians who have been elected to the legislature (in some countries mayors and some councillors may also be full-time paid and elected representatives).

The ordinary membership, as we have suggested, play only a small role in the electoral process. The activists can communicate what they see as local 'grass-roots' feeling to their local councillor or legislator or at national party meetings (conventions, conferences, assemblies, etc.). In principle in Britain, Labour and Liberal Democrat Party national meetings of activists 'make' party policy, whilst the Conservative equivalent only advises the parliamentary leader. In practice all three are dominated by the parliamentary leadership and can be ignored by it when this is thought to be politically necessary. In the United States the only real (but very important) function of the national party conventions is the selection of presidential candidates.

In Britain party professionals play only a small political role; on a local level they are almost exclusively concerned with keeping the party machine going (and paying their own salaries); on a national level headquarter professionals differ in that they are officially responsible to the (parliamentary) party leader in the Conservative Party, but to the mass party executive in the Labour and Liberal Parties. In the United States there are few real party employees with each politician employing '*ad hoc*' groups of image consultants, pollsters, public relations specialists and the like.

However, in practice in virtually all liberal democracies, nationally elected politicians firmly control the national party machinery. In Britain, the parliamentary party (i.e. its members in the House of Commons) constitutes the core of the party and for the government party in particular it is an important centre for duplex flows of information between MPs (Members of Parliament – i.e. the House of Commons) and government members, interest group representatives, party activists and ordinary 'constituents'. Government back-bench MPs seek to increase their chances of re-election by popularising the governments message to the electorate and by alerting government 'Whips' to potential and actual problems. In the United States incumbent congressmen (and women) are at an enormous advantage in having sizeable professional staffs, free postage and travel facilities and the opportunity to do individual constituents favours and build up good will.

In US parties and in more conservative parties in Europe there are often few party activists to contest control of the party machinery with elected officials and those who benefit or hope to from their patronage. Socialist, christian democratic and, to some extent, liberal parties may have larger numbers of activists, some of whom may be ideologically committed 'militants' with strong policy views. Whilst useful as enthusiastic canvassers or envelope lickers, such militants may, from the professionals point of view, be a source of internal conflict and resistance to the perhaps inevitable compromises of democratic politics. They may serve, however, from time to time, to inject an element of idealism and dynamic change into political systems.

Interest groups

A pressure or interest group differs from a political party in seeking only to influence the government – not become part of it. Thus, by definition, it can be said to be in the business of political communication. 'Interest group' may be a better term since they may well seek to influence the government more by persuasion and information than by threats of political reward or penalty. However, it would be surprising if they were not listened to more closely if they represented large numbers of voters (trade unions), influential 'opinion formers' (doctors) or wealthy potential contributors to party funds.

Where the interest is a professional or business one, then the group concerned may well have both specialised expertise which government policy-makers may wish to draw upon and the capacity to aid the acceptance and implementation of the policy. Thus, doctors' representatives (notably the American and British Medical Associations) will usually be drawn into making health policy, help to win acceptance within the health professions for an agreed policy – which will largely be implemented by their members. Most democratic governments of whatever party have tended to consult such groups and try to win them over to their policies. In Britain, post-1979 Conservative administrations have, however, on occasion seemed to make a political point of not consulting groups whom they regarded as having been 'feather-bedded' or over-influential in a liberal direction. It is worth pointing out, however, that consultation remains the rule – for instance even in an act recently passed designed to make a 'bonfire of controls' by allowing laws and regulations thought by the government to be unnecessary to be repealed by a much shortened legislative process, it is explicitly laid down that affected parties must be consulted before regulations are dispensed with.

In Britain, the links between Whitehall and such producer interest groups are institutionalised in the practice of each sector of industry having an official 'sponsoring' department. It is standard for such groups to be represented on official advisory committees and for their leaders and administrators to be on first-name terms with the corresponding higher civil servants (i.e. there are established unofficial communication patterns – weekly lunches, etc.).

Trade unions have generally speaking (i.e. post-1945), been seen within this framework – as groups who are automatically consulted, whose prominent leaders finish up in the House of Lords and are appointed to quangos etc. This was so under Conservative administrations such as those of Edward Heath and Harold Macmillan. In Labour administrations they have benefited from the historic link between the various wings of the labour 'movement'. (Most members of the Labour Party remain 'affiliated' members signed up through their trade unions who retain the majority of seats at Labour Conferences, automatic representation on the National Executive of the Labour Party and in local constituency associations.) It is not unknown for trade union leaders to be appointed to Labour Cabinets. Conversely, some on both Left and Right have argued that trade union leaders have often been too pliant towards 'their' Labour governments – sacrificing their members' economic interests to the political success of the party. However, recent Conservative Thatcherite administrations have been much less ready to accord automatic deference to trade union leaders despite their (in some cases) nominal millions of 'followers'.

In all democratic systems non-producer interest groups – residents affected by planning proposals, consumers of both private and public goods and services, housewives, carers, and so-called 'cause' groups who operate more altruistically on behalf of others – seem less effective than producer groups. In Britain groups such as the Royal National Institute for the Blind, Greenpeace working for the environment, the Consumers' Association, and more especially the many local 'cause' groups, generally have less effective and permanent communication links with Whitehall. Such groups may only hear of legislative or administrative decisions after they have been made – rather than whilst they are being considered. This then makes it much more difficult – if not downright impossible – to influence the decisions concerned. Even trying to amend a bill in Parliament when it is still under consideration is a relatively late stage to try to affect events. By this time the prestige of the government may have been attached to the bill and amendments may affect compromises reached between civil servants or ministers and other more established groups.

The mass media

Confining ourselves here to the existing conventional mass media – press, radio and television – we are mainly concerned with, by definition, broadcasting: centralised origination of simplex flows of information to large numbers of recipients whose only choice is to change channel, 'listen' or switch off.

In this framework, the important issues would then seem to be as follows. What information on political life is available to be reported? How many channels of such information are available? Who controls and edits the transmission of information by these channels in whose interests? How do potential recipients of the messages react to them? Do the mass media represent the masses to the elite?

What information on political life is available to be reported?

If the media do not know what the government is doing, then clearly it cannot be reported to the electorate. In this respect, democratic countries vary greatly in the access reporters and citizens can obtain to information on government decision-making. At one extreme the Swedish tradition of open government requires virtually all decision-making to be publicly documented. At the other, the British tradition of official secrecy made the assumption that executive deliberations will be kept private unless positive decisions are made to release information. The United States has now adopted the opposite assumption with its Freedom of Information Act which requires federal government agencies to reveal any document at the request of any enquirer unless reasons such as national security or personal confidentiality can be plausibly advanced against this. A new non-statutory Code of Practice on Access to Government Information (April 1994) has rather half-heartedly moved in the open government direction in Britain – but it allows for numerous exceptions, including advice to Ministers and anything that could be the subject of a public inquiry.

The nature of legislative decision-making will also have relevance here. In Britain effectively laws are made before being introduced into the legislature, so that the nature and extent of compromises involved may well be obscure. In the United States, and in many continental European coalition-based systems where, as we have seen, legislative compromises are reached much more on the public record in committees of the legislature, such decision-making is more open to scrutiny.

The extent to which journalists have a tradition of and are rewarded for hard-hitting investigative journalism is also of importance. In the United States there is a long tradition of such 'muck-raking' journalism culminating in the 'Watergate' investigations of Bernstein and Woodward (1974), which contributed to the ignominious resignation of President Nixon.

How many channels of such information are available?

Another problem which might be identified with political communication patterns from a democratic point of view is the relatively limited number of effective 'channels'. In Britain, for instance, there are only four terrestrial television channels, BBC Radio (these having only two news services between them), a largely a-political commercial radio sector, a dozen or so national daily newspapers and, effectively, one evening newspaper per city. The present government has encouraged the growth of more satellite TV and commercial radio channels, put out a fifth terrestrial TV channel to tender and encouraged the growth of cable TV, but the effectiveness of these as major independent sources of news seems fairly limited at present. In effect, most citizens probably rely on, at most, four major political news channels – BBC, ITN (Independent Television News), their customary national daily and possibly a local evening paper or free weekly. In principle, of course, anyone is free to set up an alternative newspaper, or to tender for an ITV franchise – in practice, anyone with several million pounds to lose!

In the United States a much greater number of television and radio channels are available, with three major groupings of television providers and also CNN providing news services by cable and increasingly over air. Public service broadcasting is also available in many parts of the country. As a result of economic and geographical factors, however, newspapers tend to be rather parochial and uncompetitive outside of major metropolitan areas.

Surely the least satisfactory arrangement from a democratic point of view is where the only effective mass communication channels are the state radio and television channels – as is still the case in a number of countries in the South.

The more 'channels' available the less we need to worry about the content and control of any one of them, since consumers can exercise influence over them by selecting them or not. Arguably, with so few effective major channels in Britain, the control and editing of those which do exist becomes a matter for greater public concern. This is especially so when we consider that, in Britain, satellite television and three of the major national daily newspapers are all under the ownership of one company grouping controlled by one man (Rupert Murdoch).

Who controls the transmission of information, in whose interests?

In Britain, because of their near monopoly situation it has been accepted for many years that the BBC and ITV TV channels should be carefully regulated to ensure that their output is reasonably politically balanced. This has mainly taken the form of ensuring that the views of the official opposition get exposure in replies to ministerial broadcasts, party political broadcasts, representation on discussion programmes, etc. Minor parties and minority groups such as gays, racial and religious minorities, have less institutionalised exposure, but there is recognition that they should have some access to publicly financed or licensed communication channels. Further controls have been thought appropriate in the interests of children (rules about what can be broadcast before 9.00 p.m.), decency (the Broadcasting Standards Council) and, until recently, anti-terrorist measures (no live interviews with the IRA).

Such a pluralist approach has been taken even further in the Netherlands, where radio and television have long been divided on a party and religious basis to ensure all substantial minorities have an opportunity to express their views.

In contrast, the newspaper industry has, in most democratic countries, been thought to be sufficiently 'regulated' by the existence of free competition and the laws of libel. In Britain only the theoretically unofficial 'D' (defence) notice system can be seen as attempting to regulate the distribution of politically sensitive information – and this is supposed to be restricted to matters vital to the security of the realm, not politically embarrassing information. From the Left, the present system in Britain seems most inadequate in its failure to secure political balance – with most national newspapers clearly editorially favouring the Conservatives and only the (wavering) Mirror Group

Labour. Since running a national newspaper is a large financial operation the owners and managers of such operations, naturally tend to favour capitalist/Conservative values. From the Right in Britain the anxiety has centred upon 'irresponsible' tabloid intrusions into the private lives of both the rich and famous (including royalty and politicians) and more ordinary people – including victims of crime and people with untypical sexual proclivities. The Press Complaints Commission (a voluntary industry body) has been urged to introduce greater self-regulation under the threat of statutory controls. One difficulty is to find a formula for protecting the legitimate privacy of ordinary people which will not prevent the media from revealing misconduct by public figures which affects their accountability for their deeds.

One defence that can be made for the present arrangements in both broadcasting and national newspapers is that the actual editing and presentation of news is done by professionals who, in order to maintain circulation/audience figures, must respect the values of a plural society and pursue 'news values' – one organisation cannot afford to neglect or distort awkward news because it will be rapidly and accurately reported elsewhere. In this respect the BBC in Britain can be seen as an important 'quality control' standard against which other organisations are judged – whilst possibility of pro-establishment bias by the BBC is reduced by the existence of maverick organisations such as the *Sun* and *Private Eye*.

There does seem to be some strength in this argument (and it must be remembered that journalists themselves are often to the political left of their managers and proprietors), but some anxieties do remain including reservations about the implications of pursuing news value (including 'scoops') in the interests of greater circulation in this way. Problems which have been raised include suggested biases against understanding (explaining events is neglected in favour of the sensational and the new) and against good news in favour of bad. The economics of capitalist journalism mean it may be a more sensible strategy to raise circulation by lotteries and price-cutting than to risk libel suits by expensive and complex investigative journalism. Many newspapers – especially local ones – do little to search out the news for themselves but rely upon a few international news agencies

(Reuters, etc.), standard public sources like the the courts, Parliament and local council meetings and a stream of 'press releases' from the public relations arms of government, political parties, commercial organisations and entertainers.

How do potential recipients of the messages react to them?

Another fascinating area of political and sociological research upon which we can only touch here is the issue of how the potential audience choose which messages to attend to, how they interpret the messages when they receive them and how important these messages are in moulding political behaviour?

Evidence derived from research on party political broadcasts and newspaper circulation patterns suggests that people tend to attend to political messages which confirm their existing ways of thinking and to interpret ambivalent political messages in the same ways. There is little to suggest that people are very influenced by party political broadcasts or newspaper editorials; much to suggest that people are influenced by face-to-face conversations with people they know.

However, much research suggests that political events are interpreted in terms of the recipient's own images of themselves (working class, black, housewife, . . .) and of the parties (caring, profligate, responsible, united . . .). These must surely be continually subtly influenced by messages conveyed in the mass media (including advertising) often on a 'subliminal' (unconscious) level.

Do the mass media represent the masses to the elite?

The popular press, in particular, is often keen to portray itself as the champion of its readers to the elite. To some extent this is clearly arrant nonsense – neither millionaire newspaper proprietors nor sophisticated metropolitan journalists are necessarily particularly well qualified to interpret the views of millions of provincial voters. However, letters columns and the very important modern innovation of the opinion poll – which is now a staple source of 'news' – do help to give politicians some clues on mass opinion. One suspects that 'informed' commentators in the broadsheets and magazines are probably still mistaken by politicians quite frequently for 'public opinion'.

Democracy and communication

In terms of our three models – centralisation, corporatism and pluralism – then, we can see the evidence we have reviewed provides some support for each of the patterns of communication we suggested they entailed. Centralisation seems supported by the evidence of centralised national parties and a centralised communication system mainly concerned with 'broadcasting'. Corporatism is supported by the evidence of a well-established pattern of legislative consultation with certain favoured pressure groups. Whilst we have found less evidence in the pattern of established institutions of political communication for pluralism, we saw that the legitimacy of consultation before decisions were taken and of any group to organise and protest are accepted. We might well have elaborated on this theme by emphasising a tradition of sturdy independence and well-established right to petition the parliament and other decision-makers in many liberal democracies. What seems inadequate to the author are the opportunities for less well-established groups to have a real chance of influence.

Recommended reading

Ball, Allan, 1988, *Modern Politics and Government*, 4th edn, Basingstoke, Macmillan. A useful introductory text on political institutions.

Bogdanor, Vernon, 1988, *Constitutions in Democratic Politics*, Aldershot, Gower. Broad survey of constitutionalism in many contemporary democracies.

Bowles, Nigel, 1993, *The Government and Politics of the United States*, Basingstoke, Macmillan. Well-reviewed and up-to-date text on the USA.

Coxall, Bill and Robbins, Lynton, 1994, *Contemporary British Politics*, Basingstoke, Macmillan. One of a number of good introductory texts available on the UK.

Gallagher, Michael *et al.*, 1992, *Representative Government in Western Europe*, London, McGraw-Hill. Impressive general description of the pattern of democratic politics in contemporary Europe.

Gladdish, Ken 1991, *Governing From the Centre: Politics and Policy-Making in the Netherlands*, London, Hirst & Co. This includes treatment of consociationalism.

MacPherson, C.B., 1966, *The Real World of Democracy: The Massey Lecture*, Oxford, Clarendon Press. Very influential essay which seeks to understand non-liberal democracy in communist and third-world countries as well as the Western liberal version.

Negrine, Ralph, 1994, *Politics and the Mass Media in Britain*, 2nd edn, London, Routledge. Mainly concerned with British Press and terrestial broadcasting but also raises more general and 'new media' issues.

Reeve, Andrew and Ware, Alan, 1992, *Electoral Systems: A Comparative and Theoretical Approach*, London, Routledge. A useful and up-to-date text.

Sakwa, Richard, 1993, *Russian Politics and Society*, London, Routledge. Includes Soviet and post-Soviet developments.

Scott, John, 1991, *Who Rules Britain?*, Cambridge, Cambridge University Press. Some clear theoretical material as well as specific evidence on classes and elites in Britain.

Wilson, Graham K., (ed.), 1990, *Interest Groups*, Oxford, Basil Blackwell. Includes both theoretical and country-based contributions including the USA and Japan.

Chapter 8

Policies

In this chapter we shall consider how, in liberal democracies, particularly Britain, public policies should be made, and implemented, how they are made, and the problems of evaluating the public policy process. In particular, by way of example, and because of its key importance, we shall be looking at welfare policy with special reference to health and education.

Rational policy-making

We saw earlier how Weber used a series of models of authority to explain the range of social possibilities and to explain the internal logic of these variations (Chapter 3, pp.55–6). These 'ideal-type' models are often a useful analytical device – his model of 'bureaucracy' is very much of this kind (Chapter 2, p.37). A good example of an ideal-type model of the policy-making process is Lindblom's (1959) 'rational comprehensive' model (see Box 19). Here Lindblom considers how decision-makers would proceed if they did so in a completely

logical and rational manner. This then serves as a bench-mark or standard against which to compare actual processes of decision-making. Lindblom's model is also very similar to the economic model of individual consumer choice.

Box 19   A rational-comprehensive model of decision-making

1 Define and rank *values*;
2 Specify *objectives* compatible with these;
3 Identify all relevant *options* or means of achieving these objectives;
4 Calculate all the *consequences* of these options and compare them;
5 Choose the option or combination of options which could *maximise* the highest ranked values.

SOURCE   After Lindblom (1959)

If such an approach to decision-making is treated as the paradigm for making public policy, then it is clear that few actual policy decisions are made in a manner which approaches it. Some attempt has been made to apply such a systematic and rational method of policy decision-making by employing the technique of cost benefit analysis (CBA) on, for instance, the decision as to where to build a fourth London airport. CBA, basically an attempt to put monetary figures on the costs and benefits accruing from an investment over time, is more widely used by strategic planners in business situations. As that example shows, however, there are problems in both establishing an agreed ranking of values and in measuring and predicting outcomes as far as most public policy decisions are concerned. Some of these difficulties derive from the fact that the model is implicitly based on how *one* individual decision-maker would approach a problem. In practice, virtually all public policy decisions are made by organisations, only some of which even claim to be 'bureaucratic' (in Weber's sense) or to be rational decision-makers.

Problems with rational policy-making

The problems of interpreting organisational behaviour as if it is the product of rational decision-making by its top managers are neatly illustrated by Allison's (1987) seminal book, *The Essence of Decision: Explaining the Cuban Missile Crisis*, to which we briefly referred in Chapter 1. He rightly suggests that most of the literature of international relations treats the behaviour of states as if it is the product of rational policy-makers, behaving much like Lindblom's rational comprehensive model suggests. (The same is true of the classical economic literature on the theory of the firm.) This is what he calls the 'classical rational actor' model (or Model 1). In practice, though, such assumptions seem to be a long way from empirical reality. For instance, in the Cuban missile crisis US policy-makers produced a series of hypotheses about 'Russian' behaviour in installing IRBMs (intermediate range ballistic missiles) in uncamouflaged soft silos – none of which were very convincing because they assumed the behaviour was part of a single co-ordinated and rational policy.

We can briefly summarise some reasons why any organisation is likely to diverge from the rational comprehensive model of policy-making, in Box 20.

Box 20   Why organisations are not always rational

Psychological limitations;
Limitations arising from multiple values;
Factored problems and fractionated power;
Information problems;
Cost limitations – blind rule implementation.

SOURCE   See Hogwood and Gunn (1984, 50–3)

By 'psychological limitations' it is meant that organisations are composed of individuals with limited knowledge and skills and imperfectly known values.

The limitations arising from multiple values are that organisations face additional problems in determining values and objectives (compared with individuals) because they are composed of individuals with different values and objectives. Whilst this may be true of all organisations, it is arguable that it is necessarily so in organisations seeking to implement political policies on behalf of the whole community and which may have been the subject of intense debate between political parties, or which remain socially contested. For instance, the British Child Support Agency has found itself torn between rival demands from groups reflecting the interests of deserted mothers and children, those representing fathers and second families and, not least, the demands of the Treasury that the Agency make a substantial reduction in the costs of Social Security.

By 'factored problems and fractionated power' is meant that the division of problems amongst specialist departments helps to overcome the first (psychological) problem but creates new ones – sub-units concerned with part of the problem treat it in isolation, elevate their own sub-goals over those of the organisation whilst their leaders seek power and influence for themselves. (In *Parkinson's Law*, Parkinson (1958) amusingly documents, for instance, how the number of Admirals in the British Navy increased as the number of battleships declined deriving the 'law' that organisations grow irrespective of the amount of work they have to do.)

Although organisations collectively possess much more information on problems than individuals (through filing systems, computer data-bases, etc.) they frequently fail to access the relevant information at the right time, thus losing one of the major strategic advantages they possess.

In order to achieve the cost benefits of 'mass producing' decisions, organisations tend to economise on searching out alternatives in making decisions. If a rule appears to apply it will be automatically operated. Subordinates can always defend an action to their superiors by referring to a rule made by those superiors. The more a bureaucracy is criticised and needs to defend itself, the worse this behaviour may get.

Incremental decision-making

Thus Allison (1987) suggests a second 'organisational process model' of decision-making which stresses that organisations normally operate without explicitly defining objectives through a *repertoire of standard operating procedures* reflecting the parochial views of its constituent departments. To put the idea more simply: departments in organisations go on dealing with standard situations in their usual set ways without relating these to overall organisational objectives.

In a non-standard situation, or if acceptable performance standards are not being met, then *incremental* (i.e. bit by bit) changes will be made. A limited search will be made for the first satisfactory solution that can be found (this is what Simon (1959) calls *satisficing* rather than *optimising* behaviour). This will usually be through a modification of standard operating procedures rather than producing a new solution from a blank sheet.

Allison also stresses organisations' preference for avoiding the disruptive effects of uncertainty and conflict by concentrating on short-term problems rather than long-term planning (which would involve discussion of goals and values), by using 'rule of thumb' decision rules based on short-term feedback and by attempting to negotiate away uncertainties in the environment.

The various authors mentioned react to this (largely shared) perception of organisational decision-making in different ways. Allison is mainly concerned to formulate a realistic descriptive model of decision-making. Lindblom (1959) tends to accept that in a pluralist society incremental decision-making may not only be inevitable but also desirable. Simon (1977) has made sophisticated suggestions for improving the management of organisations in the light of these observations.

Allison puts forward a third model which he describes as a 'governmental (bureaucratic) politics' one. To emphasise its generality and to avoid confusion with Weber, we shall refer to it as the political bargaining model. Briefly this third model of Allison's stresses that social decisions may be often more appropriately seen as *political resultants* rather than as either individual rational choices or even as organisational outputs. Essentially, policy-making is seen as the outcome of a *game* between *players* occupying positions. The outcome is the result of bargaining between players and is dependent on (among other things) their bargaining skill, their resources and the rules of the game. Just as in physics a resultant is the outcome of physical forces operating in different directions on a mass, a political resultant is the outcome of different social forces (players) which is unlikely to be identical to what any individual player desired.

Allison stresses among other things the importance of mutual (mis)perceptions, the variety of stakes held by the players and the number of different issues being considered. Because of the complexity of the game, players' actions are constantly focused on deadlines which have to be met by decisions – frequently on the basis of inadequate information. One important maxim Allison stresses is 'Where you stand depends on where you sit': issues look radically different to players from different organisations or from different levels of the same organisation. Each player, too, will have made prior commitments to others within or without the game, and will have a distinctive style of play. Another salutary emphasis in Allison's treatment of this model is on the ever-present potential for 'foul-ups'!

Although this model is formulated primarily with US foreign policy-making in mind, an increasingly strong trend in the literature on organisations is to stress similar issues. In particular, writers like Ian Mangham (1979) have stressed the extent to which people in organisations pursue their own political (career, etc.) objectives, whilst others (e.g. Karpick (1978)) have stressed that every organisation has an environment composed primarily of other organisations. Thus, by negotiating with representatives of other organisations, a more stable organisational world can be created.

Allison's political bargaining model should also remind us that many policy decisions are not taken in a bureaucratic organisational environment. At the extreme, policy decisions may be taken in a legislative assembly which characteristically works by bargaining amongst parties and factions and in which the resultant policy is not a clear expression of the values of any one group but a temporary compromise reflecting the bargaining power of the parties and the state of public opinion at the time. Frequently too, executive bodies from cabinet-level down consist of representatives of departments or even outside organisations, so that policies may be modified not only to reflect experience in execution, but also to reflect changes in the political bargaining power of the parties concerned. As we have seen, many writers, like Lindblom, view such 'incrementalism' (i.e. making policy in small steps) as not only inevitable given our limited knowledge of the social effects of policy-making, but as desirable in a democracy in which relationships between groups and individuals are freely renegotiable. He also stresses that incrementalism is a *safer* way to adjust to events given the limitations of human knowledge in relation to the complexity of the issues facing the decision-maker.

The policy process

Hogwood and Gunn (1984) offer a useful and sophisticated model of the policy process which takes into account some of the points we discussed above. They offer it not as a description or prescription of what happens in every case but as framework for understanding what does or does not happen in each particular case. Each of these stages is potentially of key importance in deciding the outcome of a policy process (see Box 21).

BOX 21 Hogwood and Gunn's model of the policy process

1 Deciding to decide (issue search or agenda setting);
2 Deciding how to decide;
3 Issue definition;
4 Forecasting;
5 Setting objectives and priorities;
6 Options analysis;
7 Policy implementation, monitoring and control;
8 Evaluation and review;
9 Policy maintenance, succession or termination.

In comparison with the rational comprehensive model discussed earlier this has some important and desirable features: it sees policy-making as a more or less continuous process; it stresses political issues of agenda-setting, decision process and definition; and it does not take the implementation of the decision for granted.

Items (1) and (9), in particular, in the model rightly suggest that policy-making is an extended process in which certain issues are picked out for attention (see our earlier discussion of Bachrach and Baratz (1970)), may be approached in different ways during the process of decision and implementation, and then may be subsumed into debates on other issues as time goes by.

Rather than a one-off decision on values, we have already stressed the extent to which policy-making often reflects compromises on values between different groups. These groups, in turn, may define 'the problem' in different ways. As we saw in Chapter 6, the question of whether a problem should be dealt with by the state, the market, voluntary action or whatever, is a crucial part of many contemporary policy discussions as demonstrated later in our discussion of health issues.

Partly as a consequence of the extended time policy-making takes and the partial nature of the consensus built up behind many policies, it cannot be assumed that decisions, once made, will automatically be implemented. Many agencies, firms and individuals and levels of government may be involved in realising a decision initially taken at one level of the state machinery. The outcome may not be recognisable to the initial policy-makers. The consequences of the policies adopted may not, in fact, be as predicted by the original analysis upon which the policy was based. For these reasons, it is sensible that policy-makers set up mechanisms to monitor the success or failure of their policies so that they may be adapted, refined or indeed abandoned, as appropriate. We shall be discussing the issues of implementation at some length later in this chapter. In the next chapter we shall expand upon the problems of predicting the future consequence of policies and the future environment in which policies will be realised.

The welfare state and the policy process

At the end of Chapter 5 we outlined a rough typology of the sorts of political issues which are likely to generate public policy initiatives – issues of identity, distribution, process and redistribution. Issues relating to identity and process are frequently resolved by processes of political compromise and negotiation which bear little relationship to the sorts of model of the policy process we have considered so far in this chapter. More elaborate and 'rational' processes are perhaps more likely to be found in relation to the issues of the provision of state services, the regulation of the economy and the redistribution of resources to the less well-off in society. In short, the 'welfare state', with its large bureaucracies and phalanxes of interested experts and client groups, seems the ideal ground upon which to examine the nature of this sort of policy-making.

A wide variety of definitions of the 'welfare state' have been put forward but it is convenient to adopt Johnson's (1987) approach (see Box 22.)

Box 22   The welfare state

Definition

A modern liberal democratic industrial state in which the state has intervened to:

1 provide a wide range of social services to the bulk of the population;
2 seek to maintain full employment;
3 nationalise or regulate a number of key industries, but in which the bulk of the economy remains in the hands of private enterprise.

SOURCE   After Johnson (1987)

One can see the welfare state as the natural consequence of the extension of democratic ideas to the social and welfare sphere. Thus, President Franklin D. Roosevelt proclaimed the Allied war aims to include four freedoms (including not only freedom of worship and of speech but also the social aims of freedom from fear and freedom from want). In wartime Britain a consensus between parties was evolved on the basis of the Beveridge (1942) Report on the need to conquer the 'four giants' of idleness, ignorance, poverty and disease. We have already referred to the social dimension of The UN Declaration of Human Rights.

Without attempting a history of the rise of the welfare state (Hill (1988 Ch. 2), Fraser (1984 *passim*)), in Britain its origins are clearly quite complex and include Conservative Party measures in the interests of national efficiency (cf. Bismarck's Germany mentioned earlier), Liberal Party pioneering of old age pensions and non-partisan measures aimed at public health and promoting local government, as well as explicitly socialist measures by Labour administrations. Both World Wars resulted in considerable moves in the direction of central planning and commitment to welfare, whilst pre-Thatcherite Conservative governments often preferred to favour British industry at the expense of free market principles. For instance, not only did Conservative governments in the 1930s adopt tariff protectionism but they created British Imperial Airways and even as late as the 1970s the Heath government was prepared to nationalise Rolls-Royce rather than see it fail.

As we have seen, generally speaking 'ideology' – the development of a coherent, comprehensive and consistent worldview – has not been popular amongst practical politicians. Pragmatism, if not anti-intellectualism, has reigned. Thus, much policy debate is notable for its specificity (lack of reference to general principles) so that Box 23 (which tries to identify alternative coherent sets of ideas) is an attempt to make more sense of debates on social policy than is, perhaps, appropriate. However, it attempts to discern the logical alternative positions from which the main stream of debate proceeds. They should not be mistaken for current party policies but, in concrete terms, (a) can be thought of as approximating to the Friedman/Thatcher position, (b) as the Titmuss/left-wing socialist perspective and (c) as the position held not only by liberal democrats, but also by many Christian and social democrats and moderate conservatives.

Nor should the very real influence of electoral politics be neglected. Democratic politicians have been naturally chary of attacking provisions like health care, child benefits and old age pensions linked to at least the cost of living, which are regarded as electoral 'sacred cows'.

Related to these general perspectives are attitudes to the selectivity or universality of state benefits or social services.

The '*laissez-faire*' (or what Titmuss calls the residual model)

Box 23   Three views of social policy

(a) Laissez-faire

Private market and the family natural mechanisms for resource allocation.

Economic demand better than professional or bureaucratic judgement as an assessment of need.

Merit, work-achievement and productivity lead to a bigger 'cake' for division between all. State to remedy market failures and rescue indigent.

(A safety net approach – liberty and efficiency valued above equity; minimum role for state)

(b) Socialist

State services based on need not market.

Rights of all to participate in social economic and political activities.

(Large state sector – equality valued at possible expense of liberty)

(c) Liberal

Civilised level of living for those dependent on state.

Limits state aid in interests of responsibility of individuals.

(Intermediate role for state)

SOURCE   After Parker (1975) and Titmuss (1968)

---

school prefers services or benefits to be targeted on a minimum size group in acute need. The argument being that benefits can be maximised for those in real need in this way whilst minimising state bureaucracy and leaving scope for private initiative, foresight and enterprise.

The socialist school (or what Titmuss calls the institutional redistributive model) argues that restricting state services to a small minority turns beneficiaries into a stigmatised pariah group, thus drastically reducing take-up of benefits even when they are needed (cf. nineteenth-century paupers who starved rather than go into the workhouse). Instead, everyone should benefit from, and contribute to, the best possible level of state services in areas like education and health, where need is unrelated to ability to pay. If the rich and powerful are allowed to contract out of such services, then two levels of service will result and they will not care about the level of welfare achieved by ordinary people.

The liberal (or what Titmuss calls the industrial/achievement performance model) school is impressed by some of the above arguments into arguing the importance of welfare rights for all rather than a highly selective hand-out to the poor only, but argues that it is unrealistic to think that a uniform standard can be imposed upon all. Some incentives to effort as well as opportunities for individual and communal initiative and charitable impulse should remain. A minimum humane standard should be available to all, as of right, with supplementary provision being open to all who show sufficient foresight and inclination.

From the point of view of the study of the policy process, these differences are very significant in that the same situation might generate a very different policy agenda, definition of key issues and proposals for deciding how to resolve them when viewed through the lens of each 'school'.

The distribution of wealth and income

Consider, by way of example, the distribution of wealth and income. In contemporary Britain the official statistics (Rose (1993), Table 5.10) on the distribution of marketable wealth are as follows:

| | 1976 | 1981 | 1990 |
	%	%	%
Most Wealthy 1%	21	18	18
Most Wealthy 10%	50	50	51
Least Wealthy 50%	8	8	7

Comparable figures for other countries are not regularly published, but a study for the UK Royal Commission on the Distribution of Income and Wealth (Harrison (1979)) produced the following estimates of percentage wealth holdings:

	Canada	USA	Germany	France	Sweden	Denmark
Most wealthy 10% own	59.8	53	45.3	51.7	50–57	63

Whilst the distribution of income is not quite so dramatically unequal, 1989 UK Official Figures (Rose (1993), Table 5.14)) still show the bottom 20 per cent of the population receive only 25 per cent of the income of the top 20 per cent *after* tax and cash benefits (£5,200 v. £21,400).

Slightly older figures on *pre-tax* incomes (World Bank (1992), *Economic Trends* (November 1987)) suggest the picture is very similar in other industrialised countries:

	Australia (1985)	Canada (1987)	Germany (1984)	USA (1985)	UK (1984)
Most Affluent 20%	42.2	40.2	38.7	41.9	46.3
Least Affluent 20%	4.4	5.7	6.8	4.7	5.8

From a Socialist point of view, such statistics suggest that policies attempting equity between individuals in the UK (and similar economies such as those of the European Community and the USA) will have to abandon the market mechanism altogether and distribute benefits direct, without regard to ability to pay. It is in this context also, that some radical socialist critiques of piecemeal welfare reforms become intelligible. Such massive inequalities are felt to be incompatible with equal rights for all in a democratic society.

A liberal approach might be to adopt some form of means testing or redistribute income on a large scale perhaps through a 'negative income tax' scheme instead of social security and means-tested benefits. In such a scheme, a minimum standard of living is guaranteed to all, with a minimum of stigmatising special treatment for the poor, by paying out income through the same machinery which collects taxes on the basis of one declaration of income and circumstances for everyone, with solutions being sought which preserve the individual freedom associated market mechanisms, whilst treating all citizens by consistent rules.

From a *laissez-faire* point of view, an uneven distribution of capital may merely be seen as enabling worthwhile investments to be made and as the results of rewards of previous risk-taking and effort. Providing the income of the bottom 20 per cent of the population is judged to be above an adequate 'safety net' level, the existence of unequal incomes is not seen as a problem for social and economic policy.

It is often thought that the 'welfare state' both through progressive taxation and the redistributive effect of its 'universal' social services has radically affected the distribution of income and wealth (especially the former after tax and benefits). A considerable academic literature exists on this (which concentrates, however, on the tax element of the equation). Summarising this brutally, the overall conclusion seems to be that taxation has had surprisingly little effect – other than to redistribute *within social classes*. Perhaps surprisingly, it seems that the social services have also had virtually no redistributive effect between classes as LeGrand (1982) clearly shows. In Britain working-class gains from unemployment benefits have been counterbalanced by middle-class gains from post-school-leaving age educational benefits – with the middle classes showing a greater capacity to benefit from the National Health Service. (Housing is a controversial area depending on the treatment of mortgage tax relief.)

Most discussions of welfare policy-making have concentrated on the *distributive* goals of social policy – seeing social services as the provision of goods and services which need to be allocated in an optimum fashion. However, the area is often presented in terms of *redistributive* goals – either as part of a socialist attempt to redistribute income and wealth between different classes within society, or at least, as a humane attempt to cushion the worst effects of an unequal society and the market mechanism.

It is important to realise, however, that many social policies are advocated wholly or partly as a means of advancing the overall *efficiency* of the economy – so that a healthy and well-educated workforce may be seen as a key factor in economic success.

Policy objectives in education

As a second illustration of the problems of defining public policy goals in a specific area of social policy we may briefly consider the case of education (see Box 24).

Box 24 Alternative policy objectives in education

a means of personal fulfilment;
an instrument of social continuity;
a mechanism for social mobility;
a means to promote equality;
an 'economic investment' for individuals and society.

SOURCE   After Maddison (1974/5)

The traditional objective of a 'liberal' education is to bring out the talents of the individual concerned. The pursuit of knowledge, the cultivation of an appreciation of the arts and sciences, the development of a moral sense and of skills such as painting, dancing and singing are seen primarily as good for their own sakes.

A more conservative interpretation of the educational process is that it enables the passing down from one generation to another of the values of a specific culture and, indeed, fitted and trained individuals for specific roles within that culture. Thus, in (say) the late-nineteenth-century, English public schools trained the ladies and gentlemen who would lead society, the grammar schools the middle ranks of society, whilst ordinary church or local council schools gave the limited indoctrination and training necessary for the bulk of the population.

A more radical interpretation (endorsed for instance by American writers like John Dewey (1916) [1859–1952]) is that in a democracy education is about promoting *equality*. Thus, some commentators stress the need for all citizens to share common values and have a more than adequate grounding of literacy and numeracy, and to be able to communicate with each other thanks to a common educational background. Others stress the apparently similar idea of *equality of opportunity*: that the schools system should recognise the talents of all within it and promote each to an appropriate level of educational achievement. However, as Michael Young (1961) graphically shows, these two ideas are in some respects quite sharply opposed in that 'equality of opportunity' can be used to legitimise a sharply unequal society in which the lower classes have demonstrated their inferiority by failing scholastic examinations.

Finally, education can be seen as an economic investment which repays individuals (or their families) with increased 'life chances' (better jobs or husbands) or, on the level of whole societies, enables whole societies to obtain an enormous 'competitive advantage' over less-educated societies.

Quite clearly, such different perceptions of the purposes of education can throw up quite different priorities and perspectives on educational issues, quite apart from the obvious differences between rich and poor, and between teachers, parents, and non-parent taxpayers.

Implementing social policy

In this section we outline some of the difficulties in ensuring accurate implementation of central policy, going on to illuminate some of the problems of the local managers of social provision.

Social policy, particularly in Britain, is often discussed almost entirely from a central government perspective. A problem is identified, a 'solution' propounded, after which the problem is assumed to be the effective and efficient implementation of the policy at local level. Indeed, many commentators on social policy – especially in the national press – scarcely consider the possibility of a gap between policy prescription and its implementation. Yet, most social policies are implemented by local agencies at various distances from the central government.

Hood (1976) introduced the concept of 'perfect implementation' for a state of affairs in which central policy-makers prescriptions were perfectly realised. The likelihood of such an eventuality in the real world is remote. For instance, studies by the National Audit Office show that even social security payments, being paid through local branches of a central ministry on the basis of relatively clear and unambiguous rules enforced through a single bureaucracy, suffer from a 35 per cent error rate. In the case of the Child Support Agency its first Annual Report referred to a study by the Chief Child Support Officer who found, of 1380 assessments checked, only 25 per cent were judged correct, 39 per cent were found to be incorrect, whilst in 35 per cent of cases insufficient information was recorded to tell if the assessment was right or wrong. When policies are implemented through a series of agencies, each of which expects to have some influence on the nature and interpretation of the policy, then clearly 'perfect implementation' becomes still less likely. Inter-organisational bargaining will doubtless affect the outcomes of policies, and with different agencies in different parts of the country, considerably different outcomes may result, as is shown in Figure 8.1.

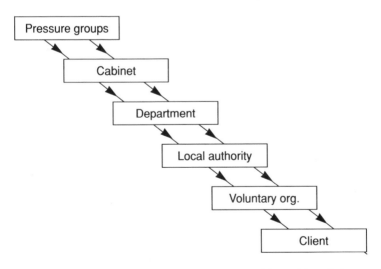

FIGURE 8.1 Example of an inter-organisational bargaining chain

Pressman and Wildavsky (1973), in an American study graphically entitled *Implementation/How Great Expectations In Washington Are Dashed in Oakland or Why It's Amazing that Federal Programs Work at All . . .*, demonstrate that if a series of administrative agreements or clearance stages are necessary for implementation, even with 99 per cent of agreement at each 'clearance', overall probability of perfect implementation falls below 50 per cent after 68 clearances.

Is 'perfect implementation' always desirable? This seems, in any case, arguable. Local conditions may differ radically from those central policy-makers had in mind in formulating their response to 'the' problem. Barratt and Fudge (1981) attack the traditional British 'top-down' approach to social problem solving, arguing that local communities can deploy scarce resources much more effectively to meet their real need rather than the centrally perceived 'problem'. Lindblom (1959), as we have seen, defended incrementalism as a policy-making procedure in cases where it is difficult to define a clear consensus on policy goals and circumstances are rapidly changing – as is the case with much social policy. If the central policy is a radical one then the analysis of Bachrach and Baratz (1970) referred to earlier may well help to explain its non-implementation. Equally, a British Conservative government may find some Labour local areas will stonewall on the implementation of economic and fiscal policies with a severe local economic impact.

In some cases it may even be the case that policies are not even intended to be implemented! Edelman's (1977) study of political language has emphasised the symbolic function of many policy declarations. A fine-sounding policy may have its origins in a political compromise at central level which was acceptable *because* it was too vague to be implemented unambiguously.

Perfect implementation, then, is not necessarily desirable – and certainly is not inevitable. To overcome the barriers to implementation may well be costly in both communication effort and need to offer sanctions/inducements to the implementor. Following R.E. Neustad (1960) the requirements for implementation seem to include:

(i) unambiguous signal of required behaviour must reach local implementor and be understood;

(ii) *either* (a) they must want to conform to new policy and have power to implement it;

or (b) costs of non-implementation must be made to clearly exceed benefits of inertia.

Managing local social policy

It may be helpful to expand upon the previous section by looking briefly at the implementation of social policy from the point of the local managers of such a service. This may help to add a realistic perspective to the problems of implementing policy prescriptions. Although such managers are in very varied circumstances, we can point to some likely common characteristics: they are in a multiple series of bargaining relationships as suggested by Figure 8.2; they have limited time and information sources; many tasks and limited resources.

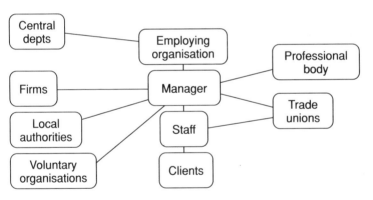

FIGURE 8.2 Managing local social service provision

A minor example of this would be the author's research on the Youth Training Scheme (Tansey (1989)), in which Training Officers within organisations were seen as having to negotiate with:

personnel and finance directors for permission to run/finance the scheme;

departmental heads to offer worthwhile placements for trainees;
Manpower Service Commission (now local Training and Enterprise Council) representatives to approve the scheme;
Careers Service officials to publicise and recruit for the scheme;
technical college course tutors on the content of off-the-job training;
industrial training boards on the acceptability of the training for apprenticeship purposes;
the trainees themselves in respect of their behaviour;
and so on.

Some major variables which may affect managers' capacity to take an independent view of how policy should be implemented will include their relationship to, and distance from clients, their relationship to local authorities/central departments, and the degree of their *dependence* on firms/voluntary organisations etc. for resources. This last point should be further clarified by Figures 8.3 and 8.4.

		Importance of resource: High	Importance of resource: Low
Substitutability of resource	Low	High dependence	Low dependence
	High	Low dependence	Independence

FIGURE 8.3 Dependency and resources

By 'substitutability' is meant the degree to which the organisation whose dependency is being assessed can easily obtain the resource provided from some other source. For instance, in my example above, a training officer's dependence on an outside organisation for good-

A's dependence
on B

		High	Low
B's dependence on A	High	Mutual dependence	Unilateral dependence
	Low	Unilateral dependence	Mutual Independence

FIGURE 8.4 Dependency relationships between organisations

SOURCE   Scharpf in Hanf and Scharpf (1978)

quality appropriate placements would depend upon the number that organisation offered and their availability from within his own organisation and from other local employers.

Evaluating public policy

Evaluation of decision-making processes on public policy can concentrate on either procedural or substantive issues. From a *procedural* point of view, we can ask whether the process of making the decision accords with the evaluative criteria to be applied (e.g. was the decision taken in a democratic manner? Did the decision-maker consider all rational alternatives and cost them?) From a *substantive* point of view we can ask was the result 'correct', set against appropriate criteria in terms of its outcome? The criteria employed may be many and various – ethical, economic, ecological, etc. (e.g. were the decision-maker's objectives achieved? did the decision promote justice?)

In fact, our earlier discussion of democracy (Chapter 7) neatly links the complex interrelationship between the two sets of criteria. For, to summarise brutally, we saw that one major controversy about democracy is whether to stress substantive or procedural criteria. The

Marxist–Leninist tradition emphasises the concept of a 'people's democracy' – governing in the interests of the people. This is interpreted as the largest class enforcing its will against the rest (i.e. government of and for the people), thus stressing substantive criteria. Whilst the Western tradition places emphasis on the free consent and participation of the governed (government by the people) – a procedural criterion. To express the dichotomy another way, democracy as achieving an equal society or democracy as a free society.

Democracy clearly relates particularly to defining values and specifying objectives, in Lindblom's terminology. It is an explicitly political concept. Assuming objectives and values to be more or less fixed, it may be possible to assess decision-making in a less controversial way. Here we may offer some more 'managerial' concepts for evaluating policy-making (see Box 25).

Box 25   The 3 'E's: managerial concepts and policy evaluation

Efficiency   can be seen as something like the physicists definition of 'the ratio of useful work to energy expended' (*Shorter Oxford English Dictionary*: Addenda). Thus, given fixed resources and a fixed objective, efficiency can be seen as achieving the maximum effect in the desired direction. The emphasis is often on implementing planned actions to specification

Economy   is clearly closely related to efficiency, but is more likely to be expressed in financial terms. It can be seen as employing minimum resources to achieve a fixed objective. It is more likely to encompass costing of alternative ways to achieve an objective

Effectiveness   can then be seen as including the choice of objectives in order to realise the values desired. The emphasis here is not on the volume of work done, but the overall impact of the work done. In economists terms, has utility been maximised?

The three concepts can thus be seen as occupying a hierarchial relationship, with efficiency the most limited concept, economy a somewhat broader one and effectiveness the most comprehensive. Economy in public administration (and more generally) may be interpreted irrationally merely as minimising financial expenditure on a particular budget. If, however, a reduction in expenditure means that the department or organisation fails to achieve its objective or if, for instance, refusal to buy capital equipment means that expensive staff time is not made good use of, then such behaviour is far from economical in the true sense.

In terms of substantive criteria, our previous discussions of justice and equality is clearly of relevance (see Chapter 3), but here we shall turn to the question of how we can measure the success of public policies – an essential part both of the monitoring and evaluation phases of the policy process in Hogwood and Gunn's (1984) terminology.

Performance indicators

Clearly, any rational monitoring and evaluation of public policy needs to measure as precisely as possible how far objectives are being achieved. In the absence of a general purpose measure of efficiency, such as profitability in the private sector, then the output of public sector organisations can only be measured in more specific terms related to their objectives. In principle, the establishment of 'performance indicators' seems unexceptionable. The attempt to define performance indicators has, however, become more controversial and central to the political process in Britain in the light of a number of political developments: the role of such indicators as part of the privatisation process; their use in the context of 'Citizen's Charters'; and their role in public sector pay bargaining.

In the privatisation process, performance indicators are important in defining the standard of service to be expected from the privatised service provider. Merely specifying a maximum level of profits or prices could encourage the provider to produce a sub-standard service (perhaps with minimal investment), allowing exploitation of a monopoly position. Thus, an electricity company is required to restore any interruptions to supply to at least 85 per cent of domestic customers within 3 hours (Southern Electric (1994, 7)). Such indicators can then be policed by an independent regulator (in this case, the Director General of Electricity Supply) with 'league tables' of the efficiency of each supplier being available and the possibility of the removal of franchises from non-performing companies. Similarly, if (say) the information technology section of an organisation is to be 'market-tested', the services it provides have to be not only defined but quantified so that bids may be made by both the in-house unit and possible outside providers of the service.

In a series of 'Citizen's Charters' the Major government in Britain has established publicly known standards of performance to which consumers/citizens are entitled. In some cases, compensation is payable for under-performance (e.g. refunds on rail season tickets if trains run persistently late). In some cases, these standards have been criticised as unacceptably anodyne (e.g. 'you will get a reply within seven days' – but the letter may merely say, 'We are looking into it').

Such standards may be linked to the appraisal of the performance of individual public servants which, in turn, may be linked ultimately to some sort of payment by results. Such moves have been opposed by most public sector trade unions as a move away from nationally negotiated common standards of pay and service towards individual contracts and as failing to recognise environmental factors which affect individual performance.

One of the major problems may be that those aspects of performance which are most easily quantified are not necessarily the most significant parts of the public sector organisation or individual's work. Yet, particularly where managers' pay or career success are felt to be crucially affected by them, such performance indicators may come to be 'the tail that wags the corporate dog'. Thus, if police officers and forces are judged by the crime clear-up rate, crime prevention and developing good community relations may be neglected. Such statistics may also be subject to manipulation – in our example, criminals may be induced to confess to a string of unsolved crimes they did not commit, or 'unsolvable' crimes may not be recorded.

Another example of the problems inherent in the use of such performance indicators can be seen in the publication of school league tables of examination and test performances. The problem here is that the environmental differences between schools are neglected – together with the starting points from which their pupils begin. Some unofficial attempts have been made to assess the 'added value' given by schools, but these have received much less attention than the misleading, crude headline figures.

Health: the policy process in action

In this final section we consider some recent debates about health policy in Britain by way of illustration of some of the points made earlier in the book.

Since the foundation of the National Health Service (NHS) in 1948 there has been a broad consensus in Britain that health services are a public good (see Chapter 6) which should be, broadly speaking, free at the point of delivery. Co-operation of doctors in the NHS was obtained by the then Labour Minister for Health, Nye Bevan, by allowing General Practitioners to retain their status as self-employed professionals and by giving leading hospital doctors (the consultants) great powers within hospitals and leaving them ample opportunities for private practice and research (Eckstein (1960)).

It is interesting to compare Britain with other developed countries in terms of health service provision. In the United States a much more market-oriented system, dominated by private health insurance schemes, has lead to much more concentration on surgical rather than preventative medicine and very high administrative costs. In continental Europe most countries have a strongly state-regulated insurance-based system with lower than US costs but with features that reflect the administrative and payment systems in place. In France, for instance, where general practitioner doctors (GPs) are paid by the consultation, visits to the doctor tend to be many and brief, whilst in Britain (where GPs are paid by the patient) consultations tend to be longer but infrequent. As a percentage of gross national product (GNP) per head British expenditure on health is low in international league table terms – with a better record in achieving health for the population than its level of expenditure would suggest (Abel-Smith (1976)).

In such circumstances, many issues might dominate the health policy agenda – the documented inequality of access to health services between different regions and social group, a decline in Britain's position from the top of league table in terms of the safety of births, the possibility of an Aids epidemic or the presence of internationally high rates of death from heart disease. In practice, however, a series of issues relating to Conservative government attempts to apply the disciplines of the market-place and introduce better managerial practices have dominated policy discussion in recent years. This approach has reflected a perceived unacceptably high and rising cost of health provision. Such proposals seem to have attained a very high political visibility, partly because Labour sees any 'threat' to the NHS as a strong political card to play, and partly because many of these changes have been seen as threatening the autonomy, status and remuneration of doctors and other health professionals.

Many of these Conservative reforms have sought to set up price-sensitive cost centres which will buy in medical services – e.g. 'contracted-out' doctors' general practices and area health authorities who purchase services from 'trust' hospitals rather than run their own hospitals. Such arrangements require far more sophisticated managerial and accounting systems than were previously to be found in the NHS and have, hence, raised the profile, influence, status and numbers of managers and information system specialists within the area. These changes mean that issues previously decided (if at all) by unco-ordinated medical professionals are, in principle, now open to more rational and co-ordinated decision-making.

It is striking, however, that these far-reaching changes seem to have been introduced without any very sophisticated evaluation of the various alternative options available for management systems in a health service, and there is little evidence of systematic monitoring of their impact. Indeed, the BMA and others have suggested, unsuccessfully, that such changes might be appropriately brought in on a trial basis in one or more regions and the comparative performance of authorities operating different regimes assessed.

In terms of the distinction we drew between efficiency and effectiveness, the following example is of some interest. A number of health authorities are reported as having achieved a more efficient use of hospital resources. More patients have been treated each week in the same operating theatres and wards as before, using the same number of doctors and nurses. The problem is that this has involved a higher expenditure on 'consumable' articles such as medicines, bandages, laundry, X-ray film, etc. Consequently, the area health authorities are deeper in financial deficit than their less 'efficient' counterparts. Does this, amongst other things, illustrate ineffective management?

In the health sphere the Citizen's Charter objectives have largely side-stepped the key objectives of a health service. The focus has been on the length of waiting lists, time spent waiting in accident departments and at out-patient clinics and so on, rather than on the effectiveness of the treatment given by hospitals and GPs. This may have been designed to prevent too immediate and great a clash with powerful doctor interests, but it does suggest that resources may have been deflected into the most visible rather than the most necessary areas of expenditure.

Recommended reading

Allison, Graham T., 1987, *The Essence of Decision*, Harper College. Develops three theoretical models of decision-making from a study of the Cuban misssile crisis. Influential in management schools as well as amongst political scientists.

Ham, Christopher and Hill, Michael, 1993, *The Policy Process in the Modern Capitalist State*, 2nd edn, Hemel Hempstead, Harvester Wheatsheaf. A standard UK public administration text with welcome emphasis on more general themes.

Hill, Michael 1988, *Understanding Social Policy*, 3rd edn, Oxford, Basil Blackwell. A thoughtful introductory discussion of UK welfare state.

Hogwood, Brian W. and Gunn, Lewis A., 1984, *Policy Analysis for the Real World*, Oxford, Oxford University Press. A general model of the policy process which can be applied in any country.

Immergut, Ellen M., 1992, *Health Policies, Interests and Institutions in Western Europe*, Cambridge, Cambridge University Press. A stimu-lating comparative discusssion of health politics.

Young, Michael, 1961, *The Rise of the Meritocracy 1870–2033*,

Harmondsworth, Middlesex, Penguin. A thoughtful well-written and amusing discussion of the political implications of equality of opportunity in form of a social history of Britain written from the viewpoint of 2033.

Chapter 9

Futures

Political change

In this last chapter we shall mainly consider three related and rather ambitious topics:

> How do political systems change?
> Can political change be predicted?
> What is politics likely to be about in the next century?

A final note considers the scope for political action by readers who are concerned about any of the issues raised in the book.

The inevitability of political change and the unlikelihood of the twenty-first century being much like the twentieth seems, from an examination of past history, almost the only certainty that it would be safe to advance in such an area. This in itself is worth stressing, since it is all too easy to assume that the future will represent a continuation of the present. Most readers of this book will probably have lived

215

all their lives in a relatively stable, prosperous and peaceful liberal democratic nation-state. Yet it is only necessary to imagine that, instead, you had been born in the Soviet Union on the same date as your own birthday or in England shortly before our own Civil War to realise how immensely and rapidly the political framework of our lives can be transformed in a lifetime.

Political change is probably thought of most readily in terms of violent and rapid transitions such as the English Civil War and the French, American and Russian Revolutions (see later in this chapter), but it is worth bearing in mind that in the English and Russian instances at least, such violent and rapid changes were largely reversed within two generations without extensive violence. Conversely, a series of piecemeal, evolutionary, changes may result in a 'new' political system based on fundamentally different principles from the old. In short, revolutionary changes need not be violent or permanent.

Thus, Britain in the eighteenth century was fundamentally still an oligarchic or aristocratic, if constitutional, country controlled by a coalition mainly of aristocrats and country gentlemen with limited participation by a few city businessmen. By the middle of the twentieth century a series of limited reforms of the franchise and in the powers of the two Houses of Parliament (and a whole host of economic and social changes) meant that Britain could claim to be a democratic country.

Indeed, much the same could be said for the United States of America whose Founding Fathers were also careful to defend their new constitution against the charge of democracy (Hamilton *et al.* (1961)) yet now the same document (with only a limited number of formal amendments) is seen by many as the very model of a democratic constitution. Major changes which helped the USA to transform its political system into a democratic one include the change from indirect election of the President by an electoral college to, effectively, direct election through national political parties; the introduction of the direct popular election of Senators; the extension of the vote to all male whites, to all women and to blacks. Most of this was done largely by state legislation, or even changes in political practice outside of the law (Amendments 15, 17 and 19 broadened the franchise, but 15 was ineffective and 17 and 19 mainly codified previous practice at state level (Morison and Commager (1962)).

Coups d'état and revolutions

We have already seen that fundamental changes in political systems are not always the consequence of violent revolutions. It should also be made clear that every use of violence (or the threat to do so) to change the political system cannot be sensibly called a revolution. The term 'revolution' (associated with the idea of a wheel turning and hence things being turned 'upside down') may be helpfully reserved for occasions when major changes in the nature of politics and society take place. An examination of the historical record suggests that such events are relatively rare whilst the use of force (or its threat) to change the government is much more commonplace. In the absence of an established tradition of election or inheritance of top offices within the state, violence has often been the usual way to power. In the ancient world, Emperors of Rome were frequently the most successful generals of their day, their bodyguard – the Praetorian Guard – effectively controlling succession. In much of Africa, Asia and Latin America, in this century, a similar state of affairs has been found, with the army constituting perhaps the most effective route to political power (Huntington (1957, Finer (1976)).

In many Latin American states there is a long history of the alternation in power of civilian and military regimes without any fundamental change in either the role of the state or the social composition of the governing elite. Although the support of the metropolitan crowd may have been drawn upon from time to time in struggles for the succession, fundamentally power has stayed with the white, educated, Spanish- or Portuguese-descended, upper/middle classes at the expense of the rural Indian/Mestizo (mixed race) groups and their descendants in the urban slums.

In contrast, full revolutions can be seen as rarer and more fundamental changes in the political system in which new social groups achieve power and the state carries out new tasks in a different way, perhaps with a different claim to legitimacy. Writers such as Crane Brinton (1965) and Lyford Edwards (1926) have perceptively analysed major revolutionary episodes such as the English Civil War and the French and Russian Revolutions and suggested that they tend to go through a series of distinctive phases. Paradoxically, the old regime often collapses in a relatively bloodless triumph of popular forces following a loss of legitimacy and a manifest failure to cope with the economic, political or military demands put upon it. This is followed, after a honeymoon period, by confusion and conflict amongst the revolutionary forces. In face of real or imagined counter-revolutionary reaction, extremist forces then often take control, launching a reign of terror, not only against declared counter-revolutionaries but also against moderate reformers. Such a situation may then be resolved by power being taken by a tyrant (Cromwell, Napoleon, Lenin/Stalin) who leads a post-revolutionary regime which may draw upon the pre-revolutionary tradition, as well as claiming descent from the revolution itself. One might add that, in the longer term, still further compromises with the pre-revolutionary tradition are likely. This is not to deny, however, that revolutions do transform societies – they are often accompanied by a major transformation in the role and power of the state, massive changes in property ownership and in the type of legitimacy claimed by the state.

From a sceptical point of view, it might be worth pointing out to potential revolutionaries that the outcome of such a process is unpredictable in the extreme, and the likelihood of the originators of the revolution finishing up in power at the end of the process seems very low.

Causes of political change

So far we have considered the nature of political change, but not its causes. Sociologists sometimes rather pretentiously speak of endogenous and exogenous social change – meaning change from within the social system and change from without. The same distinction can sensibly be drawn in terms of politics.

In terms of endogenous change, if we think of the political divisions considered in Chapter 5, then the balance of forces between regions, classes, ethnic groups or other forces may be thought of as one of dominance, stability or instability. Where an ethnic group, or even a metropolitan region, is dominant over the rest, the potential for change may seem small because of the control of the power elite over the media, the economy and other potential influences for change.

It may be, however, that in such situations gradual adjustment being ruled out, revolutionary changes become the only possibility.

Allardt and Littunen (1964) argue that the most stable political situation is where many such divisions overlap and different groups go into political coalitions for different purposes (the analogy with our earlier treatment of the Tiv segmentary lineage system may be obvious). All groups feel that they can influence the situation and thus remain committed to the system, and are forced to stress those aspects on which they agree in order to build co-operation with others. The premium on bargaining in such situations means that as new developments arise, piecemeal adjustments to them can be made and stability maintained.

Such a situation of healthy co-operation, competition and bargaining must be distinguished from the sort of situation characteristic of, say, the French Fourth Republic, in which a kaleidoscopic variety of forces fail to agree on an effective government, with governments succeeding each other with dizzying frequency – every eight months in this case (Williams (1964)).

The inherent stability of the existing political system may be tested by changes springing from the social system of which it is a part. Thus, for instance, one ethnic group may have a higher birth (or lower death or emigration rate) than the others, thus threatening the electoral arithmetic in a democratic system (Ulster may be a case in point). Economic growth may take part in one locality, but not in others, altering the balance of social, economic, and ultimately, political power. New religious movements may create fresh political groups, or processes of secularisation and urbanisation undermine the social power of existing conservative religious groups. Industrialisation and mass education may create a self-conscious 'working class' and undermine peasant parties. The railway and the motor car make possible the creation of dormitory suburbs with distinctive patterns of political behaviour.

Important as these internal changes are, the influences of external societies upon domestic politics should not be overlooked. War has clearly been one of the major determinants of political change. For instance, Germany and Japan both had liberal democratic political systems imposed upon them as part of the post-Second-

World-War settlement. Women acquired the vote in Britain after the First World War (and in France after the Second World War) partly as a result of changes in social attitudes brought about by their participation in the war effort. In West Africa, and in many other parts of the British Empire, ex-servicemen constituted the core of new nationalist movements.

Reference has already been made to the impact of colonialism on racial attitudes in the former 'metropolitan' powers and in defining the national borders in many parts of the world. Clearly, the economic influence of capitalist North America and Europe remains a potent one in many 'third world' states, as we shall discuss at more length later in this chapter. The political and economic influence of major powers is thus often a major factor in changing the internal politics of countries, even if no direct attempt is made to intervene by financing revolution, terrorism and subversion. The contribution of external encouragement and financing of such movements was often exaggerated by the threatened governments and by ideologues on both sides of the cold war – but a glance at the literature on the CIA (which is better documented than the KGB) will suggest that such accusations are not all, by any means, James Bond fantasies.

The influence of developments in other similar states, in an era of global communications, is also marked. The literature on coups in South America has documented the way in which military coups in one country seem to have encouraged the same in its neighbours (Huntington (1962)), whilst the idea of a one-party regime seems to have waxed and waned in the same way in Africa. More recently, the collapse of communism in Poland encouraged the same phenomena in other Eastern Bloc countries, whilst the same occurrence in the Soviet Union not only succeeded by example but by removing a potential external check upon the process in other Eastern Bloc countries.

Predicting the political future

Having looked at the nature of political change, we return to the question of whether the sort of changes we have discussed can be predicted. It will be recalled that in discussing the possibility of a scientific theory of politics in the first chapter, some of the difficulties in evolving reliable general predictive theories were discussed. Given the difficulties in amassing valid data, in creating usable conceptual schema, in applying experimental method and in overcoming the philosophical questions raised, the reader will not be surprised to learn that there are no generally accepted theories about the likely evolution of politics into the next century. Two particular problems about predicting future general trends should also be highlighted, before discussing some specific hypotheses of relevance to the problem.

The first problem was touched upon in Chapter 1, but is worth enlarging upon here. Any published predictions about the nature of future political developments are, in principle, immediately available to those affected by those predictions – and who may, therefore, alter their behaviour accordingly. Thus, we can consider perhaps the best-known prediction about the political future – Marx's prediction of the inevitability of proletarian revolution. On the one hand, working-class activists have been emboldened by the prediction to work harder for the revolution (as Marx clearly intended). However, on the other hand, 'bourgeois' politicians have seen the potential for instability in the exploitative economic practices described by Marx and have created welfare institutions to ameliorate their impact, introduced regulations to curb their excesses and opened up opportunities for social mobility which have 'robbed' the working classes of many of their natural leaders. Of course, it is debatable how much influence Marx's theories have had on either working-class political strategies or 'bourgeois' governments' policies, but this only reinforces the point made here, about the uncertain impact of making political predictions – that they often have (and indeed are intended to have) an effect on the events they describe.

The second problem is a related and probably more serious one, and that is the impact of scientific and technological development on future societies (Popper (1960)). It is clear that developments such as the discovery of iron and the invention of the steam engine have transformed societies in the past, changing both the balance of power between classes within societies and between states. In the past, technological developments have often, but not always, depended upon the development of new scientific theories, and this is increasingly likely to be so in the future [see 'Post-industrial politics' p.224]. Yet, by definition, we cannot predict what scientific discoveries will be made – otherwise we should have already made that theoretical development!

These general points should be kept in mind in relation to all the propositions examined in the remainder of the chapter. Here we consider some of the leading contemporary ideas about the likely shape of twenty-first-century politics. Our starting point will be what we have already described as the best-known theory about the political future – Marxism – but in the 1990s, the issues of class conflict, ideology and technology linked with this have taken on a radically different appearance. The question to be raised is more likely to be the end of Marxism than the end of capitalism which Marxism itself predicts. Similarly, whilst the impact of technology on the future has always been debated, the downside of technology in the shape of its ecological implications has now become a much more prominent debate. Later versions of Marxism correctly highlighted the importance of what, until recently, was described as the third world (now perhaps better described as the South). We shall argue that the role of this sector of the planet remains vital in considering its political future. Finally, however, we shall consider the proposition that the main difference between the politics of the next century and this one is the reduced emphasis on the (nation-)state as the main political mechanism for conflict and co-operation.

Class conflict in the twenty-first century

The collapse of the Soviet Union and the disintegration of the East European 'Communist Bloc' has generated the impression that Marxism is a failed ideology. Certainly, many Western former communist parties have now dropped their titles and even their claims to Marxist adherence. Yet it can be argued that Marxism remains one of the more impressive political theories, particularly in relation to the explanations of political change it advances (many 'democratic' political theories being oriented towards a static and idealistic analysis.) Well before the collapse of the Soviet Union, many thinking Western Marxists (i.e. the ones free to choose critically what stance to take) had taken the attitude that the Soviet Union hardly embodied

Marx's ideas, since it was difficult to reconcile these ideas with the emphasis on state machinery and centralism found in the Soviet Bloc. Indeed, the logic of Marx's theory is that socialist revolution should take place in the advanced capitalist states – not in a semi-feudal state on the periphery of Western capitalism.

Some features of Marx's theory which remain impressive are its dynamic nature and the systematic explanation it advances for political change. As we have seen, the main political actors are seen to be economic classes whose interests are in conflict. Political conflict becomes more acute as the result of both an increasing consciousness by classes of their interests and changes in their relative positions as a result of what would now be termed 'economic development'. Major revolutions such as the French Revolution and the English Civil War can be seen in terms of an old dominant class (the rural feudal aristocracy) being replaced by a new dominant class (the urban capitalist bourgeoisie). His prediction was that the capitalist system, in turn, would fail because of its in-built contradictions leading to the triumph of a new dominant class, the more numerous and increasingly well-organised and militant proletariat. The concept of the need for a 'fit' between the economic and political systems and the dynamic role of class structures both seem well founded. A somewhat paradoxical example of this might well be the fall of East European communism. Here, one might argue, the command economy, having served its purpose in aiding the forced industrialisation of underdeveloped and war-damaged economies, in conjunction with a centralised and dictatorial political system, was no longer adequate to manage a more complex affluent and consumer-oriented economy. Demands for greater political freedom thus fitted well with demands for economic reform.

More doubtful is the idea of the inevitability of a bi-polar class system in which one class inevitably becomes dominant. This idea of a historical dialectic, as we have seen earlier, was inherited by Marx from Hegel and, whilst politically convenient, seems far from justified by events. As we have seen, much academic analysis, as well as observation, suggests that much political conflict (especially voting behaviour) especially in Europe – but also to some extent in North America – can be explained in terms of class divisions. However, the trend would appear to be, in voting behaviour at least, away from the sort of clear class-based voting found in Britain in the 1950s and 1960s towards a more North American pattern in which issues, personalities, and tactical voting predominate (e.g. an increased tendency to vote for third parties in the UK, considerable fluctuation in the socialist vote in France, the desertion of both the neo-communist and Christian democratic voters in Italy). Instead of a clear commitment to parties based upon class identification, the 'floating voter' has come to rule.

Empirical studies of voting behaviour also indicate that few voters think in 'proletariat v. bosses' terms, but that Right-wing parties (Republicans, Christian democrats, Conservatives) successfully appeal to a broader concept of a 'middle class' identity, including not only the self-employed and business professionals but a whole variety of 'white-collar' occupations, some relatively unskilled, but most open to those with higher education and paying higher 'salaries' (rather than 'wages'). Increasing levels of affluence (at least amongst those employed) and, especially of home-ownership amongst traditional working class voters, also seem to have played a part in weakening traditional class allegiances. Marxists may lament these trends as an example of 'false class consciousness' and also the decline in both the numbers of trade unionists and their links with socialist parties. But it seems an unjustifiable act of faith to assume that these trends are only 'blips' distorting an otherwise inevitable process.

Post-industrial politics?

Dahrendorf (1959) and others have argued that the trends in the class system observed above mean that Marx's analysis has been outmoded. He argues that Marx wrote in an era of lone capitalist entrepreneurs and unskilled mass production workers. This simple dichotomy is no longer adequate to a production system in which the functions of capital have become divided – for instance, between shareholders and professional managers – and labour is divided between skilled professionals and unskilled labourers, between white-collar office workers and the production-line operatives, and so on. Dahrendorf goes on to suggest that 'class' divisions be reinterpreted to include any politically relevant dimension; black/white, unemployed/employed, football supporters/non-supporters, etc. and that, further, the over-lapping of all these various splits has contributed to the 'floating voter', a phenomenon referred to above, and the stability of pluralist political systems.

There is clearly some strength in these criticisms – although it can be argued that a real divergence of interests remains between 'capitalist' and labour groups, and that Dahrendorf's reinterpretation of class goes so far as to rob the term of any clear meaning.

Other writers, such as Bell (1973), have taken a rather different (even neo-Marxist) line of argument: that Marx's focus on the factory mode of production is fundamentally inappropriate to the emerging information economy. Economic development is seen as having gone through a series of stages dominated by different occupations and technologies: hunter-gatherer with stone and wood axes, bows, coracles, etc.; agrarian with simple iron craft tools; manufacturing based on the steam engine and factory production. The main division in the economy and society is now seen as focusing on the dominant technology of the late twentieth and twenty-first centuries: information technology. The emerging dominant class are thus 'knowledge workers' who control this technology.

It is indeed difficult to underestimate the economic and social importance of scientific knowledge and its manipulation through information technology at the turn of the twentieth century. In the seventeenth and eighteenth centuries inventors were often practical men influenced by the experimental and innovative temper of the age, but not necessarily using the most advanced scientific theories. More recent advances such as radio, atomic energy and electronic computing were, however, all theoretically developed before increasingly large teams of scientists and technologists realised them in practical terms. Increasingly, scientific and professional expertise is being brought to bear on business and social problems, so that the ability to co-ordinate teams of highly qualified and well-informed experts becomes crucial to success – whether in developing the next generation of weapons (say anti-missile systems) or the next generation of consumer goods (e.g. high definition television).

In addition to producing, recruiting and co-ordinating human expertise, information technology – the collection, storage, retrieval, analysis, presentation and communication of information using the microchip – is increasingly central to such operations. Every kind of scientist and professional worker has, or will shortly have, computing facilities on their desk. Information technology through the use of automated machinery and electronic networks can also be seen as rapidly replacing the need for the concentration of large numbers of factory production workers in urban centres (thus undermining working-class strength).

Already, in the most technologically advanced economies (e.g. the USA), white-collar occupations (roughly equal to 'knowledge workers') outnumber traditional 'blue-collar' workers, whilst the information sector of Western economies appears to be the major growth sector. Some economists have gone so far as to suggest that that information is a fourth major factor of production alongside the traditional trio of land, labour and capital.

Information technology can be seen as at the core of social and economic developments in the twenty-first century because it is already transforming business, society and government. It is a pervasive technology because computers are general-purpose machines which can be used to carry out any operation that can be reduced to a series of logical steps (an 'algorithm') – from navigating an airliner, through building a car, to diagnosing diseases or reading human handwriting (all of which are already being done by computers). Information technology is likely to be increasingly applied in the next century, particularly given its historical tendency to reduce in price and increase in memory power and speed.

But does this mean that a post-industrial society and an information economy are likely to bring forth an 'information polity' – a society in which power rests with the group who control knowledge and its technology? This seems a much more debatable proposition than the idea that scientific ideas and information technology will be central to the development of society. If 'those who control' is interpreted to mean scientists, professionals and technologists, and these are to become the nucleus of a new dominant class, this seems a doubtful proposition for which there is little evidence. There is no sign, as yet, of such groups developing what Marx would term 'class consciousness' or, as we have earlier described it, a sense of political identity separate from that of the middle classes as a whole. Information in the broad sense may well be a crucial source of power in the twenty-first century, but its control is as yet predominantly vested in the executives of corporate bodies like business corporations, government departments and universities. A 'new' source of power, surely, only creates opportunities for power brokers to bargain and negotiate over; it does not determine who rules.

Information technology and democracy

Fundamentally, as Youeji Masuda (1985) points out in an article entitled 'Computopia', governments and societies can use the potential of information technology either to liberate or control the individuals within it. Thus, with everyone offered free access to sophisticated information acquisition and processing systems, a democratic 'computopia' may be established in which ordinary individuals possess more information than the most sophisticated Prime Ministers could have twenty or thirty years ago.

The opposite possibility – what Masuda calls the 'automated state' – is to mobilise the power of information technology on behalf of state control and surveillance of its citizens. In the late 1940s George Orwell's (1949) idea of television sets in every household which could also monitor every household's activities (in the novel *1984*) seemed like a fantasy – now GCHQ is apparently monitoring all satellite-based international telephone calls, virtually all domestic financial transactions are recorded in the banks' computer systems (from which they could, at least, be extracted), whilst developments in road traffic control may well mean individual vehicle movements will also become centrally available over the next few years. The potential for central monitoring and control is disturbing, to say the least.

The possible relationships between information technology (IT) and types of government can be illustrated in another way: why were PCs a rarity in the former Soviet Union? Partly for the same reason that all duplicators/photocopying machines were registered with the KGB – individual citizens were not trusted by the Party with such information processing power. Decentralised information technology is a powerful force for democracy. But it can be argued that centralised information technology is as potentially destructive (literally in the case of the sort of 'Star Wars' technology deployed in the Gulf).

The argument is, then, that information technology is a powerful tool which must be harnessed by, rather than against, democratic government. But, as has also been said, the price of liberty is eternal vigilance. If choices are not deliberately made in this area, they may be taken by default, with the worst consequences.

The (sinister?) possibilities of the use of information technology in the surveillance of the population and for warfare (always described as 'defence' when employed by our side) have been already alluded to. Two other major uses of information technology in government will be briefly considered. The first is information technology's relevance to the process of electing and controlling a government; the second is its use in administering large-scale programmes such as social security or taxation.

As far as electing and controlling governments are concerned, information technology has already made a large contribution, but a still greater impact is entirely possible. Already, in many parts of the USA, complicated multi-candidate elections are routinely conducted using 'voting machines' which enable a speedy and accurate tally of the result to be made. More significantly, the whole electoral process has been transformed by the nationwide availability of information on television. Not only are presidential elections arguably decided by televised debates between the major candidates, but most US electoral campaigns now are basically electronic media events – with slick ten-second paid TV advertisements currently figuring largely in most successful candidates' strategies. In addition, the selective mailshot (also the product of information technology) has come to figure largely in the financing and tailoring of campaigns to particular constituencies of voters. The strategy and tactics of campaigns are also largely conditioned by computerised statistical analysis based upon opinion surveys (which also would be virtually impossible to conduct without computers). Finally, of course, the results of campaigns will be announced in advance with computerised graphics on television as the result of exit polls made possible by the same technology. These phenomena are clearly spreading to the rest of the democratic world (just as competitive party democracy is also, spreading across the world as never before). It can be argued that opinion polls are also making a contribution to controlling the actions of governments by making them aware of public reactions to their policies with greater accuracy and rapidity.

Potentially, the impact of information technology on democratic procedures goes much further than this since, in principle, the technology exists to enable the issues to be explained to all voters over television and for them to respond in a series of 'electronic referenda'. This has already been tried on a local level in the United States, whilst in the UK we are familiar with similar techniques used to vote for pop songs, films or talent show contestants.

The question arises, however, as to whether all this constitutes the development of a modern 'superdemocracy' (re-enacting the ancient Greek idea of democracy in which all citizens vote directly on the issues), or whether, in practice, this enables the forms of democracy to be combined with a manipulation of public opinion by the rich and powerful in society. If access to the mass media is open only to those who can pay for it (along with a similar control over the technology of campaigning), then a superficial popular 'chat show' style of pretend participation may hide a failure to critically expose the real issues.

Turning now to the government's output of services to citizens, similar problems may also apply. Information technology is already extensively employed by the public services, although less by the civilian parts of the government than by the armed forces (and to some extent the police). In Britain relatively well-known examples include the Driver Vehicle Licensing Authority at Swansea, the payment of child allowances and, at present in progress, massive projects relating to the computerisation of social security and income tax.

Again, it can be argued that computerisation is highly desirable in ensuring an efficient, economical, fast and fair service to clients of the public agency concerned. With a computerised system like cases can be treated alike, right across the country. Data on millions of people in the National Insurance or tax system seems an obvious candidate for treatment via an automated data-base. Just as private insurance companies and accountants are now extensively computerised, the same might be expected for public insurance or accounts systems. IBM, in their evidence to a recent Select Committee inquiry, has argued that the British public sector is behind equivalent private employers in these respects.

Is this process of computerisation a politically neutral one? IBM in the same evidence just quoted criticised the way in which, so far, the Civil Service has merely attempted to do the same things as before more economically with computers. Insufficient attention has been given to the possibility of giving better service using the potential of the technology. One of the problems then becomes that, from an industrial point of view, such exercises look to be merely concerned with job-cutting – and this has certainly caused problems with the social security project. It also seems that an obsession with cost-cutting computerisation has led to some of the recent reforms in social security which have reduced flexibility in the way clients are dealt with. Such an approach may end in alienating both work-force and clients by reducing the whole process to a soulless and remote form-processing operation.

However, a more imaginative use of information technology could, in contrast, help to humanise and improve administrative processes. For instance, there is much evidence that current social security decisions are frequently wrong in terms of the statutes because the regulations are very complicated, the work-force over-stretched and the clients ill-informed. The use of intelligent systems in which clients interacted directly with a user-friendly terminal, could well help to give a better service – but probably it would cost more because more clients would get the benefits they are entitled to!

Similarly, it has been suggested that a 'negative income tax' scheme (see Chapter 8) could only be implemented when both social security and income tax have been computerised – but that it would result in a much fairer benefits/tax system. In summary, a democratic welfare state can be improved – or dehumanised – with the aid of information technology.

There are many broader issues relating to what one might term the 'democratic social' use of information technology. A common theme in relation to these might, however, be that, in a democracy, ordinary people should, as Apple computers would put it, be 'empowered' by the technology rather than being its passive objects or victims.

Not being a victim involves not only data protection in the rather narrow sense current UK law gives to it, but also rights to privacy and freedom of information briefly referred to above, and possibly some sort of right to reply in the increasingly varied media.

More positively, if people are to have access to the power made possible by the technology, then positive steps to this end seem necessary. First and foremost in this respect is a requirement to ensure that everyone has the educational and training opportunities to enable them to use IT. After this, imaginative government initiatives may help to create a mass understanding of, and market for, information technology. A good example of the sort of thing that can be done is the French initiative in using their equivalent of Prestel (Minitel) as the standard telephone directory facility – compare the UK approach which has led to the wasting away of Prestel and (now) 'commercial' charging for directory enquiries.

It seems a tragedy that the UK should have the largest home micro market in the world – but that all this individual interest, knowledge and enthusiasm is not being led into economically and socially constructive channels. Without offering any 'solution' at this stage, it does seem that there must be scope for imaginative policy-making in this respect.

Unfortunately, in recent years in the UK a (correct) understanding of the crucial economic and competitive importance of information, has led to the (incorrect) idea that information is a commodity to be charged for at maximum possible price like any other. This approach fails to appreciate that, particularly from the point of view of society as a whole, information is a 'public good' (like a bridge) (see Chapter 6, pp.138–9) – that is, one person 'consuming' it does not prevent someone else from doing so, and that the cost of producing it is best capitalised upon by encouraging its consumption for the public benefit.

In conclusion, information technology will neither automatically ensure democracy nor undermine it. However, this does not mean that as democrats we can safely ignore information technology. The impact of IT on democracy will depend on the choices that are made as to how such technology is employed. These 'choices' may be made by big business or individuals in ignorance of, or ignoring, their impact on the rest of society. It may simply be that no one will make a conscious choice on some issues but, as a result of conscious or unconscious choice, or failure to consider alternatives, one future will be established for democracy rather than another equally possible future.

That the author's preference is for a future in which many individuals have access to information technology and hence democracy is a participatory reality, has been made clear. The most likely alternative future seems to be one in which all are nominally free to use information technology (as to enter the Ritz) but few have the actual resources and know-how to take full advantage of the opportunities. The most unhappy possible future in this respect is one in which the extensive powers of surveillance and manipulation offered by this technology are used, ultimately, to undermine even the fiction of democracy.

Technology and survival

Similar considerations to those just applied to information technology may be applied to the likely future influence of technological developments more generally. Too great an air of inevitability may easily be invested in predictions about both the likely development of technologies and upon their impact upon our environment. Just as information technology may be used to enslave or empower individuals, so research on the development and use of energy resources, for instance, can focus upon the employment of nuclear fission and existing fossil fuels to support existing patterns of individual and government consumption – essentially a concentration of individual consumption and strategic power in the North Atlantic area. Alternatively, new technologies may be developed of greater relevance to the problems of the South and to the survival of non-human species on our planet.

By way of illustration, let us consider three alternative scenarios in relation to the future use of the planet's energy resources (these alternatives are neither exhaustive nor exclusive). In the first, a deliberate decision by the governments and multinational corporations concerned could change our futures. In a second scenario, new energy resources of which we have little or no present conception could be developed which would change our world as drastically as the internal combustion engine has already done. A third alternative is that the gloomier prognostications of environmentalists may prove to be ill-founded as market forces fundamentally affect the consumption and use of energy resources.

In the first alternative, as a result of a successor conference to that in Rio which we briefly discussed in Chapter 4, or through the United Nations, a deliberate policy of raising taxes on fossil fuels, subsidising public transport and discouraging unnecessary private travel, investing in research and development of renewable energy resources and, particularly, discouraging the consumption of energy by rich consumers in the 'North' might significantly affect Western lifestyles and help prevent global warming and the disruption of the eco-system.

In the second alternative, a new source of clean renewable energy might be discovered – such as the simple 'cold' atomic fusion process which was recently announced, only to be found unreproduceable in other research laboratories. If the source did not require large and complex investment, this might allow the spread of a Northern lifestyle to the whole globe, besides fundamentally altering the world balance of power (reducing the influence of oil-rich areas such as the Middle East and the United States).

A third possible scenario is that, as fossil fuels become scarcer and the demand for them increases, their price will automatically rise as a result of the market mechanism. Higher prices for energy makes investment in research and development of alternative fuels more profitable and hence likely, discourages excessive use of energy, and reduces, in many cases, the disposable income of those wishing to consume energy. It might, in any case, be discovered that the 'greenhouse effect' was only a random fluctuation in the global weather pattern.

How likely are each of these alternatives? The problem about the first is clearly the need for a coherent and co-ordinated international response – a response akin to that generated by the Allies in the Second World War and which brought about the United Nations, NATO and the post-war Marshall Plan for the regeneration of Europe. So far there is no common perception of the same sort of level of danger. Major problems being that the chief beneficiary from the current system of industrial prosperity at the expense of environmental squalor is the leading actor in the international system – the United States. 'Underdeveloped' countries of the South are at present used by multinational companies as dumping grounds for polluted materials and as low-cost (partly because of low environmental standards) sources of raw materials and as mass-production sites.

The likelihood of the discovery and development of a relatively costless (in all senses) source of energy is more difficult to predict. As we have seen, logically, scientific innovation cannot be certainly predicted, but it must be clear that the likelihood of scientific innovation bears some relationship to the amount of resources devoted to research in an area. At present, expenditure on research on non-nuclear renewable energy resources is a fraction of that on nuclear and fossil fuels. Little research is devoted to energy-saving strategies. It should be borne in mind too, that it is a long way from a discovery in scientific principle to the application of an idea as a marketable product (the development process). In many cases, large skilled multi-disciplinary teams must be assembled and financed to develop the product, factories must be built, marketing of the product with the public carried out. Generally speaking only large multinational companies or the government of an affluent country are capable of such an effort. The likelihood of this scenario is limited, therefore, not only by scientific considerations (e.g. the principle of energy conservation – that the amount of energy in a closed system is fixed – i.e. nothing is for nothing) but also by the likely behaviour of governments and large firms. However, one organisation could gain an immense competitive advantage in developing such a resource.

The third scenario is difficult for non-economists and non-ecologists like the author and most readers to assess. However, it does seem likely that predictions of the environmental future which rely on extrapolating exponential curves of energy consumption and population growth are unduly pessimistic because of their neglect of price and social factors. Put simply, an exponential curve is one which rises at an ever-faster rate. (More accurately the equation describing it will have a power in it.) Extrapolating is assuming that the shape of a curve already established between two points is the same beyond those points. World population has risen faster and faster, broadly speaking, to date – but factors such as birth control, the reduced economic usefulness of children in urban industrial environments and government policies may well mean such a trend will not continue. Most industrial countries have gone through a 'population explosion' followed by stabilisation. As fossil fuels come nearer to exhaustion they are likely to rise steeply in price, thus reducing consumption. In so far as critics who emphasise points such as these are right, then there is little need for government action to restore balance to the system, since it is self-righting (homeostatic).

The serious cause for concern in this analysis, however, is the concept previously introduced of social costs and social benefits. It does seem likely that the real cost of consuming fossil and nuclear fuels will rise markedly over the next few decades – but will these costs be borne by the consumer? Will the large energy consumers have lower incomes as the result of higher energy prices?

If the consumer does pay the cost through higher prices, this will indeed be likely to cut demand. The price mechanism may, however, fail to accurately reflect the real cost of production. For instance, in the case of nuclear electricity production, there may be a hidden subsidy from the defence budget as far as development costs are concerned, whilst a major element of the full cost may be the decontamination of redundant plant and the compensation of those affected by nuclear accidents (such as Three Mile Island and Chernobyl) which may be borne by later generations or foreigners. Similarly poor non-consumers all over the globe (e.g. peasants on the flood-plains of Bangladesh) may pay a large part of the cost of American consumers' energy use, as the result of global warming.

Clearly, then, two major factors which will affect the environmental future are the balance of power between the 'North' and the 'South' and the role of multinational enterprises. Both of these deserve some more specific attention.

North versus South?

Just as the confrontation between communist 'East' and capitalist 'West' dominated the international relations in the second half of the twentieth century, it seems likely that the divisions between 'North' and 'South' will dominate the scene at the beginning of the twenty-first (Brandt (1980) *passim*).

By 'South' is meant what used to be called the 'third world', 'developing' or 'underdeveloped' countries. 'Third world' was a useful term, since it suggested the geo-strategic truth that such countries were a loose block of states who could play off the capitalist 'West' against the communist 'East' at the United Nations and elsewhere. It hardly seems an appropriate term with the virtual disappearance of the second, communist, world. China, of course, is still very much a major power, but it is not a super power, which professes to be communist. However, it cannot play the same sort of dominating role as the Soviet Union, and has adopted many features of the capitalist economic system. At the risk of being proved disastrously wrong, the author suspects the discrepancy between capitalist 'relations of production' and communist 'political and legal superstructure' will make itself felt in political restructuring before the end of the century – perhaps with the demise of its current aged leadership .

'Developing' is of course a polite euphemism for not yet developed or 'underdeveloped'. It certainly cannot be taken literally that the rate of economic growth in developing countries is greater than elsewhere. The sad truth is that the whole of Africa, on average, has actually stayed static economically or even retreated in terms of GNP per head over the last decade, as 1994 World Bank statistics show. The term 'underdeveloped' also carries something of the implication of general inferiority as against the 'developed' countries and implies an aspiration to emulate them in all respects. To assume that a sub-continent like India, with its artistic and spiritual richness, diversity and long history of civilisation, should aspire to emulate the United States of America is surely to adopt a somewhat limited perspective: consider the reply attributed to Gandhi on being asked, on a trip abroad, what he thought of Western civilisation: 'I think it would be a good thing!' (Bloomsbury (1987, 147)). (Still, clean water and modern sanitation would no doubt be very welcome in many parts of the sub-continent.) The simple terms 'rich' and 'poor' states might be adopted as descriptors of the division we are making, but perhaps politically and socially an oil-rich sheikhdom might have more in common with its poorer neighbours than with Sweden or Switzerland.

The 'South' then is a very loose term to describe the less industrialised countries of Africa, Asia and Latin America. Although such countries encompass an enormous variety of political, economic and social conditions, we can see that they share some important similarities which potentially may place them in conflict with the 'North'. In addition, in general to the problems inherent in a relatively low average standard of living, most of these countries share an experience of colonial subordination to the 'North' (often exacerbated by racialism) and a continuing position of economic subordination to a world market dominated by 'Northern' interests (e.g. the World Bank is effectively controlled by the United States). Although the military and economic dominance of the 'North' seems at this date inescapable, the coexistence of the vast majority of the world's population in poverty with a relatively small minority living in secure plenty does seem to constitute a position of extreme long-term instability.

In most areas of the 'South' the institutions of a modern independent state are relatively new (although most parts of the 'South' contain civilised cultures dating back as far as, or further than, those of Europe). New state institutions and old social values can sometimes conflict. In other cases, rapid industrialisation and new waves of migration have created new ethnically mixed communities which can be difficult to govern – or easy to disrupt with irresponsible political agitation. Transition towards new styles of government and the lack of an established democratic tradition has helped to generate greater political instability on the whole than in the 'North'. As we have seen (Chapters 2 and 7) both military governments and experiments with single-party government are much more common in the 'South' than the 'North'.

Having made some generalisations about the politics of the 'South', it is worth cautioning readers about accepting too easily generalisations put forward by 'Northern' commentators about the nature of these systems which may appear to condemn them all to a position of permanent subordination and inferiority. Employment of huge generalisations about the 'rationality' of Western forms of political organisation (Parsons (1957)) and the prevalence of 'kleptocracy' – government by thieves – in the 'South' (Andreski (1968)) may, on occasion, be little more than a mask for sophisticated ethnocentrism. It is worth bearing in mind that, as we have seen, ethnic conflicts can be found in US cities, in Northern Ireland and in the former Yugoslavia as well as in Africa or the Indian sub-continent. Corruption, too, can be observed on a large scale in apparently stable and rapidly growing political and economic systems such as nineteenth-century USA or twentieth-century Japan.

The range of social, political and economic systems to be found in the 'South' means that the prognosis for the future of these countries may well be equally varied. Already, states like Singapore and Taiwan (the 'newly industrialised countries' – NICs – of South East Asia) seem to be achieving massive economic growth. As Japan has moved rapidly up the 'league tables' of social and political indicators conversely, parts of the UK seem to be taking on many of the social and economic characteristics of the 'South' – for instance, acting as a reservoir of cheap labour for the assembly plants of the multinational enterprises discussed below.

Rather than concentrating on the domestic political systems of the 'South', it may be more relevant to a consideration of the future of the political stability of the planet to consider soberly the extent to which the 'South' faces a common economic and political environment which has the potential to drive the states of the 'South' together in an increasingly desperate and potentially aggressive alliance against the 'North'. Issues such as indebtedness to 'Northern' banks; adverse movements in the terms of trade for the primary products of the 'South'; 'Northern' monopolisation of intellectual property rights and information resources; the activities of ('Northern') multinational enterprises; the destruction of the planetary environment in the interests of 'Northern' consumption – all this could combine to create a new major 'fault line' in international relations. Many of these issues were raised by the report of the Independent Commission on International Development Issues (Brandt (1980)) to which the reader is referred. The likelihood of such a development must depend upon the extent to which the 'South' feels deliberately excluded from the affluent economy of the 'North', as opposed to the degree to which it is thought possible that individual countries will gradually be able to participate in the benefits of 'Northern' affluence. So far the dangers of the situation may be emphasised by a quotation from the Brandt report: 'It is a terrible irony that the most dynamic and rapid transfer of highly sophisticated equipment and technology from rich to poor countries has been in the machinery of death' (Brandt (1980, 14)).

Multinational enterprises, information technology and 'globalisation'

The importance of multinational enterprises in the modern world is difficult to overestimate. Some of these firms have a greater financial turnover than the GNP of a medium-size state (see Box 26)

Box 26   Multinationals and countries compared

Co. rank	Company sales (£ billions)		Gross national product (£ billions)	
			USA	3787*
			Japan	2382*
			UK	491
1	Itoh & Co	86		
6	Gen. Motors	66	Iran	64
8	R. Dutch Shell	58		
13	IBM	38	Pakistan	39
			Ireland	31
			New Zealand	27
29	Unilever	24	Bangladesh	19

SOURCES   *Times* (1993), *Economist* (1991), *Lloyd's Bank* (1993), OECD (1993)

NOTE   1991 figs except *=1992 figs

In addition, many of these corporations control vital economic resources such as oil (the 'Seven Sisters': ESSO, Texaco, BP, etc.), the automobile industry (Ford, Volkswagen) and computing (IBM, Microsoft). In some cases the world price of an entire commodity may be under the control of a multinational enterprise (e.g. De Beers and diamonds).

Virtually all multinational enterprises are clearly based in one host country, with the majority of shareholders and senior personnel from that country (the few exceptions include Anglo-Dutch operations such as Unilever and Shell). Operations in specific countries may be minority-owned and largely staffed by local personnel. In the majority of cases, significant multinational enterprises are owned in the USA, with Japanese companies second and European countries (including Britain) a poor third. It is possible that European mergers *may* lead to European-registered companies which are truly multinational.

Thus, in bargaining with governments in the 'South', a multinational enterprise is a sophisticated and richer organisation bargaining with a poorer, less skilled and less well-informed one.

Even in bargaining with a middle-rank power like the UK, a large Japanese or American corporation has very considerable bargaining power, since it has the alternative of setting up elsewhere within the European Union and exporting to the UK from there. Even a US corporation dealing with its own government can channel its funds and development projects 'off-shore' to lower labour cost countries or tax havens.

In the past, multinational enterprises often ran virtually independent operations in separate countries. (e.g. Ford in USA, UK, Germany, Australia). But they are now increasingly pursuing integrated global strategies in which financial resources can be swapped around the globe, production is planned centrally with resources coming from the cheapest country relevant to the market in mind, whilst profits are channelled to the most tax-efficient point. (Thus Ford is planning the 'world car' strategy in which all models will have interchangeable parts and components can be shipped all over the world to be assembled in models appropriate to the market in question.) This is only possible as a result of a sophisticated global use of information technology through a wide area network (WAN), often dependent upon the satellite broadcasting of data between countries and continents. Consequently, 90 per cent of satellite data-flow is intra-corporate – i.e. takes place between the branches of the same organisation. In fact, data-flow within the communication networks of individual multinational enterprises accounts for 50 per cent of all trans-border data-flow (Suprenant (1985)).

Marshall McLuhan (1964) has familiarised many people with the concept of the 'global village' in which the instant transmission of electronic images familiarises everyone instantly with the same version of events all over the world. With rapid satellite reporting and transmission of events from the bombing of Baghdad to the Olympic Games; with a shared repertoire of pop videos, international sporting events and Hollywood films; with a shared consumption of similar goods such as jeans, Nintendo games, Reebok trainers and Coca-Cola; a new shared international popular (youth) culture is thought to have been created.

Unprecedented levels of international travel – both for holidays and business, and even for education and spiritual enlightenment – have been made possible by modern technological developments. In addition, television documentaries, advertisements and films have familiarised people all over the globe with something of the ways of life of people in faraway places – especially affluent America!

On a perhaps more serious level, international publishing oper-ations (including CD-ROM and on-line data-bases – see Appendix), and the growing practice of international professional communication through journals and conferences, have made professionals in all spheres more rapidly aware of the new achievements and standards of international colleagues.

The social and political consequences of all this are immensely controversial. In countries as varied as France and Iran many of these developments have been denounced as 'creeping Americanisation'. There seems little doubt that a growing awareness of standards of living and freedom in the rest of the world was immensely influen-tial in bringing about the decommunisation of Eastern Europe.

What seems clear is that it is increasingly difficult for national governments to cut their people off from a knowledge of developments elsewhere in the globe, and that this knowledge can be political dynamite. In the USA in the 1960s a series of urban riots were said to have been incited by the urban poor's greater knowledge of the extent of their deprivation as a result of television. It is not beyond the scope of possibility that one of the greatest forces for instability and change in the next century will be a similar awareness of deprivation on behalf of the millions of inhabitants of the 'South'.

Many of the themes introduced so far are encapsulated in the concept of 'globalisation' (Luard (1990), McGrew and Lewis (1992)). This is the thesis that the increasing global interdependence of states, individuals and social and economic organisations is reducing the autonomy of individual states. Box 27 summarises:

BOX 27   Globalisation – is the nation-state doomed?

Challenges to the nation state

Internal instability	from mini-nationalisms, ethnicity, etc.;
External instability	need for regional/global security;
Economic dependence	on global economic and financial organisations;
Social integration	development of world standards for human rights, professional behaviour;
Technical integration	dependence on world communication networks and leading-edge technical developments increases vulnerability;
Ecological inter-dependence	threats of pollution, global warming, etc. insoluble within state boundaries.

The European future

It is worth relating the likely future of the European Union and Britain's role within it to some of the themes introduced earlier in this chapter. The European Union is an interesting example of the processes of political change. Clearly a reaction to the impact of two world wars on the heartland of Europe, it has developed from an organisation to co-ordinate iron and steel production in six countries to a potential continental superpower in a little over 40 years. For the most part, this has been a story of building alliances around common interests, of trading advantages against disadvantages and of seeking accommodations where national interests have conflicted.

The initial creation of the European Economic Community upon the foundations of the original Iron and Steel Community can be seen as a pragmatic bargain struck with an eye to a perhaps nobler vision. Essentially, the creation of the EEC can be seen as part of a process whereby the French government accepted the rehabilitation of (Western) Germany into the democratic community of nations in return for such a measure of economic integration in basic industries and of co-operation on defence issues through NATO that a German attempt to independently dominate Europe militarily and economically would not be feasible. In addition, French rural voters were softened in their attitude to the Community by a large element of agricultural subsidy and protection. Although the details of the Treaty of Rome were fairly prosaic, behind it lay the vision of Jean Monnet's Action Committee for a United States of Europe.

It is significant that most of the states who 'joined Europe' between 1957 and the early 1990s shared a commitment to a vision of a united and democratic Europe – the idea of Europe as a political symbol. For instance, Spain, Portugal and Greece all joined what was by then known as the European Community after ending periods of authoritarian dictatorship, seeing the move as a significant move toward joining the political mainstream of European development. Similarly, former Eastern Bloc countries such as Poland, the Czech state, Slovakia, Hungary and so on, who now wish to become members are clearly wishing to assert a long-term future as a part of a united and democratic Europe.

In contrast, the British application to join was defended domestically even by its proponents as a sensible, even essential, economic move much more than a political one. Even proponents of joining the EEC asserted that we could still maintain our special political relationships with the United States and the Commonwealth and that parliamentary sovereignty was undiminished by the move. Long after Brussels dropped the middle 'E' in EEC, the British government retained it. In the circumstances, it is understandable that France's President de Gaulle vetoed Britain's first application to join on the grounds that Britain would be an American Trojan horse undermining European unity.

Since joining, Britain has played a somewhat ambivalent role. Under Mrs Thatcher's leadership, despite expressions of reservations on the political front, Britain did show some enthusiasm for the creation of a Single European Market ('1992'). The removal of obstacles to trade in order to create a 'level playing field' throughout Europe fitted the free-market economic policies of the Thatcher government which permitted a temporarily strengthened legislative procedure to be introduced for the purpose. An exchange rate policy of maintaining a stable relationship with the Deutschmark and the franc, eventually within the ERM (European Exchange Rate Mechanism), seemed to be the precursor of closer financial unity – despite some disavowals of any idea of dropping the pound.

The Maastricht agreement reinforced the ambivalence of British government policies with a renewed nominal commitment to greater European unity and the creation of a single European currency, the strengthening of the powers of the European Parliament and of European institutions *vis-à-vis* domestic ones, being combined with an immediate UK opt-out from the Social Charter provisions, the option of a later withdrawal from the single currency provisions and the securing of general assent to the principle of subsidiarity (discussed in Chapter 6).

Since the 'failure' of the ERM (strictly speaking the ERM remains in operation, with wider permissible limits of fluctuation for most currencies), the difficulties in ratifying Maastricht in France and Denmark as well as Britain, the admission of Britain's former EFTA partners who may share Britain's more pragmatic approach and with

FUTURES

the need for flexibility to meet the needs of Eastern Bloc countries also wishing to join, the idea of the desirability, perhaps the inevitability, of a looser set of European relationships – 'a multitrack Europe' as Mr Major has described it – is not without credibility.

However, on balance, the author would stress a number of considerations which suggest both that a United States of Europe is highly likely in the long term and that, however reluctantly, Britain will continue to be a part of the Union. One set of considerations, which suggests that the conspicuous trend to strengthen the central institutions of Europe will continue, are the arguments rehearsed in Chapter 6 as to why central governments in federal structures tend to gain power.

Another set of considerations links back to our discussions of information technology and of multinationals – crucial technological developments are likely to require massive investments probably by multinational companies and states with massive economic resources. Effectively, the United States and Japan are the only political and economic systems with big enough tax-bases and consumer markets to develop on their own massive technological innovations such as space research, genetic engineering or super computer networks with built-in artificial intelligence. Individual European countries left to compete on their own (with the possible exception of the new united Germany) will become (as to some extent they already are) merely important subsidiary areas of competition between US and Japanese 'multinationals'. Only if Europe is a real single market and its research and development effort is genuinely pooled can it hope to remain an area where first-rank scientific, technological and hence industrial development on a substantial scale takes place.

Politically, too, the existence of a directly elected European Parliament can hardly be reversed. Once constituted, given the dominant traditions of representative democracy, the European executive, must, in the long term, become responsible to it (or to the people directly). A democratically constituted European executive will find itself the focus for enormous expectations for a peaceful prosperous and united Europe. Already the EU is being expected to play a peace-making role in the former Yugoslavia – even though Yugoslavia has never been a part of the EU.

It is possible that Britain might withdraw from the 'United States of Europe'. This is, however, unlikely since the majority of its trade is with the EU and virtually all the inward investment it attracts is because Britain is inside the EU trading area (just as if a European currency is established, London could hardly hope to remain the prime European financial centre if sterling were retained).

Finally, an analogy can be drawn between European developments at the present time and American history in the period 1776–89. Following the Declaration of Independence in 1776, the thirteen former American colonies agreed to a 'Confederation'. Because of an insistence on the sovereignty of the individual states, Congress was without adequate executive, judicial or financial machinery with which to attempt to manage the security and economy of North America. Congress's failure to meet the expectations its very existence generated led to the adoption of the present constitution in 1789.

Taking political action: where do I go from here?

> The philosophers have only *interpreted* the world differently – the point is to *change* it.
>
> Karl Marx, *11th Thesis on Feuerbach*
> (Marx and Engels (1962, Vol. II, 403))

Every reader of this book about politics will, after reading it, go on to practise politics in the all-encompassing sense we defined it in Chapter 1. The most private of individuals will, none the less, inevitably need to work with, and on occasion come into conflict with, others in social situations. At every point upon the globe some state will claim jurisdiction over your actions. It is hoped that this book will, at a minimum, have given some sense of the processes at work and have suggested some sources of further information when they are required (for more see 'Recommended reading' at chapter ends and the Appendix on sources).

It is hoped that some readers not already enrolled on politics courses may have been inspired to do so. A section in the Appendix gives further details on courses available for British readers.

Politics is not only a spare-time or academic activity, however.

There is truth in the feminist slogan 'the personal is political'. It is worth reviewing your personal relationships and professional activities (or plans) to see if they are in accord with political principles you profess (although this can be rather sobering).

No sensible author would urge all their readers to go out and become professional politicians, but this author does share Aristotle's conviction that it is a mark of civilisation to wish to join in the political life of the community. There is great satisfaction to be had, not only in discussing political issues in the abstract but in helping to build a better world through membership of voluntary organisations which attempt to influence events – from GreenPeace through to Unidentified Flying Object enthusiasts. Almost everywhere, local party organisations tend to fall over themselves with eagerness in welcoming new members, and many have congenial sections specifically for young people. Independently, readers may actually exercise real influence through writing to newspapers and to their elected representatives.

If politics is thought of only in terms of the activities of the nation-state, then the scope for ordinary citizens is necessarily a limited one. But the argument of this book has been that important political decisions can be made at the level of work, educational and leisure organisations, by local and regional authorities, voluntary interest groups and by international co-operation. The scope for individual action is already large and should, in the author's view, be made larger.

Recommended reading

Luard, Evan, 1990, *The Globalization of Politics: The Changed Focus of Political Action in the Modern World*, New York, New York University Press. Takes a slightly narrower view than the author of the nature of 'globalization'.

Masuda, Youeji , 1985, 'Computopia', in Forrester, Tom, *The Information Technology Revolution*, Oxford, Blackwell. Seminal essay by one of Japan's most influential critics and policy-makers.

Moore, Nick and Steele, S., 1993, *Information-intensive Britain*, London, Policy Studies Institute. The impact of information technology on the economy, government and organisations in Britain, the regulation of information.

Nugent, Neill, 1994, *Government and Politics of the European Union*, 3rd edn, Basingstoke, Macmillan. A useful standard text.

Rice, E E, (ed.), 1991, *Revolution and Counter-revolution*, Oxford, Basil Blackwell. Broad-ranging collection of conference papers on the politics of revolutionay change.

Sources on politics

This guide is mainly intended for use by British students on under-graduate courses with access to a university library and JANET (the Joint Academic Network – a British 'branch' of the Internet). Some of the obscurer sources mentioned would perhaps only be likely to be used by students writing dissertations – but could earn extra credit if used in ordinary assignments. Large city libraries may also provide many of the same resources and increasingly owners of personal computers with modems can gain access via the Internet to much of the world's knowledge. Non-university readers may not realise that most academic libraries will admit non-members of the university for reference access with very little formality (although you are less likely to be able to borrow directly). Most public libraries can also obtain items not in stock on inter-library loan at minimal cost to the reader.

Books

Too many students search for material by going to what they think is the right shelf in the loan section of the library, finding little or nothing and then reporting back to their tutor in all seriousness, 'There is nothing on it in the library'! If you have some authors and titles in mind (for instance, references from the 'Recommended reading' sections of this book), look these up in the catalogue – they may not be where you think – and view adjacent entries in the catalogue and on the shelves. The catalogue may lead you to restricted loan collections, reserve stacks or departmental collections which may not always be obvious. You should also check the subject catalogue trying to think of related terms ('Labour Party' as well as 'socialism', 'Russia' as well as 'Soviet Union', etc.).

Consider also the possibility of using the Reference shelves. Much valuable material can be found in sources like the *Encyclopaedia of Social Sciences*, Kogan and Hawkesworth (1992), and various specialised dictionaries (e.g. Evans and Newnham (1992), Riff (1990), Roberts and Edwards(1991)). Most useful statistical sources will probably also be in the reference section.

An important part of the reference section will be a collection of specialised bibliographies which will give you further ideas for books and journal to look for – for example Royal Commission on Historical Monuments (1982), Shaw and Sklar (1977).

Newspapers

Much valuable and (especially) recent material is to be found in newspapers and magazines. The problem is to find it! When, for instance, did the last election in France take place? If you do not know, you cannot easily find reports on it in quality daily newspapers such as *The Times*, the *Guardian*, the *New York Times*, or *Le Monde*. *Keesings Contemporary Archives* is a valuable and clearly indexed summary of contemporary events which can help you with this as well as providing much useful information in its own right. Several newspapers such as *The Times* also print quarterly or annual indexes (see also below for electronic versions/searching).

Journals

University libraries also contain extensive collections of (usually quarterly) academic and professional journals. They often cover the points you are looking for in a pithier and more up-to-date fashion than do textbooks. Key British academic journals include *Talking Politics*, *Political Studies*, *Politics*, *Political Quarterly*, the *British Journal of Political Science*. Other important journals include the *American Political Science Review* and the *Revue Français de Science Politique*. In addition to articles, these journals usually carry very useful book reviews – excellent for supplying telling critical points about books recommended by your tutor!

The same problem applies to journals as to newspapers – finding the relevant article. To some extent their titles may help – public administration in *Public Administration*, etc., but serious use of journals requires you to master the bibliographical tools available. Examples of these are the *International Political Science Abstracts* (six per annum), which indexes and summarises most relevant academic journals, and the annual *International Bibliography of Political Science*.

Official sources

British government publications may be kept in a separate sequence from other publications and may not be individually catalogued alongside the book collection. This can lead students to miss very valuable information. Most important central government publications are published by Her Majesty's Stationery Office, and HMSO catalogues are a valuable way to track down recent publications in this category.

HMSO publications come in four main categories. First, *Hansard* the daily record of parliamentary debates, which are subsequently bound and indexed. References to *Hansard* will normally refer to which House (Commons or Lords), the parliamentary session (e.g. 1995/6), possibly the date of the debate, and certainly to the 'column' in which the remark quoted is reported (each page being divided into two columns). Debates often read better than they sounded because MPs can 'correct' Hansard's reporting. Second, 'parliamentary papers' are numbered in order of publication during a session (e.g. HC 213 1994/5) and include the reports of Select Committees – these often contain interesting interviews with Ministers, civil servants, industrialists, academics and others about the workings of government policy. Third, are a series of Command Papers (i.e. issued theoretically by command of Her Majesty) the most important of which are White Papers stating government policy in a particular area. Others are consultative Green Papers. In addition to this, HMSO issues a host of more specialised publications by government bodies.

Unfortunately for scholars, many government publications are not published by HMSO, but by the departments of agencies concerned and are therefore more difficult to track down. Some useful documents may be lodged only in the library of the House of Commons or the department concerned (e.g. reports on the tendering out of parts of their work). All publications by local government bodies and nearly all by quangos are also, naturally, published by the individual bodies concerned, in an uncoordinated manner. For local government see Nurcombe (1992) and Snape (1969).

European Union documentation is as complex as that of the British government (see Thompson (1989)), United States government publications more so (see Swarzkopf (1994), Schmekebier (1969)).

Other printed sources

Politically relevant bodies like the Confederation of British Industry and the Trades Union Congress, major pressure groups and the political parties all publish numerous reports and papers which can often only be obtained by writing to them direct.

Unpublished student theses and conference papers may also contain valuable information. Some of these are catalogued by the British Library and may be obtained from them on inter-library loan.

Videos/television/radio

Electronic mass media sources can be valuable but are difficult to identify, capture and use. The BBC monitoring service does provide some bibliographical assistance to academics. For undergraduates the most useful source is your own library's catalogue. The single most useful source of video material in UK higher education is the Open University, which does publish catalogues and provide broadcasting calendars to the general public.

CD-ROM

All major libraries now have collections of material on CD-ROM (compact disk – read only memory) and facilities to view them. Most of these so far are either bibliographic data-bases, or electronic versions of reference works such as encyclopaedias, dictionaries, company information, etc. The systems concerned are usually reasonably 'user-friendly' and should not take someone used to operating a video or consulting Oracle or CeeFax information on television long to master.

The big advantage of CD-ROM sources is that they can be searched far more easily and in far more sophisticated ways than conventional printed versions of the same material. For instance, a set of academic journal articles or abstracts can be searched for any mention of both say 'information' and 'politics' in the same article or abstract – or within so many words of each other.

On-line data-bases

Just as there are so many journals that no library is likely to have every one on a given subject, there are now so many bibliographic data-bases that no library is likely to have all of them either in printed or CD-ROM versions. Fortunately, most academic libraries now have access via the telephone lines to literally hundreds of data-bases held at computer centres like DIALOG in California. These 'on-line' systems are somewhat less user-friendly than the CD-ROM versions mentioned earlier, so you may have to ask a librarian to search for you, but this does mean that, in a sense, the resources of most of the world's major libraries can be searched from any one of them.

Not only bibliographic data-bases are accessible in this form, but also a number of 'full-text' data-bases are available including, for instance, the full text of the *Harvard Business Review* and recent issues of the *Guardian* and other quality newspapers. Thus, a required article can be down-loaded onto your own computer and quotations from it pasted into the assignment you are writing. Where the full text is not available, a fax of any article indexed can usually be sent.

The Internet

Computer-literate students can use direct access to JANET to search campus information systems and libraries almost anywhere in the world for relevant information. Some information facilities, like DIALOG, are commercial operations to which you must pay a subscription, but many are open free to all. For instance, you can access the Library of Congress catalogue direct free of charge. By way of example, some useful Internet addresses complete this section (see *Guardian* 'On-line' section and Carver (1994)):

Library of Congress Catalogue	telnet locis.loc.gov
Law and Politics Book Review	mzltov @nwu.edu [or e-mail command 'subscribe lpbr-I your name' to listserv @nwu.edu]
Political Science and Research Teaching List	polpsrt @mizzou1.missouri.edu
Social Science Information Gateway	e-mail command 'subscribe mailbase@mailbase.ac.uk
to e-mail US President	president@whitehouse.gov
info on White House activities	publications@whitehouse.gov [message: 'send info']
CIA Web-server	http://www.ic.gov
Paddy Ashdown	PaddyAshdown @Libdem.compulink.co.uk
Labour Party	http://www.poptel.org.uk/labour-party
The Author	stansey @ bmth.ac.uk
USENET message-boards include:	bit.listserv.politics alt.politics.libertarian eunet.politics

Courses on politics

Any British reader not already enrolled on a politics course who is inspired to do so is recommended to read a useful pamphlet produced by the CRAC biannually which outlines full-time degree courses available in Britain. Most further education colleges and university extramural departments provide part-time courses suitable for the beginning student, as does the Open University. Increasingly, even full-time courses have a fair proportion of 'mature' students, so that older readers should not dismiss the possibility of pursuing their interest in this way. Although somewhat dated, an article by the author (Tansey (1981)) does suggest the wide variety of courses available in Britain in addition to single-honours politics degrees.

Undergraduate 'politics' courses in Britain are marked by, if anything, an increasing diversity. A recent report (CNAA (1992, 55–8)) found that the author's expectations of core studies in French, US, UK, Soviet politics alongside political behaviour and political philosophy in each degree were not sustainable. 'Diversity is more the pattern'. Most courses include some British politics and some political theory (but this was interpreted in different ways). There was a trend towards recognition of the increasing importance of the European dimension. Beyond this, students who wish to explore in depth international relations, public policy and administration, the politics of a particular area (e.g. the South), or even the history of political thought, should ensure that these options are available on the course they are contemplating.

Recommended reading

CRAC, 1993, *Degree Course Guide to politics including International Relations*, Cambridge, Hobsons. These pamphlets are often found bound in two-volume sets of Degree Course Guides covering all subjects in reference libraries.

Englefield, D. and Drewry, G. (eds), 1984, *Information Sources in Politics and Political Science World Wide*, London, Butterworth.

Levine, John and Baroudi, Carol, 1993, *Internet for Dummies*, IDG.

Mardall, B., 1976, *How To Find Out in Politics and Government*, London, LLRS Publications.

References

Abel-Smith, Brian, 1976, *Value for Money in Health Services* London, Heinemann.

Algar, Hamid, (trans and Introduction), 1980, *Constitution of the Islamic Republic of Iran*, Berkeley, Calif., Mizan Press.

Allardt, E. and Littunen, Y., (eds), 1964, *Cleavages, Ideologies and Party Systems*, Helsinki, The Westermarck Society.

Allison, Graham T., 1987, *The Essence of Decision*, Harper College.

Almond, Gabriel and Coleman, James (eds), 1960, *The Politics of Developing Areas*, Princeton, N.J., Princeton University Press.

Almond, Gabriel and Verba, Sidney, 1963, *The Civic Culture*, Princeton, N.J., Princeton University Press.

Andreski, Stanislav, 1966, *Parasitism and Subversion, The Case of Latin America*, London, Weidenfeld & Nicholson.

Andreski, Stanislav, 1968, *The African Predicament, A Study in the Pathology of Modernisation*, London, Michael Joseph.

REFERENCES

Arendt, Hannah, 1967, *The Origins of Totalitarianism*, 2nd edn, London, Allen & Unwin.

Aristotle, (ed. Ernest Barker), 1946, *The Politics of Aristotle*, Oxford, Clarendon Press.

Arterton, C. F., 1987, *Teledemocracy*, London, Sage.

Atkinson, Anthony. B., 1985, *The Economics of Inequality*, 2nd edn., Oxford, Clarendon Press.

Bachrach, Peter and Baratz, Morton S., 1970, *Power and Poverty*, New York, Oxford University Press.

Banfield, Edward C., and Banfield, L. F., 1967, *The Moral Basis of a Backward Society*, Glencoe, Ill., Free Press.

Barker, Sir Ernest, 1961, *Principles of Social and Political Theory*, Oxford, Oxford Universty Press.

Barrett, Susan and Fudge, C., 1981, *Policy and Action*, London, Methuen.

Bell, Daniel, 1960, *The End of Ideology*, New York, Basic Books.

Bell, Daniel, 1973, *The Coming of Post Industrial Society*, New York, Basic Books.

Benedict, Ruth, 1935, *Patterns of Culture*, London, Routledge & Kegan Paul .

Berlin, Isiah, 1958, *Two Concepts of Liberty, An Inaugural Lecture*, Oxford, Clarendon Press.

Berlin, Isaiah, 1969, *Four Essays on Liberty*, Oxford, Clarendon Press.

Bernstein, Carl and Woodward, Bob, 1974, *All the President's Men*, New York, Simon & Schuster.

Beveridge, William, (Ch.), 1942, *Report of the Committee on Social Insurance and Allied Matters*, London, HMSO, Cmnd 6404.

Blair, Tony, 1994, *Socialism*, London, Fabian Society.

Bloch, M., 1961, *Feudal Society*, London, Routledge & Kegan Paul.

Bogdanor, Vernon, 1988, *Constitutions in Democratic Politics*, Aldershot, Gower.

Bohannan, Paul, 1965, 'Social and Political Organisation of the Tiv', in Gibbs, J.L. (ed.), 1965, *The Peoples of Africa*, New York, Holt, Rinehart & Winston.

Bottomore, T.B., 1964, *Elites and Society*, Harmondsworth, Middlesex, Penguin.

Bradshaw, J., 1972, 'A Taxonomy of Social Need', in Mclachan, G., 1972, *Problems and Progress in Medical Care*, Oxford, Oxford University Press.

Brandt, Willy (Ch.), 1980, *North–South: A Programme for Survival*, London, Pan.

Brinton, Crane, 1965, *The Anatomy of Revolution*, London, Johnathan Cape.

Bryce, James B., 1921, *Modern Democracies*, London.

Burke, Edmund, 1907, *The Works*, Oxford, Oxford University Press (World's Classics).

Campbell, Peter, 1965, *French Electoral Systems and Elections Since 1789*, revised edn, London, Faber & Faber.

Carver, Terrel, 1994, 'Gopher @ U.R COMMAND', *PSA News*, Spring, 10,.

Cater, Douglas, 1965, *Power in Washington: A Critical Look at Today's Struggle to Govern in the USA*, London, Collins.

CNAA, Committee for Social Sciences, 1992, *Politics and International Relations: A Review of Undergraduate Provision within UK Higher Education*, London, Council for National Academic Awards.

Coulborne, Rushton (ed.), 1956, *Feudalism in History*, Princeton, N.J., Princeton University Press.

Cranston, Maurice, 1954, *Freedom: A New Analysis*, London, Longmans Green.

Cranston, Maurice, 1962, *Human Rights Today*, London, Ampersand Books.

Crick, Bernard, 1993, *In Defence Of Politics*, Harmondsworth, Middlesex, Penguin.

Dahl, Robert A., 1961, *Who Governs?*, New Haven, Conn, Yale University Press.

Dahl, Robert A., 1971, *Polyarchy*, New Haven, Conn., Yale University Press.

Dahrendorf, Rolf, 1959, *Class and Class Conflict in Industrial Societies*, London, Routledge & Kegan Paul.

Dalton, Russell J., 1988, *Citizen Politics in Western Democracies*, Chatham, N.J., Chatham House.

Dawson, Richard E. and Prewitt, Kenneth, *et al.*, 1977, *Political Socialization*, Boston, Little Brown.

de Crespigny, Anthony and Minogue, Kenneth (eds), 1976, *Contemporary Political Philosophers*, London, Methuen.

de Jouvenal, Bertrand, 1963, *The Pure Theory Of Politics*, Cambridge, Cambridge University Press.

de Tocqueville, Alexis, (eds J.P. Mayer and Max Lerner), 1966, *Democracy in America*, New York, (trans.12th edn of 1848), 2 Vols, Harper & Row.

Derbyshire, J. Denis and Derbyshire, Ian, 1991, *World Political Systems, An Introduction to Comparative Government*, Edinburgh, Chambers Political Spotlights.

Deutsch, Karl, 1963, *Nerves of Government*, Glencoe, Ill., Free Press.

Dewey, John, 1916, *Democracy and Education*, (1955 reprint) London, Macmillan.

Djilas, Milovan, 1966, *The New Class*, London, Allen & Unwin.

Dowse, Robert E., 1969, *Modernization in Ghana and the USSR*, London, Routledge & Kegan Paul.

Dowse, Robert E., 1972, *Functionalism in Political Science*, World Politics,.

Duff, Andrew (ed.), 1993, *Subsidiarity Within the European Community*, London, Federal Trust for Education and Research.

Duverger, Maurice, 1972, *The Study Of Politics*, London, Nelson.

Easton, David and Dennis, Jack, 1969, *Children in the Political System*, New York, McGraw-Hill.

Easton, David, 1979, *A Framework For Political Analysis*, Chicago, University of Chicago Press.

Eberhardt, Wolfram, 1977, *A History of China*, 4th edn, London, Routledge.

Eckstein, Harry, 1960, *Pressure Group Politics*, London.

Economic Trends, 1987, HMSO, November.

Economist, The, 1991, *World in Figures 1991*, London, The Economist.

Edelman, M., 1977, *Political Language*, London, Academic Press.

Eisenstadt, S. N., 1969, *The Political System of Empires: The Rise and Fall of Historical Bureaucratic Empires*, London.

Enloe, Cynthia, 1986, *Ethnic Conflict and Political Development: An Analytic Study*, Collier-Macmillan.

Evans, Graham and Newnham, Jeffrey, 1992, *A Dictionary Of World Politics: A Reference Guide To Concepts Ideas And Institutions*, London, Harvester-Wheatsheaf.

Eysenck, Hans J. and Kamin, L.J., 1981, *Intelligence: the Battle for the Mind*, London, Pan.

Fainsod, Merle, 1963, *How Russsia is Ruled*, Cambridge, Mass., Harvard University Press.

Finer, Samuel E., 1976, *The Man on Horseback*, 2nd edn, London, Pall Mall Press.

Firestone, Shulamith, 1971, *The Dialectic of Sex*, New York, Bantam Books.

Fischer, Michael, 1980, *Iran: From Religious Dispute to Revolution*, Cambridge, Mass., Harvard University Press.

FitzJames Stephen, J., 1873, *Liberty, Equality, Fraternity*, London.

Fogarty, M. P., 1957, *Christian Democracy in Western Europe*, London, Routledge & Kegan Paul.

Forrester, Tom, (ed.), 1985, *The Information Technology Revolution*, Oxford, Blackwell.

Forster, E.M., 1972, *Two Cheers for Democracy*, London, Edward Arnold,.

Fortes, M. and Evans-Pritchard, E.E., 1961, African Political Systems, Oxford, Oxford University Press.

Fraser, Derek, 1984, *The Evolution of the British Welfare State*, Basingstoke, Macmillan.

Friedman, Milton and Friedman, Rose, 1980, *Free To Choose*, Harmondsworth, Middlesex, Penguin.

Friedrich, Carl J., (ed.), 1964, *Totalitarianism*, New York, Grosset & Dunlop.

Frissen, Paul, 1994, 'The Virtual Reality of Informatization in Public Administration', London, Conference on ICTs in Public Administration, 30 September.

Gbadamosi, T.G.O., 1978, *The Growth of Islam Among the Yoruba, 1841–1908*, London, Longman.

Gerth, H. and Mills, C. Wright (eds), 1948, *From Max Weber: Essays In Sociology*, London, Routledge & Kegan Paul.

Gluckman, Max, 1965, *Custom and Conflict in Africa*, Oxford, Blackwell.

Goldman, Emma, 1915, *Anarchism and Other Essays, USA*, Mother Earth Publishing Association.

Gorovitz, 1976, '*John Rawls: A Theory of Justice*', in de Crespigny, Anthony and Minogue, Kenneth (eds), *Contemporary Political Philosophers*, London, Methuen.

Gramsci, A., 1969, *The Prince*, New York.

Green, Thomas H., 1941, *Lectures on the Principles of Political Obligation*, quoted in Milne, A.J.M., 1962, *The Social Philosoply of English Idealism*, London, George Allen & Unwin.

Greenleaf, W.H., 1983, *The British Political Tradition*, London, Methuen.

Hamilton, A., Jay, J. and Madison, J. (Rossiter, C. ed.), 1961, *The Federalist Papers*, New York.

Hanf, K. and Scharpf, F.W., 1978, *Inter-organisational Policy-Making: Limits to Co-ordination and Control*, London, Sage.

Harrison, Alan, 1979, *The Distribution of Wealth in 10 Countries*, London, HMSO, Royal Commission on The Distribution of Wealth Background Paper 7.

Hayek, F.A., 1979, *Law, Legislation and Liberty*, London, Routledge & Kegan Paul.

Hegel, George, Dyde, (trans), 1896, *The Philosophy of Right*, London.

Hershey, Marjorie R. and Hill, David B, 1975, 'Watergate and the Benevolent Leader', Chicago, MidWest Political Science Association Proceedings.

Hess, Robert D. and Torney, Judith V., 1967, *The Development of Political Attitudes in Children*, Chicago, Aldine Press.

Hitler, Adolf, (trans R. Manheim), 1969, *Mein Kampf*, London, Hutchinson.

Hobhouse, Leonard, 1964, *Liberalism*, New York, Oxford University Press (reprint of 1911 edn with new introduction).

Hogwood, Brian W. and Gunn, Lewis A., 1984, *Policy Analysis for the Real World*, Oxford, Oxford University Press.

Hood, C., 1976, *The Limits of Administration*, London, Wiley.

Horowitz, Irving L., 1964, *The Anarchists*, New York, Dell Publishing.

Huntington, Samuel P., 1957, *The Soldier and the State*, Cambridge, Mass., Harvard University Press.

Huntington, Samuel P., (ed.) 1962, *Changing Patterns of Military Politics*, Glencoe, Ill., Free Press.

Irving, R.E.M., 1979, *The Christian Democratic Parties of Western Europe*, London, George Allen & Unwin.

Jansen, J.H., 1979, *Militant Islam*, London, Pan.

Jennings, Sir Ivor 1957, *Parliament*, Cambridge, Cambridge University Press.

Johnson, Norman, 1987, *The Welfare State in Transition*, Brighton, Wheatsheaf.

Jones, Maldwyn A., 1960, *American Immigration*, Chicago, University of Chicago Press.

Karpik, Lucien, 1978, *Organisation and Environment*, London, Sage.

Keynes, John Maynard, 1936, *The General Theory of Employment Interest and Money*, London.

Knight, Barry, 1993, *Voluntary Action,* London, Home Office. Reprinted 1994, London, Centris.

Kogan, Maurice and Hawkesworth, Mary (eds), 1992, *Encyclopaedia of Government and Politics*, London, Routledge.

Kuhn, T., 1970, *The Structure of Scientific Revolutions*, Chicago, University of Chicago Press.

Kurian, G.T., 1985, *A New Book of World Rankings*, Facts on File.

Lambert, Wallace E. and Klineberg, Otto, 1967, *Children's Views of Foreign Peoples*, USA, Irvington,.

Lane, Erik *et al.*, 1991, *Political Data Handbook: OECD Countries*, Oxford, Oxford University Press.

Lasswell, Harold, 1936, *Politics Who Gets What, When, How?*, reprinted, London, Peter Smith.

LeGrand, Julian, 1982, *The Strategy of Equality: Redistribution and the Social Services*, London, Allen & Unwin.

LeMarchand, Rene (ed.), 1977, *African Kingdoms in Perspective*, London, Frank Cass.

Lenin, V.I., 1917, *The State and the Revolution: Marxist Teaching on the State . . .*, in Marx, K., Engels, F. and Lenin, V.I., 1960, *The Essential Left: Four Classic Texts on the Principles of Socialism*, London, Unwin Books.

Lewis, Paul G. *et al.*, 1975, *The Practice of Comparative Politics: A Reader*, 2nd edn., London, Longmans.

Lindblom, C.E., 1959, 'The Science of Muddling Through', *Administrative Review*, 19: 79–88.

Lipset, Seymour Martin, 1979, *The First New Nation, The USA in Comparative and Historical Perspective*, Norton.

Lloyd's Bank, 1993, *Economic Profile of GB 1993*, London, Lloyd's Bank.

Lovelock, James, 1979, *Gaia*, Oxford, Oxford University Press.

Luard, Evan, 1990, *The Globalization of Politics: The Changed Focus of Political Action in the Modern World*, New York, New York University Press.

McClellan, D., 1986, *Ideology*, Milton Keynes, Open University Press.

McGrew, Tony G. and Lewis, Paul G., 1992, *Global Politics*, Cambridge, Cambridge University Press.

Machiavelli, 1961, *The Prince*, Harmondsworth, Middlesex, Penguin.

McKenzie, W.J.M., 1958, *Free Elections*, London.

McKibbin, R., 1983, *The Evolution of the Labour Party 1910–1924*, Oxford, Oxford University Press.

McLuhan, Marshall, 1964, *Understanding The Media: The Extension of Man*, London, Routledge & Kegan Paul.

MacPherson, C.B., 1966, *The Real World of Democracy: The Massey Lecture*, Oxford, Clarendon Press.

Maddison, Angus, 1974/5, 'What is Education For ?', *Lloyd's Bank Review*.

Mangham, Ian, 1979, *The Politics of Organisational Change*, London, Associated Business Press.

Marcuse, Herbert, 1964, *One-dimensional Man*, London, Routledge & Kegan Paul.

Marshall, L, 1961, 'Sharing Talking and Giving: Relief of Social Tensions among the !Kung Bushmen', *Africa*, March.

Marx, Karl and Engels, Frederich, 1962, *Selected Works* (2 volumes), Moscow, Foreign Languages Publishing House.

Marx, K., Engels, F. and Lenin, V.I., 1960, *The Essential Left: Four Classic Texts on the Principles of Socialism*, London, Unwin Books.

Masuda, Youeji, 1985, 'Computopia', in Forrester, Tom (ed.), *The Information Technology Revolution*, Oxford, Blackwell.

Michels, Robert, 1915, *Political Parties*, (1959 reprint), New York, Constable.

Milgram, Stanley, 1965, 'Some Conditions for Obedience and Disobedience to Authority', *Human Relations*, 18: 57–74.

Miliband, Ralph, 1969, *The State in Capitalist Society*, London, Weidenfeld & Nicholson.

Miliband, Ralph, 1984, *Capitalist Democracy in Britain*, Oxford, Oxford University Press.

Mill, John Stuart, (ed. A.D. Lindsay), 1910, *On Liberty, Representative Government*, Utilitarianism, London, Dent.

Mills, C. Wright, 1956, *The Power Elite*, New York, Oxford University Press.

Millward, Robert, 1971, *Public Expenditure Economics*, Maidenhead, McGraw-Hill.

Milne, A.J.M., 1962, *The Social Philosophy of English Idealism*, London, George Allen & Unwin.

Mitchell, Duncan, 1959, *Sociology, The Study Of Social Systems*, London, University Tutorial Press.

Morgan, Michael L. (ed.), 1992, *Classics of Moral and Political Theory*, Indianapolis, Hackett.

Morison, Samuel Eliot, and Commager, Henry Steele, 1962, *The Growth of the American Republic*, New York, 5th edn Oxford University Press.

Mosca, Gaetano, (ed. A. Livingstone), 1939, *The Ruling Class*, New York, McGraw-Hill.Nettl, Peter, 1966, 'The Concept of System in Political Science', *Political Studies*, XIV, 305–38.

Nett, Peter, 1966, 'The Concept System in Political Science', *Political Studies*, XIV, 305–38.

Neustadt, R.E., 1960, *Presidential Power: The Politics of Leadership*, New York, John Wiley & Sons.

Norris, Pippa, 1994, 'Political Science in Britain and America: The Decline of a Special Relationship?', *PSA News*, Autumn, 15–17.

Nove, Alec, 1980, *The Soviet Economic System*, London, Allen & Unwin.

Nurcombe, Valerie, 1992, *Local Authority Information Services: A Guide to Publications, Databases and Services*, London, SCOOP (The Library Association Standing Committee on Official Publications).

Oakeshott, Michael, 1962, *Rationalism in Politics and Other Essays*, London, Methuen.

OECD, 1993, *OECD in Figures 1993*, OECD.

Orwell, George, 1968, 'Politics and the English Language', in *Collected Essays* Vol. 4, Harmondsworth, Penguin.

Orwell, George, 1949, *1984*, London, Secker & Warburg.

Pahl, R.E., and Winkler, A.M., 1975, 'The Coming Corporatism', *Challenge*, March/April, 28–35.

Pareto, Vilfredo, (ed. S.E. Finer), 1976, *Sociological Writings*, Oxford, Blackwell.

Parker, Julia, 1975, *Social Policy and Citizenship*, London, Macmillan.

Parkinson, C. Northcote, 1958, *Parkinson's Law: Or The Pursuit of Progress*, London, Murray.

Parsons, Talcott, 1957, 'The Distribution Of Power In American Society', *World Politics*, 10, 123–43.

Pennock, J. Roland and Chapman, John W., (eds), 1978, *Anarchism: Nomos XIX*, New York, New York University Press.

Plato, (eds Davies and Vaughan) 1866, *The Republic of Plato*, London, Macmillan.

Popper, Karl, 1960, *The Poverty of Historicism*, 2nd edn., London, Routledge & Kegan Paul.

Popper, Karl, 1962, *The Open Society and its Enemies*, London, Routledge.

Poulantzas, Nicos, 1973, *Political Power And Social Classes*, London, New Left Review Books.

Prawer, J. and Eisenstadt, S.N., 1968, 'Feudalism' in Sills, David L. (ed.), *International Encyclopaedia of Social Sciences*, New York, Macmillan, Vol. 5, 393–403.

Pressman, J.I. and Wildavsky, Aron, 1973, *Implementation: How Great Expectations In Washington Are Dashed in Oakland*, Berkeley and Los Angeles, University of California Press.

Rae, D.W., 1967, *The Political Consequences of Electoral Laws*, New Haven, Conn., Yale University Press.

Raphael, D.D., 1990, *Problems of Political Philosophy*, 2nd edn., Basingstoke, Macmillan.

Rawls, John, 1971, *The Theory of Justice*, London, Oxford University Press.

Reischauer, Edwin 1956, 'Japanese Feudalism', in Coulborne, Rushton (ed.), *Feudalism in History*, Princeton, N.J. Princeton University Press.

Rendell, Michael J., 1978, *Introduction to Political Thought*, London, Sidgwick & Jackson.

Review of International Studies, 1989, Special Issue on 'The Balance of Power', 15 (2).

Ridley, F.F., 1975, *The Study of Government: Political Science and Public Administration*, London, Allen and Unwin.

Riff, Michael, (ed.), 1990, *Dictionary Of Modern Political Ideologies*, Manchester, Manchester University Press.

Roberts, Geoffrey and Edwards, Alistair, 1991, *A New Dictionary of Political Analysis*, London, Edward Arnold.

Rose, P. (ed.), 1993, *Social Trends 23: 1993*, London, HMSO.

Rose, Richard, (ed.), 1969, *Policy Making in Britain*, London, Macmillan.

Rousseau, Jean Jacques, (ed. G.D.H. Coles, 1913, *The Social Contract and Discourses*, London, J.M. Dent & Sons.

Rowbotham, Shiela, 1972, *Women Resistance and Revolution: A History of Women in the Modern World*, New York, Random House.

Royal Commission on Historical Monuments, 1982, *Papers of the British Cabinet Ministers 1782–1900*, London, HMSO.

Runciman, W.G., 1969, *Social Science and Political Theory*, Cambridge, Cambridge University Press.

Russell, Bertrand, 1938, *Power: A New Analysis*, London, George Allen & Unwin.

Rutter, M. and Madge, N., 1976, *Cycles of Disadvantage: A Review of Research*, London, Heinemann.

Said, Edward, 1987, *Orientalism*, Harmondsworth, Middlesex, Penguin.

Sartori, Giovanni, 1970, 'Concept Misinformation in Comparative Politics', *American Political Science Review*, (54): 1033–53, reprinted in Lewis *et al.*

Sabine, George, 1951, *A History of Political Theory*, 3rd edn. London, George G. Harrap & Co Ltd (later edn available).

Saward, Michael, 1993, 'Direct Democracy Revisited', *Politics*, 13 (2): 18–24.

Schapiro, Leonard, 1965, *The Government and Politics of the Soviet Union*, London, Hutchinson.

Schattschneider, E.E., 1960, *The Semi-Sovereign People*, New York.

Schmekebier, Lawrence F., 1969, *Government Publications and Their Use*, 2nd edn, Brookings Institution.

Seale, Patrick and McConville, Maureen, 1968, *French Revolution 1968*, Harmondsworth, Middlesex, Penguin.

Shaw, R. and Sklar, R.L., 1977, *A Bibliography for the Study of African Politics*, Walthon, Mass., Cross Roads Press.

Sherif M. *et al.*, 1951, 'A preliminary study of intergroup relations' in Rohrer, J.H. and Sherif, M., *Social Psychology at the Crossroads*, New York, Harper.

Simon, Herbert A., 1959, 'Theories of Decision Making in Economics and Behavioural Science', *American Economic Review*, 49 (3): 253–83.

Simon, Herbert A., 1977, *The New Science of Management*, Englewood Cliffs, N.J., Prentice Hall.

Singer, Peter, 1973, *Democracy and Disobedience*, Oxford, Clarendon Press.

Sklar, Richard L., 1963, *Nigerian Political Parties: Power in an Emergent Nation*, Princeton, N.J., Princeton University Press.

Smith, Gordon, 1989, *Politics in Western Europe: A Comparative Analysis*, Aldershot, Gower.

Snape, Wilfred E., 1969, *How to Find Out About Local Government*, Oxford, Pergamon Press.

Southern Electric, 1994, *Caring for Customers*, Maidenhead, Southern Electric plc.

Stoate, Deborah, 1994, 'Socialism, however, is obviously a word with more than one meaning', *Fabian Review*, Vol. 106, No 4, August.

Suffian, Tun Mohamed and Lee, H.P., *et al.*, 1978, *The Constitution of Malaysia: Its Development 1957–1977*, Kuala Lumpa, Oxford University Press.

Suprenant, Thomas T, 1985, 'Global Threats to Information', *Annual Review of Science and Technology*, Vol. 20, Section 1.

Swarzkopf, LeRoy C., 1994, *Government Reference Books 92–3: A Biennial Guide to US Government Publications*, Englewood, Libraries Unlimited Inc.

Tajfel, H. and Turner, J., 1979, 'An integrative theory of inter-group conflict', in Austin, G. and Worschel, S. (eds), *The Social Psychology of Inter-group Relations*, Montery, Calif., Brooks/Cole.

Tansey, Stephen D. and Kermode, David G., 1967/8, 'The Westminster Model in Nigeria', *Parliamentary Affairs*, Winter, 19–37.

Tansey, Stephen D., 1973, *Political Analysis: A Report On a Project of Syllabus Development*, London, Birkbeck College, M.Sc. Report.

Tansey, Stephen D., 1981, 'Politics Courses in Higher Education', *Teaching Politics*, 10 (1): 13–26.

Tansey, Stephen D., 1989, *Employers Reactions to the Youth Training Scheme*, Bath, University of Bath M.Phil. Thesis.

Tawney, R.H., 1938, *Religion and the Rise of Capitalism*, Harmondsworth, Middlesex, Penguin.

Taylor, C.L. and Jodice, D.A.A., 1983, *World Handbook of Political and Social Indicators*, 3rd edn, New Haven, Conn., Yale University Press.

Thomas, Hugh, (ed.), 1959, *The Establishment*, London, Anthony Blond.

Times, The, 1993, *Times Top 1000 Companies 1992–3*, London, The Times.

Titmuss, Richard M., 1968, *Essays on the Welfare State*, London, Unwin.

Trotsky, Leon, 1937, *The Revolution Betrayed*, London.

Tullock, Gordon, 1965, *The Politics of Bureacracy*, Washington D.C., Public Affairs Press.

Verba, Sidney and Pye, Lucian, 1965, *Political Culture and Political Development*, Princeton N.J., Princeton University Press.

Verney, Douglas, 1959, *The Analysis of Political Systems*, Glencoe, Ill., Free Press.

Vincent, Andrew, 1992, *Modern Political Ideologies*, Oxford, Blackwell.

Walt, Stephen, 1986, *The Origins of Alliances*, Ithaca, N.Y., Cornell University Press.

Weiner, Myron, 1962, *The Politics of Scarcity: Party Politics in India*, Princeton, N.J., Princeton University Press.

Wheare, K.C., 1951, *Modern Constitutions, Oxford*, Oxford University Press.

Wheare, K.C., 1963, *Federal Government*, London, 4th edn Oxford Universty Press.

Williams, Philip, 1964, *Crisis and Compromise*, Harlow, Essex, Longmans.

Williams, Gavin, (ed.), 1976, *Nigeria: Economy and Society*, London, Rex Collings.

Wittfogel, K., 1957, *Oriental Despotism*, New Haven, Conn., Yale University Press.

Wollstonecraft, Mary, 1985, *A Vindication of the Rights of Women*, Harmondsworth, Middlesex, Penguin.

Woodcock, George, 1975, *Anarchism*, Harmondsworth, Middlesex, Penguin.

World Bank, 1992, *World Development Report*, Washington, World Bank.

Young, Michael, 1961, *The Rise of the Meritocracy 1870–2033*, Harmondsworth, Middlesex, Penguin.

Index

Note: entries denoting key concepts are in **bold**.